11599673

The Economic Law of Motion of
Modern Society

The Economic Law of Motion of Modern Society

A Marx–Keynes–Schumpeter Centennial

edited by

H.-J. WAGENER

and

J.W. DRUKKER

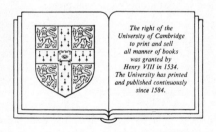

The right of the
University of Cambridge
to print and sell
all manner of books
was granted by
Henry VIII in 1534.
The University has printed
and published continuously
since 1584.

CAMBRIDGE UNIVERSITY PRESS

Cambridge
London   New York   New Rochelle
Melbourne   Sydney

Published by the Press Syndicate of the University of Cambridge
The Pitt Building, Trumpington Street, Cambridge CB2 1RP
32 East 57th Street, New York, NY 10022, USA
10 Stamford Road, Oakleigh, Melbourne 3166, Australia

First published 1986

Printed in Great Britain at the University Press, Cambridge

British Library Cataloguing in Publication Data

The Economic law of motion of modern society
a   Marx–Keynes–Schumpeter centennial.
1. Economics—History
I. Wagener, H.-J.   II. Drukker, J.W.
330.1   HB75

ISBN 0 521 30092 4

Library of Congress Cataloging in Publication Data

Main entry under title:
The Economic law of motion of modern society.
Papers presented at the Marx–Keynes–Schumpeter
Symposium held September 7–10, 1983 at the
Rijksuniversiteit of Groningen, Nietherlands; organized
by the Faculty of Economics.
Bibliography: p.
1. Economics—Congresses.   2. Marxian economics—
Congresses.   3. Keynesian economics—Congresses.
4. Schumpeter, Joseph Alois, 1883–1950—Congresses.
5. Capitalism—Congresses.   6. Entrepreneur—Congresses.
I. Wagener, Hans–Jürgen.   II. Drukker, J.W. (Jan W.)
III. Marx–Keynes–Schumpeter Symposium (1983:
Rijksuniversiteit te Groningen)   IV. Rijksuniversiteit
to Groningen. Faculteit der Economische Wetenschappen.
HB21.E243   1985   330.1   84–29369

ISBN 0 521 30092 4

TM

Contents

Contributors

M. Blaug, *London*

Y.S. Brenner, *Utrecht*

M. Bronfenbrenner, *Tokyo*

L.E. Davis, *Pasadena*

J.W. Drukker, *Groningen*

J. Glombowski, *Tilburg*

R.M. Goodwin, *Siena*

D.J. Harris, *Stanford*

R.A. Huttenback, *Los Angeles*

P. Kalmbach, *Bremen*

P.W. Klein, *Rotterdam*

J.A. Kregel, *Groningen*

S.K. Kuipers, *Groningen*

H.D. Kurz, *Bremen*

A. Maddison, *Groningen*

J.A.H. Maks, *Groningen*

H.P. Minsky, *St Louis*

J. Pen, *Groningen*

W. Pfaffenberger, *Oldenburg*

L. Preneel, *Louvain*

K.W. Rothschild, *Linz*

B. Schefold, *Frankfurt*

J. Starbatty, *Tübingen*

P. Sylos-Labini, *Rome*

R. Tilly, *Münster*

H.-J. Wagener, *Groningen*

Acknowledgements

This book is the final result of the Marx–Keynes–Schumpeter symposium held 7–10 September 1983 at the Rijksuniversiteit of Groningen, Netherlands. The symposium had been organized by the Faculty of Economics. It could not have taken place without the generous financial support of Stiftung Volkswagenwerk, Hannover.

During the symposium and during the period of preparation of the book the hard work of Cathy Drenth and Diana Vrijenhoek contributed to the final result. We thank them and all others who helped us with the project.

H.-J. WAGENER *and* J.W. DRUKKER

1 Introduction

HANS-JÜRGEN WAGENER AND JAN
W. DRUKKER

I

In the course of centuries there are those rare years when the death of a hero of human civilization is compensated for by the birth of a new one. One such year was 1642, watching Galileo's death and Newton's birth. The year 1883 was another: Karl Marx died, J.M. Keynes and J.A. Schumpeter were born. A more prosaic mind will consider this coincidence rather accidental. But it can hardly be disputed that these three eminent social scientists have more in common than just a benchmark year of their lives.

At first sight, of course, it is difficult to imagine a greater difference than that between the Jewish emigrant intellectual who 'preferring the mud to the fish, extols the boorish proletariat above the bourgeois and the intelligentsia who, with whatever faults, are the quality of life and surely carry the seeds of human progress' (Keynes 1972: IX, 258) and the British upper-middle-class 'consultant administrator' (a term from Schumpeter's vast reservoir of qualifications) who was always 'at home' and who wanted to preserve the system that fed his class which he considered to be the progressive. And while these two were positively concerned about the future of mankind, the third man from Vienna was a pessimistic erudite who lived 'in exile', since his was a past world and he foresaw a future which he certainly would not have liked to live to see. No, as far as personal background, ideology and message (if they had any: Schumpeter had none) are concerned, our three men of 1883 have little in common.

Background, however, is accidental and ideology in the first instance a matter of environment and preference. And in the history of thought it is not the message which counts, but the vision. As social scientists Marx, Keynes and Schumpeter developed influential structures of economic thought, visions of the way of functioning and the historical development of the capitalist system. This is a growth-oriented but demand-constrained system coordinated by markets and run by capitalist entrepreneurs who are motivated mainly by profit expectations. Each of them contributed a special aspect to our understanding of this system and overcame a certain theoretical ossification by revolutionizing economic thinking and economic practice. (It may be due

1

to the fact that Schumpeter had no explicit message that one does speak of a Marxian revolution and a Keynesian revolution but not of a Schumpeterian revolution.)

When J. Robinson (1975: 125) writes about the Keynesian revolution, 'On the plane of theory, the revolution lay in the change from the conception of equilibrium to the conception of history', with equal right the same could be said about Marx and Schumpeter. In any case, this should not be misunderstood as implying abandonment of equilibrium as a centre of gravitation in the continuous process of development and as a point of departure for theoretical reasoning. All three accepted history as the ultimate object of their theories. Not logical elegance (of which, it is true, Schumpeter was charmed and for which Marx, rather vainly, strived) is then the correct test of economic theory but historical relevance.

Of course, history meant different things to all three of them and the cast of their plays showed different heroes and villains. Nevertheless, the stories they told us resemble each other amazingly in terms of general vision as well as in certain details, and where they don't they can quite often be used as complements.

So it seems legitimate to ask how the visions of the three eminent economists can be compared and, eventually, combined into one interpretation of the historical process of development of modern capitalist society. This was the objective of a centenary symposium held at Groningen in September 1983 of which this book is the final result. There is no lack of specialized assessments and criticisms of Marxian, Keynesian and Schumpeterian theories (for the latter see e.g. Heertje 1981, Frisch 1982 and Seidl 1984). It is therefore the comparative aspect and the eclectic synthesis which stood out at the Groningen symposium.

Surprising as it may seem, the economics profession is still very much divided about the theories and forecasts of all three of our celebrated economists. There are 'neo-Marxist', 'post-Keynesian' and even 'neo-Schumpeterian' approaches. But on the other hand we learn 'Marx is dead', 'Keynesian macro-economics has failed', we read of 'the ultimate refutation of Schumpeter's main thesis'. If our magnificent three are such eminent social scientists as we are inclined to assume, how does it come about, then, that their theories do not belong to the universally accepted core of the science of economics? First of all, it may be questioned whether such a core exists at all, which has something to do with the political implications of this science. But secondly an explanation may be found in their way of reasoning. The following quotation could refer to any of the three:

1. His work was rarely formally complete or consistent. He only constructed the basic tools for the job at hand – no more. The rest he left to time, experience and the collaboration of a number of minds often with unintended consequences.
2. Even where his work might have been formally correct in the round, [his] methods of exposition and habits of thought required a high degree of sympathetic

cooperation from his readers. This plainly left his work open to a wide number of interpretations.

3. [His] wide reading, plus his formal neglect of his predecessors while writing meant, when coupled with the industry of the academic world that it was, and is, possible to find a precursor for almost every idea of his work.

The quotation is from Moggridge (1975: 75) and is hence directed to the work of Keynes.

A third reason for the ambivalence of the profession about Marx, Keynes and Schumpeter may be found in their critical attitude about the future of capitalism. For they analysed capitalism as an epoch, a culture or a style which is a historical phenomenon and will, some day, be gone. Marx and Schumpeter, rooted in continental intellectual traditions, did so in a romantic disposition – Marx by welcoming the end of human prehistory and Schumpeter by mourning the fall of a culture with only cold rationality replacing it. Keynes, on the other hand, had a more practical, more British attitude towards systematic change: he looked for the means to confine it. But by doing so he advocated institutional changes which constituted a new mixed economy far removed from laissez-faire capitalism.

The ultimate disappearance of capitalism meant to all three of them the vanishing of 'economy' as the fundamental function of human life. Marx (1964: III, 828) described this process as the transition from the realm of necessity to the realm of freedom. Keynes (1972: 331) spoke of the step 'out of the tunnel of economic necessity into daylight'. And Schumpeter (1976: 370) was convinced that socialism meant the 'liberation of life from the economy'. Satisfaction of basic needs and the supply of capital are then an affair of full rationality (something which other schools of thought ascribe already to the present system) and a purely administrative task. This also implies the end of capitalist exploitation (Marx), the euthanasia of the rentier (Keynes) or a zero rate of interest (Schumpeter), not only as theoretical possibility, but as a historical fact.

Keynes was even so specific as to forecast that this stage of development would come about in roughly one hundred years, of which more than fifty have already passed by. It would not be entirely meaningless to discuss the present difficulties of the Western economic system in terms of the labour pains of the new epoch to come. The symposium, however, confined itself to the analysis of the capitalist system, as did the three celebrated economists in their theories.

II

The opening contribution by Professor Goodwin is an essay synthesizing the approaches of Marx, Schumpeter and Keynes into one system, the M-K-S system. The long-run theory of structural stability is classical. Within this frame Schumpeterian innovations create disequilibrium. They propel the system to new levels. This does not, however, provide an explanation for the cyclical development of capitalism. Neither Schumpeter's swarms of innovation, nor the Ricardo–Marx assumption of the profit squeeze, are fully convincing. Here, Keynes' theory of effective demand comes to explain how the working of the accelerator mechanism alters a steady stream of innovations into the cyclical ups and downs of economic activity. The M–K–S system, thus, is a supply-and-demand-oriented system with no systematic tendency to produce full employment.

In a conference which justly can be called a symposium discussion will be ubiquitous and hence cannot properly be reproduced for, alas, the organizers, and later editors, were not themselves ubiquitous. Space constraints do the rest to veil the contribution of the discussants to the intellectual effort of the symposium. Just to render the flavour of the debate in this introduction we will cite some of the formal comments of the discussants.

Commenting on Goodwin, however, Professor Pen remained informal as usual. He did not want to dismiss Schumpeter's theory of the cycle so rapidly and looked for a reason why innovations run in clusters. He found a possible explanation in the growth-sensitivity of technical progress: technical progress is partly autonomous and partly related to the growth rate. This is due to the fact that the diffusion of new methods and new products requires investment and profits and both depend upon the growth rate. Big jumps are thus easily understood. Of course, Pen was aware of the fact that such a sensitivity may be hard to ascertain.

Being born in the year when Marx died, Keynes and Schumpeter had to live with the Marxian tradition. Keynes openly disliked the man and his theories, but tacitly reacted to them rather favourably while Schumpeter did the opposite: he made an intellectual hero of Marx and showed at the same time that all of his theories were mistaken. But he was always – as Minsky observed – 'writing with "Marx" as the hidden subject'. In his contribution Professor Bronfenbrenner evaluates this attitude of Keynes and Schumpeter by introducing the term 'rich man's Marx', meaning somebody who provided an answer to Marxian theories or an alternative to Marxism. Thus Schumpeter's creative destruction is opposed to the tendency of the rate of profit to fall and Keynesian harmonious full-employment capitalism is confronted with Marxian class conflict.

Professor Brenner made some critical comments to this interpretation:

I believe that in the light of recent history Keynes has in fact become a 'poor man's Marx'. The reason for my belief that today Keynes poses an even greater threat to the establishment has two main causes. Firstly, because traditional Marxism has lost credibility by its transformation from a moral system with essential economic aspects into an economic system with too little concern for the Western ethical traditions. Secondly, Keynes poses a threat to the modern capitalist establishment because the idea that society is or ought to be responsible for full employment is simply irreconcilable with the system.

Why the capitalist establishment cannot in the long run accept this Keynesian compromise is obvious: In the first place it deprives it of its unchallenged social hegemony. If effective demand is shown to be on equal footing in the stimulation of employment and welfare with the 'animal spirits' of the 'captains of industry' what then remains of the latters' claim to their elevated position in society? The second, and more important, reason for the establishment's inability to live with the Keynesian compromise is that it deprives it of its most essential instrument to enforce work-discipline to serve its own interests, namely the workers' fear of destitution and starvation.

The point is that half a century of welfare has shown that Keynesian economics can work. It showed that if continued it would of necessity lead to the kind of social and economic reality which Marx rather than Keynes envisaged for the good of mankind. And this, too, is the reason why I think that today Keynes has become the 'poor man's Marx'.

Brenner has shown how easily Marxian and Keynesian traditions can be combined and thus he has implicitly underlined the question which is now asked by Professor Kregel: 'Where have all the "conservative" Keynesians gone?' Kregel, in his turn, is convinced that their resurrection may be vitally important to our economic and political systems. He explores the role of the state and the role of the market in the development of capitalism by comparing the debate in the U.K. – mainly between Hayek and Keynes – with the irrelevance of Keynesian ideas for the conception of the New Deal. The identification of Keynes as a radical liberal (in the American sense of the word) is due, according to Kregel, to a misinterpretation of Keynes' attempt to integrate the structural stability of the market and the disequilibrating forces of development: the law of the market and the law of motion of modern society. In the discussion Professor Blang added a gloss to Kregel's paper:

The peculiar American association between Keynesian economics and political liberalism only emerged gradually during World War II and is beautifully exemplified by the appearance of Samuelson's *Economics: An Introduction* in 1948, the first successful elementary textbook exposition of Keynesian economics. To underline Professor Kregel's point about the American identification between Keynesian economics and the rejection of free markets and private enterprise, consider an American best-seller like William Buckley's (1950) *God and Man at Yale*: one of its chapters argued that Yale economic students were being systematically indoctrinated to believe in socialism because the Yale department of economics had adopted Samuelson's textbook in introductory economics courses and that book, he then proceeded to demonstrate, was full of the ideas of that British radical, Keynes. Such an attack simply could not have been published at the time in Britain.

The late 1930s and particularly the early 1940s witnessed the gradual acceptance of Keynesian ideas by all political elements in British public life. The eager adoption of Keynes by the Labour Party and the manner in which the concept of the welfare state was married to that of Keynesian demand management may suggest the same identification of Keynes with left-wing politics that we noted in the American case. But right-wing political objections to Keynes in Britain were never as strident as they were in America: in Britain, Keynes was too much an establishment figure to give the Tory Party much to bite on. Suffice it to say then that a mythical Keynes was gradually fashioned in both countries but the British Keynesian myth was a very different sort of thing from the American Keynesian myth: the British scene made room for both radical and conservative Keynesians, whereas the American scene allowed only liberal Keynesianism.

III

The next four chapters continue to discuss the relation of the law of the market and the law of motion of capitalism. The integration of a stability principle – static theories of competitive equilibrium or the normal state of the system – and a disequilibrating, propelling force – dynamic theories of long-run evolution of competitive economies – is at the core of this discussion. Kregel's conclusion that neither Marx nor Schumpeter were any more successful than Keynes in this endeavour is confirmed. They provided, however, elements which may help such an integration and point in the direction of the generalized M–K–S system suggested by Goodwin.

Professor Harris' contribution examines the question of whether there are macroeconomic laws of motion which are imposed upon the decisions of the individual economic agents. He uses as an example Marx's tendency of the rate of profit to fall, since this was thought by Marx to show the internal limits of the capitalist system. The validity of the tendency as a general law is disproved. In the course of the argument we gain insights into the Marxian theory of technical progress and employment which will be further elaborated in the following chapter. Professor Glombowski's comment on Harris was in fact a paper in itself and Professor Harris suggested we include it as an appendix to his contribution.

In chapter 6 Professors Kalmbach and Kurz take up the problem of technical progress and employment again. Like Harris, they start from the classical (Ricardian) position and then compare what Marx and Schumpeter have made of it. The essential problem in this context is the question of how the labour-displacing effects of innovation are compensated. Marx, of course, did not share Ricardo's optimism that due to the accumulation drive of the capitalist system all the displaced workers will be reabsorbed. His criticism of Say's law which has a 'Keynesian flavour' is relevant here. Since Schumpeter did not grasp the concept of effective demand, he accepted Say's law and advocated a theory of automatic compensation. After all, Schumpeter was a pure supply-sider.

In his remarks Professor Starbatty made clear that, out of the set of our three great economists, for a liberal (European meaning of the word) only the supply-sider Schumpeter seems to be acceptable: competitive markets plus entrepreneurial innovation:

If we change in Marx's system the premise of the falling rate of profit, it is impossible to deduce the existence of a growing industrial manpower reserve caused by technical change. In addition Marx explicitly considers the case that the entrepreneurs pass on to capital-saving technical progress and hence jobless workers can be employed again.

Discussing the work of Keynes, we are back in a stationary system. Keynes' main concern was disequilibrium in the sense that savings and investment could differ from each other. In Schumpeter's view this was a necessary part of the capitalist development. Keynes pleaded for comprehensive action by the government, as he thought this to be the only way to reach the goal 'social justice'. Schumpeter believed that such actions by politicians would only restrain the process of development. So the system which is presented in the *General Theory* finally turns into a completely stationary one or in Domar's famous words, the Keynesian wonderland, where there is continuous investment and at the same time the capitalists don't grow bigger. Let me quote Schumpeter's last words on Keynes and the consequences of a policy based on his system: 'The stagnationists are wrong in their diagnosis of the reasons why the capitalist process should stagnate; they may still turn out to be right in their prognosis that it will stagnate – with sufficient help from the public sector.'

This is the last sentence of the 'March into Socialism' (Schumpeter 1950a: 425). Being Schumpeter's vision of the fall of capitalism, most liberals, quite naturally, can do without it (cf. Heertje 1981). The quote shows that Schumpeter disapproved of the doctrine of fading investment opportunities which some American Keynesians advocated. It has been said that he even identified Keynes with this doctrine, which was the reason for his difficulties with the theory of effective demand. It is quite amusing, however, to note that at Chicago Schumpeter was thought to be one of the godfathers of American Keynesianism. So in 1943 H.C. Simons of Chicago wrote in a letter to Keynes: 'I sometimes suspect that you may not be much more tolerant than I am toward that weird amalgam of your doctrines and Schumpeter's preposterous *Entwicklungstheorie* which constitutes the extreme "American Keynesianism"' (quoted in Patinkin 1979: 232; the reference is clearly not to Schumpeter's *Theory of Economic Development* but to *Capitalism, Socialism and Democracy* which had just appeared in 1943).

It seems appropriate by now to analyse somewhat more deeply the Schumpeterian system and its relation to Marx and Keynes. This is done in chapter 7 by Professor Schefold. Schumpeter's two great heroes in our profession were Karl Marx – as already noticed – and Léon Walras. What Keynes thought of the first we have already seen. He took even less notice of Walras, only mentioning in the *General Theory* that Walras' theory of interest is in the classical tradition (Keynes 1973: 176–7). Minsky (in the following chapter) holds: 'Walras and Keynes are like oil and water; they don't mix'; he finds the explanation in their respective theories of money. Does this imply that the Walrasian Schumpeter and the Marshallian Keynes are like oil and water too? Nothing of the like seems to be the case. Schefold shows the areas of disagreement and the areas of contact; Schumpeter's monetary theory, despite its being Walrasian, belongs to the latter area. A similar impression is given by Schumpeter himself (1954: 1016–26), who takes great pains to prove that Walras cannot be accused of a veil-of-money approach: 'the Keynesian analysis of the *General Theory* (not of the *Treatise* of 1930) is but a special case of the genuinely general theory of Walras' (ibid.: 1082). In the discussion Professor Maks corroborated this interpretation:

Walras brings his analysis precisely up to the point where the motion of an economy starts with his concept of the continuous market. Walras' vision of the continuous market is beautifully described in the following quotation:

Such is the continuous market, which is perpetually tending towards equilibrium without ever actually attaining it, because the market has no other way of approaching equilibrium except by groping, and, before the goal is reached, it has to renew its efforts and start over again, all the basic data of the problem...having changed in the meantime.... The diversion of the productive services from enterprises that are losing money to profitable enterprises takes place in various ways, the most important being through credit operations, but at best these ways are slow...just as a lake is, at times, stirred to its very depths by a storm, so also the market is sometimes thrown into violent confusion by crises which are sudden and general disturbances of equilibrium. (Walras 1954: p. 382)

Since in this quotation the storm that stirs the lake and the violent confusion of the economy is introduced as a sudden, general and unexpected disturbance, one has a good case in interpreting this phenomenon, relating this disturbance to the basic data, as implying disappointed expectations. The impression is reinforced by the explicit mentioning of changing utilities of goods and services. These considerations indicate that an all future market approach or, alternatively, a (contingent) perfect foresight idea is *not* embedded in Walras' theory.

The axiom of reals seems to be less in Walras than in his followers. This discussion leads us over to the next chapter, since the axiom of reals plays a prominent role in Professor Minsky's contribution. For he gives Keynes the full credit for having abandoned it. This is essential for the understanding of capitalism. The economic system of capitalism is characterized by fragility and resilience. Keynes' analytical structure helps to understand and cope with fragility and Schumpeter's entrepreneur helps to understand resilience. We end up with a Schumpeter–Keynes–Kalecki vision of the system which in Minsky's interpretation sometimes seems to read: only money matters. At least this was the impression of Professor Kuipers, who opposed such an interpretation:

My arguments against the monetary view of the trade cycle are the following:

1. Stocks or portfolio decisions are assumed to be independent of flow of income–expenditure decisions. As Tobin (1982) and Buiter (1981) explained recently, flow decisions are not independent of stock decisions. Asset prices and current output prices are determined by a system of simultaneous equations. There does not therefore exist a one-way causality from asset markets to output and employment.

2. Proper modelling of the economy means that the 'axiom of reals' still holds. Minsky does not distinguish between neutral money and money illusion. No money illusion is a necessary condition for neutral money. It is not a sufficient condition, however. One of the other conditions for monetary neutrality is that expectations come true and that all markets are cleared. The last need not be the case. Although the 'axiom of reals' still holds, money is not neutral under these circumstances. Changes in the financial sphere will therefore influence the economy when it is out of equilibrium. When equilibrium is restored only the price level will appear to be influenced.

3. There are no theoretical indications that deep depressions are ultimately caused by developments in the monetary and not by developments in the real sphere. Empirical research has to answer the question which of the two factors is responsible for it in a concrete situation. One may conclude that the present-day difficulties are essentially real in nature. More particularly these difficulties seem to originate from the

supply side. Of course, it may happen that some banks may take unwarranted risks, as some Western banks have done with their lending to some South-American countries. They then may go bankrupt.

IV

The last four chapters of the book deal mainly with historical and sociological problems. Marx, Keynes and Schumpeter have been praised for their knowledge of history (economic history and history of economic thought) and they have been praised for their historically oriented theories (see the quotation from Joan Robinson at the beginning of this chapter, see p. 2). It is, however, not always equally clear what 'history' means in the context of their theories.

In his contribution Professor Tilly alludes to the economist's ahistorical habit of interpreting a given set of temporarily simultaneous circumstances as a complete system. This approach is confronted with the economic historian's tendency (healthy in the eyes of Tilly) to interpret the development of a given period as result of changes of a previous one. Certainly, he does not advocate a simple *post hoc propter hoc* argument. The problem of the theorist is how to open his closed system for historical influences and build a 'general theory' at the same time.

Marx's economic theory was explicitly contingent upon the capitalist mode of production (economic theory as a historical ideal-type). But within that mode of production he postulated, for instance, the tendency of the rate of profit to fall as a general law. Yet, as Harris has shown, it can claim validity only as a contingent historical condition. For the economic theoretician this is a final verdict – not so for the economic historian who might find it useful in certain situations. Schumpeter's solution was to separate pure theory from history. The reason why the dynamic part of his pure theory is so little satisfactory may be found perhaps in the fact that the Schumpeterian entrepreneur is a historical personage for whom there is no room in pure theory. With Keynes the change from equilibrium to history means above all the good Marshallian tradition of concrete concepts and an orientation towards 'the economic society in which we actually live' (Keynes 1973: VI 3).

If it is not a purely abstract logic of decision, any economic theory is modelled upon certain historical experiences. And many an opposition in theory can be reduced to different facts of experience. The economic historian will be the first to detect such divergence and by investigating the multitude of experiences he will foster doubts about the existence of a general law. In the debate Professor Sylos-Labini called the principal teaching of Marx and Schumpeter 'the idea that economic theory is historically conditioned, so that, when the "slice of history" changes, we have also to modify the theoretical model intended to explain some of its features.' The problem of a general dynamic theory, then, seems to be to identify individual 'slices of history' and the transition from one to the next. It is certainly safe to hold that this problem has not yet been solved.

A good example of historical anatomy is the contribution of Professor Tilly. He carries on with the problem posed by Minsky and tries to answer the question how much money matters. In Marx's interpretation industrialization was not constrained by financial problems. Schumpeter's interpretation was quite different: here credit plays the crucial role in making innovation effective, the banker becomes 'the capitalist par excellence'. This role, however, can only be played if an innovating entrepreneur exists separately. Schumpeter's position is contrasted by Hilferding, who modified Marx's rather simple views in his *Finanzkapital*. In Hilferding's opinion financial institutions are ruling the roost in the development of modern capitalism. All three approaches are not 'general theories' but are modelled on different 'slices of history'. By comparing British and German industrialization, and the London and Berlin capital markets, Tilly provides evidence for the view that money matters. However, he refrains from any conclusions as to how much it does so.

Stressing the historical approach, Professor Klein added some Dutch experience in the discussion:

I wonder whether the similarities and differences between British and German financing of industrial enterprises could not to some extent be traced back to their pre-industrial experience. Let me use Dutch banking and finance in the nineteenth century as a case for presenting the idea that specific pre-industrial developments and experiences may still be decisive for the ways and means of industrialization. As far as I am able to judge Dutch history beats anything economists might call sane and normal. In a word it is history, pure and proper.

Dutch industrialization arrived rather late, in earnest not before the end of the nineteenth century. Its financing was actually full of similarities with the earlier experiences of British and German enterprises. The great difference, however, is that Dutch railroad-building did next to nothing for initiating the development of a national capital market. The construction of Dutch railroads really began only in the 1860s and it was mainly financed by the state and foreign investors. Dutch banking and Dutch finance were keeping themselves more or less aloof.

For a very long time economic historians have taken all this as a sure sign and evidence of Dutch economic backwardness. Nowadays it is realized that the Dutch economy actually had been growing substantially ever since the early 1830s. This growth was not a matter of industrialization, but mainly due to the extension and improvement of traditional activities in agriculture, commerce, shipping and, most decidedly so, in finance. Differing in role, functioning and organization from German as well as British banking, Dutch banks adapted themselves to the changing conditions of the Dutch pre-industrial economy. When industrialization had finally got underway and banking began to show active interest in manufacturing, it still kept its distance from industry and remained more or less true to its pre-industrial origins.

The London capital market also figures prominently in the next chapter. Professors Davis and Huttenback are less interested in how well it served British industry than in how well it served British investors, and who these investors were. Such questions are important in the context of the theory of imperialism which brings, again, the same contestants into the theoretical arena: Marx, the neo-Marxists led by Hilferding, and Schumpeter. Which social groups, which classes support imperial activities? Is imperialism an episode of capitalism or its highest stage? And again, the facts of evidence do not allow for a conclusive answer, which left room for an animated discussion opened by Professor Preneel. It centred, however, round the historical facts and hence contributed less to our main topic.

This was pursued by Professor Rothschild. After investigating the importance of capital, and the question of how much money matters, it is only legitimate to ask what is the role of the capitalist in the economic system of capitalism and who is standing behind that character-mask. Queer as it may sound, classical and neoclassical economists seem to do without that figure and are satisfied with an automatic process of adaptation. The capitalist as the general undertaker has several functions and thus has different parts to play: supplier of funds, innovator, decision-maker, coordinator.

In Marx, the classical tradition is still to be seen: his capitalist cannot but accumulate. He is the instrument of autonomous forces of development. Methodological individualism opens degrees of freedom for Schumpeter's entrepreneur who is not shaped by the system, but on the contrary imprints his mark upon it. With Keynes the capitalist is the investor, the man who according to his expectations about the uncertain future composes a portfolio of real and financial assets. The survival of the capitalist system hinges on the survival of the capitalist and, as we have seen already, neither Marx, nor Schumpeter, nor Keynes thought that he would survive forever.

In the discussion Professor Sylos-Labini emphasized the different functions of the capitalist as saver in the neoclassical and the M–K–S system:

For the neoclassical economists the capitalist is seen essentially as a saver. Marx, Schumpeter and Keynes agree that saving *as such* is not important in the process of economic growth. Marx, in agreement with the classical economists, thinks that the acts of saving and those of investment largely coincide, though he recognized that the financing of the accumulation process is supplemented by the funds supplied by the monetary capitalists and by the banks. If we read Marx carefully, we realize that he is well aware of 'credit creation', a phenomenon that would be better defined as 'creation of bank money' and that plays an important role in Schumpeter's theory. Marx's capitalists save only in view of investment and thus there is no problem – there can be no problem – of saving as such. Schumpeter recognizes the importance of such decisions simultaneously to save and to invest, but he gives a great emphasis to the creation of bank money, which can be said to determine 'forced' saving.

Saving as such plays an important role in Keynes, but this role can be negative: if saving is not offset by a corresponding investment, growth is hampered. On the other hand, if there are unutilized resources, an additional investment gives rise to the saving that will finance it. In the place of Say's law we have Keynes' law according to which 'investment creates the saving for its own financing'. All this means that savers, whoever they are, in contrast with the crucial role that they have in the neoclassical theory, play either a very secondary or even a negative role in Marx, Schumpeter and Keynes.

The position of the capitalist in modern society is challeged more and more by the state, the interventionist state, the planning state, the welfare state. And neither Marx nor Keynes were innocent with respect to this development. Sylos-Labini stressed the point in the discussion by giving mainly Keynes the credit for recognizing and advocating the role of the state:

Marx and Schumpeter pay very little attention to the role of the state in economic activity. For Marx, the spread of the large enterprises makes the control by the state inevitable, and the large enterprises organized in the form of stock companies become quasi-public units where ownership and administration are increasingly separated (Marx 1964: III, 454). Schumpeter, apart from very general remarks, recommends state intervention not to try to avoid recessions, but to prevent a recession degenerating into a deep depression.

Keynes, in his famous pamphlet *The End of Laissez-Faire*, reproposes the quoted ideas of Marx, though it seems that he had not studied Marx and in that pamphlet has even nasty words about him. As for the role of the state in economic activity, however, he has devoted a systematic attention to this fundamental problem of our time. In fact, *The General Theory* can be seen as a great intellectual effort to find the ways through which state intervention can save capitalism by making it work in a socially acceptable way.

As far as the interventionist state is concerned, Sylos-Labini is certainly right. The problem with Marx and Keynes, however, is that they both seem to think of the interventionist state or the planning state in a-political terms, or, in Engels' words (1964: 308): 'the public functions will lose their political character and turn into simple administrative functions taking care of the true social interests'. This fiction is the main point of liberal critique against the interventionist state (cf. Buchanan and Wagner 1977). And exactly as Schumpeter (1950a) did, the liberal critics see perennial inflationary pressures as the most probable outcome of state intervention.

Apart from the interventionist state there is the welfare state which Marx saw rising beyond the class state of his time. Social security payments and expenditures for education and health 'will grow in principle considerably compared to the present society and will increase by the same rate with which the new society develops' (Marx 1958: 15). The development of the welfare state is the subject of the last chapter, by Professor Maddison. If Bismarck figures more prominently here than either Marx or Schumpeter or Keynes, we should remember Kregel's call for conservative Keynesians and his hint of the possibility of conservative Marxists. Bismarck was, so to say, a conservative Marxist: the German anarchist Mühsam has coined the word 'Bismarxism' to describe modern state paternalism.

The central hypothesis of Maddison is Schumpeter's (1976: 346, 351): 'The tax state should not take away so much from the people that they lose financial interest in production.' 'The financial capacity of the tax state has its limits.' Maddison is convinced that history has disproved any such hypothesis. This conviction was opposed in the discussion by Professor Wagener:

Bismarck's state was a class state. Calling the last hundred years the Bismarckian era, one has to face the question: is the modern state a class state or a democratic state? The transition from the one to the other implies structural changes in government expenditure as they have been predicted by Marx.

The analysis of Schumpeter's hypothesis, on the other hand, is a test of the existence of capitalism itself. For, if it does not make any difference for economic performance whether 50 or 100 per cent of GDP are the direct income from private enterprise or are chanelled through the state budget and distributed according to political decisions, then capitalism as a separate social formation with specific behavioural patterns and rules of the game does not exist. It is one thing to say that Schumpeter's hypothesis is not valid. It is a different thing to say that capitalism – for which slice of history it still can be valid – is disappearing and removed by a new system where, in principle, total GDP can be redistributed by political decisions. The transition from capitalism to the latter system was called by Schumpeter the march into socialism.

V

The symposium has treated Marx, Keynes and Schumpeter as outstanding representatives of the economics profession. To summarize we may ask: what makes a great economist? It has repeatedly been stressed by the contributors that all three of them exhibit theoretical shortcomings and historical constraints: they did not really accomplish what they were setting out to do, i.e. to find the general law of motion of the modern economic system. Apparently, to be a great economist is not a matter of forecasts which, at least to a certain degree, come true. Nor is it a question of applying advanced calculus to economic problems. It seems to demand a vision of history and the forces that make it. And it demands the personality to impose that vision upon the profession. Then, later generations can tackle the task to reshape the vision into operational theories.

There can be little doubt that Marx, Schumpeter and Keynes considered themselves to possess the required personality. 'The teaching of Marx is almighty, because it is true', was one of the slogans in the streets of East Berlin at the time of the centenary conference, and one may presume that he himself would not have objected. No such slogans were to be read, of course, in the streets of Cambridge on the corresponding occasion. Always being at home and the most influential economist of his time, Keynes felt no necessity to advertise himself. But exactly like Marx ('je ne suis pas un marxiste') he could not resist underlining the great numbers of his followers by parting from them in a slightly conceited way: 'I am not a Keynesian'.

As for Schumpeter, Professor Rothschild reminded us of the famous anecdote of his three wishes. This anecdote has been transmitted in a number of different versions. The one Professor Sylos-Labini reported to the symposium, however, seems most pertinent:

The story is that, when Schumpeter was a little baby, a gipsy saw him and said to his mother: 'This child will become the greatest lover in Vienna, the greatest horseman in Europe and the greatest economist in the world.' Schumpeter – who was endowed with a good continental sense of humour and, so I was told, was himself reporting this anecdote – commented: 'That's funny: I never learned how to ride!'

2 The M–K–S System: The Functioning and Evolution of Capitalism

RICHARD M. GOODWIN

What I wish to sketch is an analytic system consisting of selected elements, suitably combined, of the concepts of the three great economists Marx, Keynes, and Schumpeter. What a strange conjunction of the stars which could combine the dates of three such totally disparate individuals: Jewish intellectual revolutionary, English liberal reformer, and Central European reactionary. Incompatible though they are, I have found in each of them the most illuminating insights: furthermore, whilst their integral systems are quite incompatible, certain central elements from each seem to me to be essential to the understanding of the behaviour of industrial capitalism. Marx had the particular advantage of being totally hostile to capitalism whilst accepting the necessity of understanding it the better to foretell its passing. Schumpeter approved of capitalism but agreed, though for different reasons, that its dynamism would bring it to an end. Keynes wanted nothing better than to save capitalism from its own irrational behaviour, though he did foresee the euthanasia of the rentier. Marx, and like him Schumpeter, were deeply concerned with the wider social aspects of capitalist evolution: I shall, however, limit myself to the narrowly economic side.

In my view it is illuminating to regard capitalism as an example of perpetual morphogenesis: the first volume of *Capital* appeared in the same year as Darwin's *Origin of Species* and Marx felt they were fellow adventurers in uncharted territory (a feeling not reciprocated). Were he alive today, would he not hail René Thom as a fellow spirit? Seeing capitalism not as timeless wonder but rather as an evolving system, which has to be seen as an intermittent but persistent generator of changing morphology. The analysis cannot be of the familiar dynamics of a given system, but rather of a system characterized by continuing alteration of its essential technological structure.

Darwin missed joining our astrological group by only one year; but he must be considered an honorary member, since he did for natural history what Marx did for social history. Beyond the essential point of view of evolutionary morphology, all similarity ends: Marx was a critical admirer of Darwin but did not fall victim to a simple-minded translation of his concepts; he was, of course, violently hostile to the social Darwinism of bourgeois apologists. As

Schumpeter carefully puts it: 'Marx may have experienced satisfaction at the emergence of Darwinist evolution. But his own had nothing whatever to do with it, and neither lends any support to the other' (Schumpeter 1954: 441).

The problem, then, is how to conceptualize the evolutionary aspect of capitalism. The economic structure of previous societies changed, if at all, very slowly. In industrial capitalism there are elements of structural stability along with instability: they must be kept distinct and both are needed analytically. Human economic behaviour has shown many examples of continuity over long periods. By contrast the striking characteristics of the bourgeois revolution was laissez-faire: the potent harnessing of man's greed to the generation of new forms of production. Never before has there been such rapid and profound alteration of inherited ways of working and living, carried out with ruthless disregard for the effect on the lives of those involved. Biological concepts can be no more than suggestive for the study of social systems: thus one might consider the familial structure, father to son and mother to daughter, as the genetic programming which gave continuity for so long to earlier social structures. Bourgeois society has seriously emasculated the family and substituted innovative, extra-familial education for the traditional ways.

To model this problem, I assume that there are costs that vary linearly with prices, and demands that vary linearly with outputs: these constitute dual transmission mechanisms. Then there are given costs and demands which vary autonomously over time. For any set of given costs and demands, there will exist a set of equilibrium prices equal to total costs, and outputs equal to total demands. I assume that the transmission mechanisms are asymptotically stable.

Schumpeter elaborated Marxian theory by investigating the impact on such a system of innovations, broadly defined as any new, cost-reducing process, consisting of either a new method of producing an existing good or service, or a new good, better than existing ones. A single innovation, becoming operational, constitutes a shock to the system, shifting the equilibrium position, thus creating a disequilibrium state. In a competitive system there will ensue a distributed lagging reaction, a long train of adjustments, as prices fall (or fail to rise), leading to falling costs, and so on. If the innovation is quantitatively important, e.g. in energy (steam, electricity, oil, nuclear) or in transport (railways, canals, steamships, motor cars, airplanes), it will affect seriously a large number of industries. Some of them, in view of the changing constellation of input costs, will then be led to making an induced change in production processess. Reality is not, of course, so simple. Most important innovations occur at first in crude form and only subsequently, in the course of a long series of small improvements, reach their full potential.

Marx was the first economist seriously to study the cyclical aspect of capitalism, and to point out that fluctuations were an essential, not peripheral, feature of the functioning of the system. Although he phrased it differently,

Schumpeter took the same view. Unfortunately Marx never got around to formulating a unified, explicit theory of the cycle. Schumpeter did, and it posed for him, as it would have for Marx, a difficult problem. If, as is surely the case, technical innovation consists of a large number of small changes, why does it not result in the steady state growth so beloved of orthodox economists? Schumpeter tried to deal with this by his conception of 'swarms', but, in my opinion, it is all too frail a construction to bear the weight of explaining fluctuations in the general level of activity.

The issue is a central one in dynamical analysis. No linear theory, like the transmission mechanism, can explain the generation and maintenance of oscillations. Both Marx and Schumpeter firmly maintained that cycles were endogenous to the system, and that they did not come from the weather, bad government, misbehaviour of the banking system, etc., but that they were an inherent consequence of the very nature of capitalism. It follows therefore that in the structure of capitalism itself must be found the source of fluctuations.

One of the most illuminating ways to view oscillators is as frequency convertors. A steady source of energy or action is converted into a pulsating response. Therefore what Schumpeter needed was an analysis of how a roughly steady stream of innovations, along with their many improvements, got altered into the ups and downs of capitalism. For me, Keynes's theory of effective demand supplied the missing link in Schumpeter's model. To make an innovation operational requires prior investment outlays. The transmission mechanism magnifies and distributes this demand amongst the other sectors. Thus occurs a general, as distinct from a sectoral, rise in outputs, which will in turn help the expansion of the new process. If the innovation and its secondary effects are large enough, the economy may be lifted to the region of full capacity. Then the accelerator becomes effective, which constitutes a *bifurcation* of behaviour, changing the transmission mechanism from stability to instability. To put it as simply as possible, in aggregative real terms:

(1) $\varepsilon Y = I - S = I - (1 - \alpha)Y$

where I is real innovational investment plus all other real outlays independent of output, Y, with α and ε as constants. The accelerator introduces a new dynamic term, βY, where $0 < \varepsilon < \beta$, yielding:

(2) $\varepsilon Y = I + \beta Y - (1 - \alpha)Y$

so that:

(3) $(\beta - \varepsilon)Y = (1 - \alpha)Y - I$

and the system becomes unstable. Beyond this point we are treading on the Harrod–Keynes razor's edge. The economy grows at a rate which gradually reduces the Industrial Reserve Army to low levels, which will make it impossible to continue at the same rate of expansion. After a time the growth rate necessarily decelerates, which cuts out the accelerator and inhibits any remaining innovational investment. The economy relapses either to a lower growth rate or declines, but in the new equilibrium state it will have a different structure and a higher productivity, thus renewing the Industrial Reserve Army.

As a young economist I felt this Keynesian-type cycle theory was the natural, essential completion of Schumpeter's 'vision'. I spent much effort to convince him of it. About cycle theory he was reasonably open-minded, and even went so far as to agree that, if I would give a course of lectures on mathematical cycle theory, he would attend – which he did (along with Gottfried Haberler). But on the subject of Keynes's *General Theory* his mind was closed: nothing would convince him that it was anything but clever nonsense. I was baffled then and still am, to some extent: how could so acute and so unprejudiced a mind be so blind? I offer some possible explanations. Keynes's grasp of economic orthodoxy, never great, especially of the continental variety, had become ossified: it had, happily, been replaced by some sense of the real functioning of capitalism. By contrast, Schumpeter, having begun as an outrageous, semi-Marxist rebel (ejected from Böhm-Bawerk's seminar and denied a job in the university), had, by the 1930s, so immersed himself in teaching what academics wrote that he was quite unable to conceive of anything radically different. For example, he firmly believed that Walras was the greatest of all economists because of his methodology and in spite of his essentially trivial dynamics. Whilst Schumpeter, unlike Wicksell, did not explicitly assume full employment, nonetheless the cast of his thought was that technological progress, not effective demand, determined the variations of output as controlled by resources.

In an unpublished lecture on Ricardo, given in Japan, he developed one of those brilliant half-truths, maintaining that Ricardo had four unknowns, for which he needed to solve four equations: but being, like Schumpeter himself, no mathematician, he reduced the problem to one unknown. The wage level he took as fixed by the Malthusian iron law; profits disappeared into rents and were determined by them. This left output, the level of which he simply did not discuss, instead concerning himself solely with distributive shares in output. Distributive shares, since they add to unity, yield inverse relations necessarily: if one goes up another goes down. One can find this strain of thought in Marx, deeply influenced as he was by Ricardo, and it is still visible, in all its purity, in the work of Sraffa. Accumulation drives wages up and profits down, leading to crisis, depression and the search for labour-saving innovations. This is true for shares but not for levels of wages and profits. After Keynes we all know that, on the contrary, with unemployed resources, higher wages can, and usually do, lead to higher profits: or higher profits can, and usually do, lead to higher wages. Profits depend not only on the difference between prices and wage costs, but even more potently on the scale of output relative to capacity. The neoclassical assumption of market-clearing and the determination of output by resources, not by effective demand, disastrously confused a whole generation of economists. However, once the region of full employment is reached, the Ricardo–Marx assumption becomes operative.

The impact of Keynes was to produce a new form of denial of the Marxian breakdown theory. The existence of a steady-state, exponential growth path was established, for which it seemed that all that was needed was a sophisticated demand management which could realize it. The quite exceptional post-war boom gave strong support to the view of its feasibility. Marx is, however, not so easily dismissed: long before Keynes he attacked Say's Law and the facile optimism which maintained that it guaranteed full employment. The post-war maintenance of near full employment brought a growing intensity of the conflict between worker and employer over the shares of product – a conflict which has only been resolved either by inflation or by massive unemployment. It is by now clear that the Industrial Reserve Army has all along played the essential role in capitalism that Marx ascribed to it: the economy needs unemployment to restore labour 'discipline' and the conditions for further growth.

Once the economy has collapsed into depression, the question arises as to what will bring about a recovery. Keynes has no answer: Marx has one or two, not altogether convincing ones. The growth of the Industrial Reserve Army weakens the bargaining power of labour: the difficulty is that this does not restore profits, since they depend on output as well as cost. Then he refers to the irrational drive to accumulate – but accumulate for what? Here we need Schumpeter. It is rational to accumulate and profitable to invest in an innovation, even if excess capacity exists and even if demand is low; there ensues 'creative destruction' of capacity.

By calling in economic history to be an essential part of economic analysis, Schumpeter, like Marx, made a profound change, though one not too much to the liking of either economic historians or economic theorists. As an aspiring young theorist, I was much upset to discover, after his unexpected death, that Schumpeter's last paper urged economists to study the records of the great business enterprises! Superficially very un-Marxian, it is in fact very much in the line of the master's thinking: the industrial tycoon, unappealing though he is, is the dynamo of capitalism and the generator of new social structures. In this way, and in this way only, we can explain the total lack of any form of strict periodicity, hidden or overt, in economic time series. If an innovation is small, or if it has already been substantially completed, when the economy collapses, it may 'bump along the bottom' for some considerable time before rising again. On the other hand, if, following the collapse of a boom, a large innovation still has much development left in it, then, though the slump will temporarily inhibit investment, it will quickly be resumed when the economy ceases to decline. In this manner it is possible not only to explain the variable periodicity, but also the so-called 'long waves'. There can be no question of establishing the existence of Kondratieff cycles, since the run of data is too short. Indeed it may be pointless to try to develop a theory of long cycles. On the other hand, technological history, being mainly exogenous to the economy, can explain everything. Thus a big thing like the railways can explain why a relatively long span of time will have vigorous booms and short, sharp slumps; the lack of such an event will explain why other periods have weak booms and prolonged stagnations.

I agree with Schumpeter that in Marx it is not in the detail of his analytic apparatus but in his over-all 'vision' that his greatness and his unique contribution lies. He saw society as a system evolving historically along a path determined dynamically by, and determining, its productive structure. Starting from this evolutionary viewpoint, he avoided the errors of the 'vulgar' economists who gave a rosy, timeless view of capitalism.

Particularly important, and unique to him, was the conception of the Industrial Reserve Army. Connecting this with distributive shares – or more polemically, exploitation – he saw that if wages were too high, accumulation slackened; the urge to save labour increased and the demand for labour weakened. Consequently there follows a period of wages lagging behind productivity; profitability increases and accumulation accelerates again, leading back to the initial situation of rising demand for labour, rising wages and declining reserves of unemployed. Thus capitalism chases but never finds a 'natural', or dynamically equilibrated, level of unemployment. Again, Marx, unlike most economists, took the simple view, fully borne out by later statistics, that profits, not some intertemporally maximized utility, were the source and explanation of most saving and investment.

A great deal depends on whether the system is constrained exogenously by factor supply, or endogenously by demand. Generally, capacity, natural resources and labour supply, if fully employed, constitute parametric constraints. However, unfortunately for orthodox theory, most of the time the system is not so constrained: the problem is to sort out how and when the constraints do and do not operate. Capacity, of course, is not at all a constraint in the long run, nor, much of the time, in the short run: this has to be resolved by the Marxian accumulation analysis. Natural resources, contrary to the classical view, have not proved to be a serious constraint (though this may change in the future). Labour is the crucial element, much more complex: it is sometimes a constraint and sometimes not. In the course of a vigorous expansion, the supply of trained and disciplined labour tends to be exhausted. But in the longer time-span it has not been so: capitalism has been able to grow exponentially for two centuries, uninhibited by labour shortages. To begin with it inherited the endemic, rural surplus population; then came the natural increase through falling death rate, then large-scale migration, and, finally, the extraordinary technological efflorescence, which 'liberated' workers for the expansion of production. On the other hand, there clearly have been periods when demand pressed heavily on the labour supply, and others where it was not so. Thus whilst in the short run there is always an upper limit to growth, given by the effective labour supply, in the long run there is little or no limit:

labour becomes more or less an endogenous variable, growth being set by the rate of accumulation. As Marx indicated, labour shortage and high wages are a potent stimulant to the search for labour-saving innovations, and these stretch the labour supply to accommodate more growth. This complex behaviour of labour supply clearly transforms the problem and the solution: we get *no* limit to growth except the rate of accumulation, which thus helps to explain the great variations in the growth rate of capitalist economies.

Taking a simple view, one might characterize the history of industrial capitalism as follows: in the previous century capitalists enjoyed a highly elastic, cheap labour supply from agriculture, handicrafts and domestic labour. In our own century the rate of accumulation has been sufficiently large to exhaust this source, leading to a tendency for rising real wages to press on profits, with sharpened conflict over distribution. With the gradual introduction of automation, it is conceivable that there may be a reversion to the earlier condition. The original industrial revolution consisted essentially in the substitution of natural energy for human and animal energy. Animals were eliminated but not man, needed as machine-minder: now machines can mind machines. Though it is too soon to say, it is possible that a substantial portion of the labour force may be set 'free', thus creating a truly formidable Industrial Reserve Army.

Precisely this danger was foreseen, over thirty years ago, by Norbert Wiener, one of the principal creators of control theory:

Perhaps I may clarify the background of the present situation if I say that the first industrial revolution ... was the devaluation of the human arm by the competition of machinery.... The modern industrial revolution is similarly bound to devalue the human brain at least in its simpler and more routine decisions.... I have said that this new development has unbounded possibilities for good and for evil.... It gives the human race a new and most effective collection of mechanical slaves to perform its labour. Such mechanical labour has most of the economic properties of slave labour, although unlike slave labour, it does not involve the direct demoralizing effects of human cruelty. However, any labour that accepts the condition of competition with slave labour, accepts the conditions of slave labour, and is essentially slave labour. (Wiener 1948: 27)

This scenario raises the spectre of really massive unemployment and with it a new and more violent form of class conflict. The climate of the labour market under these conditions would probably be very different from that in the nineteenth century. Having finally tasted power and high wages, the working class is not likely to be as weak as formerly. On the other hand the great wealth of the modern world may and probably will be deployed to blunt protest by lavish social subventions.

Without attempting an explicit model, I will summarize what I have been trying to say. By combining elements from all three of our thinkers, one attains one good schema for the analysis of capitalism as a system in variable states of turmoil.

(1) Marx – the law of Moses and the prophets is profits and accumulation. But accumulation by itself would lead to falling profits, so another aspect of his theory was elaborated by

(2) Schumpeter – the driving force of capitalism is innovation in production (not in consumption, which is passive).

(3) The economic transmission mechanism is substantially constant over shortish periods, so that we can analyse its reactions to
   (a) new processes and goods and the resulting changes in relative prices, and
   (b) how other sectors shift to lower-cost processes in response to the changes in relative prices. Thus innovations, particularly in energy and transport, gradually infect the whole economy. Also necessary is

(4) Keynes, who taught us that effective demand, as well as, and more often than, the existing resources, determines the level and rate of change of output. This supplies the essential ingredient to Schumpeter's elaboration of Marx, showing how particular technological progress becomes generalized into a broad upsurge in the whole economy, though at very different rates for each sector.

The upper turning point creates little difficulty: we meet the accelerator in the middle of the upswing, so that the system becomes unstable. This means growth rates which cannot be sustained. The system becomes constrained by resources, by high relative prices for labour and for raw materials. Simultaneously, the growth rate decelerates and the real cost of production rises, which leads directly to inflation as the reaction of producers. This masks but cannot remove the real trouble which is deceleration. So investment is cut, expectations collapse dramatically, and the economy becomes stable downward to the level set by unsystematic expenditures, e.g. government outlays, foreign trade. There the economy sits until the arrival of a new innovation large enough to get it off the bottom. In this way we explain the historical specificity of each fluctuation. These movements are not strictly speaking cycles; they appear to be similar because the capitalist drive for profit means an eternal search for cost-reducing innovations, so that sooner or later growth is always renewed; but then it proceeds too rapidly and breaks down.

3 Schumpeter and Keynes as 'Rich Man's Karl Marxes'

MARTIN BRONFENBRENNER

By a 'rich man's Karl Marx' I mean an intellectual authority regarded by his followers, and usually by himself, as having provided a sufficient answer or alternative to Marxism over a significant portion of those social sciences – including history and philosophy as social sciences – over which Marx's own scholarship and insight had itself ranged. I also mean a man whose views are on balance substantially less threatening to the Establishment than those of Marx himself; hence the term 'rich man's Marx'. The term should not be taken to imply any 'selling out', even unconscious, to the upper classes, or any necessarily conservative, reactionary, or Fascistic slant to any of the doctrines in question. And finally, by a 'rich man's Marx' I mean someone at least superficially familiar with or at least knowledgeable about what has been called 'expository Marxism', whether or not Veblen's 'idle curiosity' or Joan Robinson's 'frivolous scholarship' had led him to plumb the Marxian *corpus* to its depths.

So I am specifically excluding thinkers, writers, and statesmen contemporary with or antecedent to Marx, who seem to have used proto-Marxian analysis of capitalism in support of doctrines far removed from Marxism. These range from G.W.F. Hegel in favor of the benevolent dictatorship of an organismic State, which may or may not have been patterned on the Prussian monarchy of his own day, to John C. Calhoun in defense of slavery in the American South, which he considered more benevolent than the capitalist labor market.[1]

I have presented elsewhere a partial and impressionistic listing of 'rich man's Marxes' from Eugen Dühring through Herbert Spencer and Vilfredo Pareto to Karl Popper and Talcott Parsons (Bronfenbrenner 1982: 97–8). Except for Schumpeter and Keynes, I shall go no further with that list. Instead, I propose to attempt three tasks:

First, to discuss the peculiar pervasiveness of the 'rich man's Marx' phenomenon in Western intellectual history – a pretentious and presumptuous activity for an obsolescent general economist with lily-white amateur standing as an intellectual historian.

Second, to consider whether Schumpeter, and more particularly Keynes, deserve the title of 'rich man's Marx'. (I shall conclude that they both do, and try to explain why.)

And third, let us assume that Marx was right about the self-destructive tendencies of capitalism as he saw it, and also that I understand in elementary fashion both what these tendencies were and how Marx saw capitalism. Then, how well do the Schumpeterian and Keynesian alternatives meet the Marxian challenge or modify the Marxian conclusions? Are they, in other words, any better, and if so how?

As for our first task: the literature abounds in polemics, often highly personal. Likewise in alternate systems and anti-systems. But how often do we find the two combined – and combined in different ways, and combined over and over again during a century or more? Anti-Machiavellianism has been the middle-class morality of political theory through the centuries, but where is a 'moralist's Machiavelli' to correspond to the 'rich man's Marx'? In economics, historicism, largely German, has been, with its American institutionalist descendant, an alternative to the Ricardian system of deductive classicism for perhaps 150 years, but personal and racial attacks on Ricardo, while by no means unknown, were in poor taste both before and after Hitler, and again, no 'Gentile's Ricardo'. One might call St Thomas Aquinas 'the Christian Aristotle' as well as 'the Angelic Doctor' – but in the sense of synthesis, reconciliation, possibly even syncretism between the theological doctrines of the Church and the philosophical principles of Athens. Even as one peruses the venomous history of religious disputation in the sixteenth and seventeenth centuries, it was the institutions of the Papacy and Inquisition, with their doctrinal underpinnings, rather than individual Popes and Inquisitors, on which the Protestants centered their fire. The Catholic side concentrated at times on arch-heretics along with heresy in general, but the identity of the arch-heretics varies from time to time and place to place – Luther, Calvin, Wyclif, Zwingli, Hus, Knox, and so on. Could one call St Ignatius Loyola 'the Catholics' heretic' for his counter-Reformation leadership (which I doubt), he certainly was never 'the Catholics' Luther' or 'the Catholics' Calvin'. Why are Marx and the Marxian case so different?

The principal reasons, I should like to suggest, are three. The first reason is the extent to which the Marx–Engels team towers over other collectivist thinkers like Rodbertus and Lassalle among the Socialists, or Proudhon and Bakunin among the Anarchists. The second reason is the manner in which Engels, a giant in his own right, contented himself to playing second fiddle or piano accompanist to Marx throughout their 40-year relationship and collaboration. The third and least important reason is Marx's own liking for sarcasm and invective.

Had Lassalle, for example, lived longer and developed further in the direction of modern Social Democracy, or had the relations between Marx and Engels come to approximate those between Lenin and Plekhanov, not only might 'scientific Socialism' have been a somewhat different body of doctrine, but little or no literature would be directed so pointedly against any one individual's ideas as we find directed against Marxism. To be blunt, Marx simply dominated Socialist thinking, although not Socialist practice, in a way that neither Luther nor Calvin dominated Protestantism, either in theology or in religious activities.

Passing on to my second task, I anticipate little disagreement with my 1980 inclusion of Schumpeter among the 'rich man's Marxes'. But the case of Keynes is very different. There was a red-baiting pamphlet entitled *Keynes at Harvard* dating back from the McCarthyite 1950s, in which certain influential Harvard alumni regarded Keynesian economics as a kind of stalking horse for the Marxian variety.[2] And of course Joan Robinson, Piero Sraffa, and their 'post-Keynesian'[3] followers at Cambridge and elsewhere use Keynes as a bridge to Marxism. I would therefore not myself have classified Keynes as a 'rich man's Marx' in 1980, but do so now after the receipt of a thus-far-unpublished manuscript by William Thweatt (Thweatt, s.a.), questioning the standard assumption among doctrinal historians that Keynes, unwilling to expend sufficient time and effort to 'make head or tail of Marx', let alone understand him, ignored him instead.[4] Thweatt agrees that 'Keynes' contempt for Marx was unmitigated,' reaching the point of claiming that 'the future will learn more from the spirit of [Silvio] Gesell than from that of Marx' (Keynes 1936: 355).[5]

But not only has Keynes read at least portions of *Das Kapital*, he referred to the second volume's C–M–C' and M–C–M' sequences in an early (1933) draft of the *General Theory* and engaged in epistolary controversy with the dramatist George Bernard Shaw on 'Marx's picture of the capitalist world, which had much verisimilitude in its day, but is now unrecognizable'. Keynes also hopes explicitly that, in overthrowing classical economics, the *General Theory* will knock away 'the Ricardian foundations of Marxism'.[6]

So I conclude as of 1983 that Keynes was indeed a 'rich man's Marx'. There is nothing original about the conclusion itself, for many Marxists seemingly thought as much from the outset. There was in the American radical press of the later 1930s considerable journalistic jargon reducing the *General Theory* to the creation of 'fictitious capital' as a means of cutting real wages, quite as though the word 'fictitious' settled any real issue. One of many and more reasoned statements include Mattick's *Marx and Keynes:*

Keynesianism merely reflects the transition of capitalism from its free-market to a state-aided phase, and provides an ideology for those who momentarily profit by this transition. It does not touch upon the problems Marx was concerned with. As long as the capitalist mode of production prevails, Marxism will retain its relevance. (Mattick 1969: 333)

The final task I set myself was to comment on both the Schumpeterian and Keynesian systems, not in themselves but as replies to Marx, and not in relation to each other. The task obviously transcends both the compass of this short essay and the abilities of its writer. What follows are little more than scattered notes, which will hopefully contribute more positively than negatively to the discussion.

Schumpeter: Three points, I believe, stand out in evaluating Schumpeter's 'rich man' rebuttals and modifications of Marxian economics on the domestic level.[7] These three points are: (1) intellectual *versus* the proletariat as prime mover of capitalist stagnation and/or collapse; (2) 'creative destruction' *versus* 'Marx's Law' of falling profit rate; (3) the truth or falsity of one or another form of Say's Law.

Ad (1): to rephrase the issue: suppose that *all* certified intellectuals without exception were 'Establishment intellectuals' – in economics, 'apologists for capitalism', 'vulgar economist', 'hired prize-fighters', etc., in the grand tradition of 'Thing-um-Bob, and What's-His-Name, and likewise, Never-Mind'. What difference would it have made? To Schumpeter, it would save capitalism, if I read the crucial chapter 13 of *Capitalism, Socialism, and Democracy* correctly (Schumpeter 1950b). To Marx, it would make no difference at all, except conceivably one of timing. The oppressed proletarians would create their own intellectuals, or proceed without any intellectuals at all. My suspicion is that, of these two exaggerated extremes, the Marxian is the less wrong, but the evidence is lacking.

Ad (2): Marx recognizes Schumpeter's 'creative destruction' – of capital, as a consequence of innovation – in all but name among the 'counteracting causes' impeding the operation of the 'Law of the Falling Tendency of the Rate of Profit' (Marx 1909: III, chapters 13–15).[8] But he does not, I think, consider the case which Schumpeter would later consider the historical norm, in which 'creative destruction' keeps both interest and pure profit both positive and reasonably constant over the long term as well as during sporadic booms. In this case, the 'counteracting cause' battles the 'law' to a standstill. Capitalism remains as exploitative as ever you please, but where are its contradictions and whence comes its breakdown? Here, it seems to me, Schumpeter has somewhat the better of the argument, unless 'creative destruction' on the Schumpeterian scale can be ruled out of court for the long term.

Ad (3): whatever may happen to the value of total output produced and its division between economic classes, where is demand to come from? Say's Law, that aggregate supply creates its own demand, is very much in point here. Marx denounces Say's Law in all its forms in no uncertain terms; Schumpeter has little to say about it other than as an aspect of the *History of Economic Analysis* (Schumpeter 1954: 618–25). There he denies it as an identity (independent of the price level), but appears to accept it in the attenuated form that at some positive price level – the equilibrium level, which may or may not be the current one – aggregate supply and demand are equal. Since, pathological cases apart,[9] I too accept Say's Law in this sense, I naturally agree with Schumpeter under a regime of price and wage flexibility. (But such a regime may of course be politically or socially unacceptable in a risk-averse 'fix-price' society!)

Keynes: I shall concentrate on only two points in evaluating Lord Keynes's 'rich man' alternative to Marxism, less completely on the domestic level. These two points are: (1) 'the preconceptions of Harvey Road' as to the consequences of guaranteed full employment, and (2) the political economy, as distinguished from the formal economics, of 'Keynesian' fiscal policies.

Ad (1): full employment – and then what? Keynes does not discuss the issue at length; not surprisingly, in the mid-1930s. He appears to believe that, with full employment guaranteed at money and real wages constant in the short term and rising gently over time in line with the national income, workers would be satisfied and class-harmony maintainable indefinitely.[10] This complacent hope has been called (originally, I believe, by Keynes's biographer, Sir Roy Harrod) 'the preconceptions of Harvey Road', which is the upper-middle-class street in Cambridge where Keynes spent his childhood,[11] and which represents no particular locality but Western middle-class intellectual thinking in general. Marx, on the other hand, can be interpreted as anticipating Samuel Gompers's confidence that workers would never be satisfied and would always want 'More!', so that it would be class-conflict or at least class cold-warfare that would persist indefinitely.

Marx seems thus far to have been obviously right (even in Socialist countries), to the discomfiture not only of anti-inflationary Keynesians but also of those post-Keynesian devotees and devisors of 'incomes policies' who have not 'gone Marxist' to the extent of 'socializing the flow' of non-labor income by degrees.[12] If unemployment, or the credible threat of unemployment, may not be used to hold the claims of particular workers – or the claims of 'labor' as a whole – in line, the substitute seems to be a propaganda monopoly from the cradle to the grave, enforced by martial law or the credible threat of martial law.[13]

Ad (2): let us now suppose (*pace* Monetarism and the Supply Side) that Keynesian fiscal policies as propounded by such first-generation Keynesians as A.P. Lerner and Alvin Hansen are capable by themselves of reaching and maintaining full employment without inflation. Marxian opposition, led in America by Paul Sweezy and the journal *Monthly Review*, still inquires as to the nature and the welfare implications of those policies themselves. This Marxian opposition sees Keynesianism as distorted in practice into the financing of imperialism and the war machine. I quote from what I believe to be Sweezy's initial published statement of this position:

The critique of Keynesian theories of liberal capitalist reform starts not from their economic logic but rather from their faulty (usually implicit) assumptions about the relationship, or perhaps one should say lack of relationship, between economics and political action. The Keynesians tear the economic system out of its social context and treat it as though it were a machine to be sent to the repair shop, there to be overhauled by an engineer state.

The presumption of liberal reform is that the state in capitalist society is an organ of society as a whole which can be made to function in the interests of society as a whole.

Now historically the state in capitalist society has always been first and foremost the guarantor of capitalist property relations. In this capacity it has been unmistakably the instrument of capitalist class rule. Again speaking historically, control over capital accumulation has never been regarded as a concern of the state; economic legislation has rather had the aim of blunting class antagonisms so that accumulation could go forward smoothly. All this presupposes relatively unlimited opportunities for capital to expand. When this condition no longer obtains, is it not possible that the norms of state policy should change? Hence our problem can be reduced to the form: is it possible for the state within the framework of capitalist society to act against the interests of capital provided such action is desirable in the interests of society as a whole?

It must be emphasized that we have to do here with a deliberate policy of restricting accumulation and raising consumption with a view of benefitting the producers. Capitalists could not be expected to adopt such a program as their own, so long as another way out exists – and another way out always does exist along the path of foreign expansion. 'Where', as Lenin bluntly asked, 'except in the imagination of sentimental reformers, are there any trusts capable of interesting themselves in the condition of the masses instead of the conquest of colonies?' Until this question has been answered, we assume that capital will, if it has the choice, decide for imperialist expansion as against internal reform. Moreover we must assume that capital and its political representatives will actively oppose any movements designed to realize liberal reform. (Sweezy 1942: 340–50)[14]

What is one to make of all this? Or rather remake, for the argument is middle-aged, with paunch and whiskers?

For one thing, the welfare-state aspects of Western capitalism have been on the rise; no one could now call them merely cosmetic. To that extent, Sweezy has been wrong and so, by implication, has Marx.

But whether more or less than the 'social spending' budget, the military budget has been rising too. The 'Brandt Report' of 1980 puts the issue in real terms and in a foreign-aid context (Independent Commission on International Development Issues 1980: 14).[15]

The military expenditure of only half a day suffice to finance the whole malaria eradication programme of the World Health Organization.

A modern tank costs about $1 million; that amount could improve storage facilities for 100,000 tons of rice and save 400 tons annually; one person lives on just over a pound a day. The same sum could provide 1000 classrooms for 30,000 children.

For the price of one jet fighter ($20 million) one could set up about 40,000 village pharmacies.

One half of one per cent of one year's world military expenditure would pay for all the farm equipment needed to increase food production and approach self-sufficiency in food-deficit low-income countries by 1990.

Western military spending, in particular, simultaneously responds to a real Soviet threat and reinforces the real Soviet fear – remember 1812, 1854, 1914, and 1941! – which has itself been partially responsible for the threat in the first place. (Some call this a vicious circle; others *Catch-22*. Both are correct.)

Here is an unthinkable thought-experiment for a Man from Mars, whom we presume to be a Marxist of the Sweezy (underconsumptionist) persuasion: The U.S.S.R. takes some giant step toward unilateral disarmament. The U.S.

follows at least half way. If one takes underconsumptionist Marxism seriously, there is a depression in the U.S. What happens next in the U.S.? Keynesian forecast: expansion of U.S. civilian spending and/or reduction in U.S. taxes. Some sort of welfare-state *cum* private-sector revival. Leninist (surely also Marxist) forecast: there may be a collapse and then a Socialist take-over in the U.S..[16] But the more likely outcome is that the U.S. manufactures some sort of threat to world peace (from the U.S.S.R. or a Soviet ally) somewhere in the world, raises military spending again, and blackmails the U.S.S.R. or its ally to do whatever the U.S. desires – all for the sake of world peace. The Best Possible Outcome (no war!) from the Soviet viewpoint: a return to the predisarmament *status quo* on a basis somewhat more favorable to the U.S., somewhat less favorable to themselves, than if they had not 'let their guard down'.

Now an unthinkable question for the unthinkable thought-experimenter: would you, as a Marxian Man from Mars, advise the U.S.S.R. to take this chance and begin a disarmament race? (On the basis of considerable subordinate experience during World War II in an intelligence branch of the U.S. Armed Services, I could hardly advise 'them' to trust 'us' and take that first major unilateral step. And why then should I, or Sweezy, advise 'us' to trust 'them' to the extent of disarming first as a test of Marxian dynamic theory?)

Until some such unthinkable thought-experimentation can in fact be justified by 'the other answer' to our unthinkable question, it seems quite impossible to confirm or disconfirm this vital evaluation issue in the 'Marx–Keynes' debate. Whether one's personal views are nearer to Marx than to Keynes, this is an unhappy note on which to end my share of this discussion, which I shall nevertheless do, becoming even less happy in the process.

Notes

1   Calhoun is in fact called 'the Marx of the Master Class' by Richard Hofstadter on the basis of his hostility to Northern capitalism (Hofstadter 1948: chapter 4).

2   Not a difficult task for anyone who 'sees Communists under the bed', in view of Keynes's views in chapters 23 and 24 of the *General Theory* on the distribution of income and wealth, 'euthanasia of the rentier', public investment, public control of private investment, etc.!

3   To me at least, the Cambridge post-Keynesians owe less to Keynes than to Michal Kalecki. Kalecki had derived (in Polish, and from a Marxist background) a Keynesian-type macroeconomic system independently of the one Keynes had worked out from his own Marshallian background. Kalecki may or may not have temporal priority over Keynes; his system is mathematically more sophisticated. Its influence in the West dates from the 1940s when he was in England as a refugee. On Kalecki, see Feiwel 1975: especially chapters 1 and 2; and Joan Robinson 1976.

4   Keynes may, however, have relied on Cambridge associates, particularly Piero Sraffa, for his knowledge of *Das Kapital*, rather than on his own first-hand explorations. But one of the first things I personally learned from the *General*

Theory, because it was a footnote on the first page of chapter 1, was that the term 'classical economics' comes from Marx (Keynes 1936: 3n.).

5 For Gesell, see Keynes 1936: chapter 23, section 6. The main features of Gesell's *Freiland-Freigeld* proposal were the shifting of taxation to land value (Henry George, modified) and the abolition of interest on money by a 'stamped-money' plan which imposed carrying charges on its holder and therefore reduced 'liquidity preference' for money over physical capital. (The term 'liquidity preference' is not itself in Gesell.)

6 These quotations are from Keynes, and were amplified as follows: 'I know that [*Das Kapital*] is historically important, and I know that many people, not all of whom are idiots, find it a sort of Rock of Ages and continuing inspiration. Yet when I look at it, it is to me inexplicable that it can have this effect. Its dreary, out-of-date, academic controversialism seems so extraordinarily unsuitable.... I feel just the same about the *Koran*. How could either of these books carry fire and sword around half the world? It beats me.' (To which Shaw replied: 'Lord help you, you know nothing ... and Cambridge had convinced you that you know everything ... the typical university result.') Thweatt digests all this and much more from vol. 28 Keynes's *Collected Writings*.

7 The international dimension, including imperialism and war, I omit.

8 I refer especially to the 'destructive' aspect of innovation, which lowers, at least temporarily, the organic composition of capital.

9 The principal 'pathology' I have in mind is the non-positive elasticity of the aggregate demand function with respect to the price level – which many Keynesians consider not pathological at all, but the normal state of affairs!

10 A situation known in contemporary China as 'the iron rice bowl'!

11 Several participants at the Groningen symposium pointed out that Keynes died in April 1946, well before 'Harvey Road' had been disconfirmed by wage pushfulness in Britain, America, or elsewhere. Keynes tended, in his policy recommendations, to deal with one complex of problems at a time, and aggregate demand had been the pressing problem of the 1930s. It may therefore be unfair to ascribe to him, as my text does, helplessness in the face of cost-push inflation, which was to become the pressing problem of the 1950s.

12 'Incomes policy can be ineffective or even self-defeating, and is always either an instrument for the preservation of the *status quo* or out-rightly iniquitous. In the current experience of advanced capitalist countries, the striking class connotations of incomes policy are hidden under the guise of appeals to the "national interest".... To add insult to injury, this kind of policy can only be enforced and is being enforced by governments commanding popular and union support' (Nuti 1972: 441). (Nuti is a post-Keynesian on the Marxist fringe; the policies he is attacking are strictly Keynesian ones with no 'socialization of the flow'.)

13 This paper does not develop further the above allusion to the harshness of allegedly Socialist societies operating *pod Zamenem Marksizma*, 'under the Marxist Banner'. Professor Y.S. Brenner, my discussant at the Groningen symposium, wondered whether this harshness might be causing Marxism to lose its appeal, to the extent that Keynesian ideas might now be more threatening to the Establishment (in North America and Northern Europe) than those of Marx. (This might make of Keynes 'a poor man's Marx' and Marx 'a rich man's Keynes'.) This is suggestive for a possible future, even though Marx was neither Stalin nor Marshal Jaruzelski. But it is surely wrong for the past and present, particularly in the Third World.

14 In later presentations of the thesis, military spending (with cost-plus contracts to safeguard capitalist profits) is presented as the only permissible vehicle for more-than-cosmetic fiscal expansion of the Keynesian type, and foreign expansion takes

second place (Baran and Sweezy 1966: chapter 7). Sweezy's (currently) latest treatment of Keynes is relatively favorable, since Keynes is given credit for concern with long-term issues while his 'orthodox' followers have allegedly reduced his insights to one more business-cycle theory (Sweezy and Magdoff 1983).

15 'World' figures of course include both Socialist and capitalist countries.

16 Not an exclusively Left forecast. During the summer of 1975, my class at the University of Colorado Economic Institute (all non-Americans, most from Third World countries) were taken to visit defense plants in the Denver area. (I was unable to accompany the class.) It so happened that I had just been lecturing on stagnationism, including the Marxian theory of Baran and Sweezy's *Monopoly Capital*. My enterprising students asked their guides the probable economic results of U.S. disarmament. They were told, they said, that disarmament would send the U.S. back to the Great Depression – precisely the Marxist answer, from management people in the military–industrial complex!

4 Laws of the Market and Laws of Motion: An Essay in Comparative Social History

JAN A. KREGEL

> The issues which Keynes had raised were not, in England, a source of political division; in America they were. It was quite easy, in England, to be a conservative Keynesian; that, on the whole was where I stood myself. But in America (at least in 1946) if one was conservative in one's politics, one must be anti-Keynesian in one's economics. (Hicks 1963: 311)

> A man may accept Marx's analytical work entirely and yet be a conservative in practice. (Schumpeter 1954: 133, n. 18)

The aim of my discussion is to try to explain Hicks' statement by reference to the economic discussions of the inter-war period in the U.K. and the U.S. The current relevance of such a discussion derives from the fact that it indirectly raises the question: 'Where have all the "conservative" Keynesians gone?'; for our current economic predicament may be traced most directly to the extermination of that species of Keynesian. Their resurrection may be vitally important to any hope of permanent recovery of our economic and political systems.

I

As the argument is complicated it may aid understanding to trace its broad outlines before providing details. Its basic message is that economies tend to go wrong when there is a predominance of professional opinion in favour of either the law of the market or the law of motion. The great economists, and in particular the three we seek to assess here, never lost sight of the importance of the combined operation of these two laws. If they erred, it was in underestimating the difficulties of their successful combination.

In the U.K. the inter-war economic discussion centred on Keynes and Hayek. At the time it appeared to be primarily a *political*, rather than *theoretical* discussion. Keynes' opinion, advocating evolutionary change in order to preserve the democratic capitalist system, found favour with the socialist parties. Hayek and Robbins accused Keynes of supporting *national-socialist* policies. They proposed instead the 'proper' operation of the international gold standard.

31

This debate, as it developed, became more and more concerned with points of pure economic theory – the laws of motion vs. the laws of the market of my title. Keynes' position was predominant in this debate, and it became established with the immediate post-war dominance of the Labour party. In simple terms Keynes and Hayek were divided on the choice of *le plus grand mal* threatening the capitalist system. For the former it was unemployment, for the latter it was *inflation*. They also disagreed on remedies; Keynes preferred an all-seeing government capable of stabilising a sufficiently high level of investment to preserve the 'Law of motion' according to which the capitalist system is doomed if it cannot grow sufficiently rapidly to provide employment for its labour force. If the problem was not solved by democratic means, Keynes was certain that other less acceptable ways would be found. He had already seen them at work in the Soviet Union. Hayek preferred an automatic counter-cyclical mechanism which would preserve the 'law of the market'. If this law could not be preserved, and with it private property and initiative, the solution to the breakdown of the democratic state that would be caused by hyper-inflation could be seen in the rise in the 'corporate state' dictatorship of Germany and Italy (cf. Parquez 1981).

Hayek was eventually convinced that something had to be done to the operation of the system to preserve the level of output. The dispute became a technical question over what and how. In the event the political victory of the Labour party turned Keynesianism into a justification for the Welfare State, shifting emphasis from Keynes' idea of the State as the 'investor of last resort' to the 'employer of last resort'. In 1946 Hicks could be a conservative Keynesian, twenty years later this implied a political decision similar to that which Hicks found in the U.S.; Keynes, the sceptical liberal of the 1930s, had become the champion of the working class.

In the U.S. developments were rather different as the Depression had voided the political argument of substance. Hoover, a Republican, had clearly failed to stop the slump, Roosevelt and the Democrats offered a new approach. For those not familiar with U.S. political history President Reagan's penchant for quoting Roosevelt in support of his budget measures must have raised doubts about the political affiliation of the new administration's policy. In fact, Roosevelt believed in balanced budgets and continued to do so until the setback of 1937. He was also elected on a platform supporting the gold standard. To be generous to Roosevelt's economic policy one can say that he was catholic – he tried everything, not from idealism but more from frustration. On the other hand, the most ardent 'Keynesian' in the administration was a private banker whom Roosevelt appointed head of the Federal Reserve, Marriner Eccles, responsible for the 1935 Bank Act – and certainly no wide-eyed radical. Thus U.S. policy was not the result of theoretical debate in which a clear position concerning the role of government in the economy emerged, nor did Keynes have any great emphasis on U.S. economic policy. The difference between Hoover and Roosevelt was purely political and the Democratic party became associated with those aspects of Roosevelt's policy,

WPA, etc., which epitomised 'big government' intervention and spending deficits. In the U.S. Keynes thus came to be associated with a particular *political* position that evolved without theoretical discussions similar to those of the U.K. It is interesting to note that when Eccles suggested that government expenditure should be reduced in step with recovery towards normal capacity levels, he was countered by the Treasury and eventually relieved of his position when he suggested spending should be reduced and attempted to counter continued Treasury borrowing. The famous Fed 'accord' was not a monetarist declaration of independence, but rather a Keynesian declaration of independence from populist democratic policies! Nonetheless Schumpeter's position in 1946 (the last sentence of the quotation from Hicks at the beginning of this essay refers to Schumpeter) was clearly one of political preference which implied a theoretical position (cf. Hicks 1963: 311 and n. 1). It was only in the 1950s and 1960s, some 30 years after the U.K., that the U.S. had its theoretical debate, which was won, just as in the U.K., by the Keynesians, by now under the euphemism of the 'neo-classical synthesis' to appease McCarthyites: 'Now the new American economics (it is sufficient to think of the work of Samuelson and Leontief) has not, in its most characteristic respects, been particularly Keynesian; and the rest of the Cambridge tradition has been even more foreign to it' (Hicks 1963: 312).

Thus in 1946 Hicks found in the U.S., in difference from the U.K., a perfect identification between a political and economic position. After 30 years of Welfare State in the U.K. the same position was to emerge (despite the fact that Keynes' theory was not practised consistently in this period) and Hicks as a conservative Keynesian must have become a very lonely figure. In the U.S., the 1960 infusion of the neo-classical synthesis into the Democratic party of the New Frontier and the Great Society meant that the U.S. never had a period in which one could be a 'conservative' Keynesian (aside from the interval between Nixon's 1971 statement that 'we're all Keynesians now' and his impeachment!). At the same time, Hayek's primordial preoccupation with inflation became more timely so that political and economic conservatism was forced into a coherent position, capable of exploiting the inflationary conditions of the early 1970s leading them to political power, but without the important concession Hayek had made concerning the necessity of a properly functioning international adjustment mechanism. The wheel had come full circle, and world economic discussion returned to 1930. But this time there were no conservative Keynesians (or even radical Hayekians) to warn against the extremes of the law of the market. The depression that has resulted rivals the 1930s.

II

The debate was born and was conditioned by two factors of experience, inflation in post-war Germany and a number of other European countries in the 1920s (cf. Bresciani-Turroni 1937; Keynes 1971: IV) and the depressed trade conditions and rising unemployment. The predominant policy issue was discussion of the return to gold. For Keynes

the fluctuations in the value of money since 1914 have been on a scale so great as to constitute, with all that they involve, one of the most significant events in the economic history of the modern world. The fluctuations of the standard, whether gold, silver or paper, has not only been of unprecedented violence, but has been visited on a society of which the economic organisation is more dependent than that of any earlier epoch on the assumption that the standard of value would be moderately stable.

But 'since 1920 those countries which have regained control of their financial situation, not content with bringing the inflation to an end, have contracted their supply of money and have experienced the fruits of deflation' (Keynes 1971: IV, 1–2).

Keynes concluded by recommending active control of 'the supply of currency and credit with a view to maintaining so far as possible, the stability of the internal price level' (ibid.: 141), a position which was also maintained by Cassel as early as 1921 (cf. Cassel 1921 and 1936). It was also suggested by Sraffa (1920). It does not seem, however, to have had much success in the U.S., where the gold parity has been maintained with the exception of Roosevelt's experiment with a random float in 1933–4.

As most commentators recognised, what was in question was the survival of the gold-standard mechanism of international adjustment. 'In truth, the gold standard is already a barbarous relic.... A regulated non-metallic standard has slipped in unnoticed. *It exists*' (Keynes 1971: IV, 138). From this point of view a return to the gold standard was already impossible in the 1920s. Events proved Keynes and Cassel to be right.

After the breakdown of the British attempt to return sterling to its pre-war gold parity Keynes shifted his policy position from promotion of public works and tariffs to advocating a low long-term rate of interest (an argument that was impossible under the gold standard given the limited use of the rate of interest for internal policy). The Ottawa Conference of 1931 which created the sterling bloc rejected a return to gold as premature and endorsed a policy of price raising via cheap money lent for purely 'commercial' purposes. (Cf. Moggridge and Howson 1974: 234; Keynes 1972: IX, 139, 243–9; Keynes 1971: V, VI). Drummond describes the intricate process which produced this agreement, showing that the determination of the Bank of England's definition of 'domestic' sterling 'management' included the Empire (Drummond 1981). It is at this time that Keynes gave up support of policy to restrict trade which he had defended along with public works policies under the gold standard.

Keynes' policy position was based on his theoretical arguments in his *Treatise on Money*, which contained a detailed analysis of the gold exchange standard and recommendations for its replacement with a system of domestic monetary management to stabilise domestic prices and set the exchange rate at the level compatible with those prices. (Cf. Keynes 1971: VI, 211–408, especially chapters 31 and 36.)

Thus, in the immediate aftermath of the Wall Street Crash and the British abandonment of the gold standard, Keynes' position was identical to that of the British government as expressed at the Ottawa Conference. This position not only rejected an early return to the gold standard, it placed most of the blame for the U.K.'s continued trade depression on it. In its place Keynes had recommended direct management of monetary policy to keep long-term interest rates low enough to make investment attractive.

This position was sharply criticised, first by Lionel Robbins and then by Hayek (who had arrived in the U.K. in 1931). Robbins' *The Great Depression* (1934) provides an explanation of the depression in terms of a change in the relation between the money and natural rates of interest which first produced an inflation which, when brought to a halt, produced depressed conditions. Robbins presumes that money rates had fallen below the natural rate (although it is not clear which moved relative to the other). This caused plans for new investment to run ahead of available savings: a 'Hayek process' whereby the investments could not be completed because saving was insufficient, hence the Crash (Robbins 1934: 46–8). Robbins presents statistical data for his argument and claims to find support for his position in all his statistics except the price data:

> the price-level was almost stationary – if anything, tending to fall slightly. At first sight this appears to be incompatible with the suggestion of an inflationary boom, and there can be no doubt that it was the more or less stable condition of the price-level which blinded contemporary observers to the real nature of what was going on at the time. So long as the price-level remains stationary, they urged, there can be no fear of inflation. A little reflection, however, should show that this belief is fallacious. A stationary price-level shows an absence of inflation only when production is stationary. When productivity is increasing, then, in the absence of inflation, we should expect prices to fall. Now the period we are examining was a period of rapidly increasing productivity. The comparative stability of prices, therefore, so far from being a proof of the absence of inflation is a proof of its presence. (Robbins 1934: 48–9)

He goes on to support his position by quoting 'Mr J.M. Keynes', who 'was one of the chief influences in the world calling for more and more cheap money' and who had written in the *Treatise*: 'whilst there was probably no material inflation up to the end of 1927, a profit inflation developed sometime between that date and the summer of 1929'. (Keynes 1971: VI, 170)

Robbins presents evidence to show that it was Federal Reserve Policy in 1927 to bring down interest rates due to the large inflow of gold prior to that date that caused the final stage of the boom.[1] It was the excessive optimism of this boom, leading to investment decisions in excess of available savings, that made the crash inevitable. Keynes' support of easy money thus contributed to the severity of the depression by aggravating the excessive investment of the boom. Robbins identifies this policy as 'socialist', but notes that

> such a policy is not confined to the Socialists ... their opponents, the dictators and the reactionaries, are inspired by the same ideas. It is a complete misapprehension to

suppose that the victory of the Nazis and the fascists is a defeat for the forces making for the destruction of capitalism. They have the same fanatical hatred of economic liberalism, the same hopes of a planned society.... The policies which at present prevail have been adopted, not because they have been forced on politicians by the masses, but because the masses have been taught to believe them. The masses, as such, do not think for themselves; they think what they are taught to think by their leaders. And the ideas which, for good or for bad, have come to dominate policy are the ideas which have been put forward in the first instance by detached and isolated thinkers. If the direction of policy ... today is overwhelmingly socialist ... it is because men of intellect, with powers of reason and persuasion, have conceived the socialistic idea and gradually persuaded their fellows. It is the same with monetary policy. The measures of the last decade have been the result ... of the influence of a number of men whose names could be counted on the fingers of two hands. We do not appreciate fully the tragedy of this aspect of the present situation unless we realise that it is essentially the work of men of intellect and good will. In the short run, it is true, ideas are unimportant and ineffective, but in the long run they can rule the world. (Robbins 1934: 197–200)

To my knowledge no one has ever commented on the clear criticism of Keynes' position or the clear relation between this passage and what must be considered as Keynes' reply in his subsequent book (the *General Theory*) defending this position. Keynes' passage is sufficiently well known not to be quoted here.

In a series of lectures at the Graduate Institute of International Studies in Geneva (published in 1937) Hayek returned to the charge, attacking the idea of a managed currency as 'monetary nationalism' and identifying the 'name of their leading exponent, Mr J.M. Keynes' (Hayek 1937: 2). One does well to recall that the tri-partite currency agreement dates from late 1936, while Germany had established currency restrictions in 1931 and bilateral trading emerged in 1933,[2] in assessing Hayek's concern for Keynesian policy, which was 'largely responsible for the particular intensification of the last depression which was brought about by the successive breakdown of the different currency systems' and 'is likely to deal a fatal blow to the hopes of a revival of international economic relations' (Hayek 1937: 3). Although careful not to accuse Keynes of 'any sort of narrow nationalism' and claiming interest only in 'the arid regions of abstract theory' (ibid.: 2–3), he was 'profoundly convinced that it is an academic discussion of this sort which in the long run forms public opinion and which in consequence decides what will be practical politics some time hence' (ibid.: p. xii). The equation between cheap-money policies and authoritarianism (either national socialism or communism) and economic planning is clear. It should not be necessary to point out that the discussions of allocative efficiency under socialism involving Mises, Hayek, Lange, Taylor, Lerner, Knight, etc., reached their height in precisely this period; Hayek's *Collectivist Economic Planning* appeared in 1935 (Hayek 1935).

Hayek's lectures were meant not only to show that the policy of managing the currency so as to stabilise the price level was impossible because a stable price level was neither desirable nor conceivable, but also to trace the ideal policy. This involved re-establishing the gold standard and abolishing fractional reserve banking so as to allow it to work properly. Only in this way could disturbing changes in the *general* price level be avoided (both inflation *and* deflation) and the relative price mechanism operate to produce economic efficiency via the market mechanism.

With stable money the constraint of the balance sheet would give clear guidance for structural adjustment: profit and loss automatically produce adjustment without need for government intervention. Those making losses are driven out of the market while the profitable enterprises attract competition. This 'law of the market' would give an objective and automatic mechanism which would adapt to change in external conditions without the instability that had been experienced under the inappropriate operation of the gold standard in the 1930s.

Keynes replied directly to this challenge in the final passages of the last chapter of the *General Theory*. First, he discards Hayek's and Robbins' political argument by an outright rejection of socialism (Keynes had visited Stalin's Russia in 1925 and 1928 and the famous exchange with H.G. Wells on the Soviet Union predates the *General Theory*) stating clearly his preference for free markets over detailed planning: 'But if our central controls succeed in establishing an aggregate volume of output corresponding to full employment as nearly as it is practicable, the classical theory comes into its own again from this point onwards' (Keynes 1973: VII, 378). In case there is any doubt that Keynes means the free-market *mechanism* (and not classical theory per se) by his reference to 'classical':

I agree with Gesell that the result of filling in the gaps in the classical theory is not to dispose of the 'Manchester System', but to indicate the nature of the environment which the free play of economic forces requires if it is to realise the full potentialities of production. The central controls necessary to ensure full employment will, of course, involve a large extension of the traditional functions of government. Furthermore, the modern classical theory has itself called attention to various conditions in which the free play of economic forces may need to be curbed or guided. But there will still remain a wide field for the exercise of private initiative and responsibility. Within this field the traditional advantages of individualism will still hold good. (ibid.: 379–80)

Finally, Keynes warns against the position that things will improve if left to themselves:

the authoritarian state systems of to-day seem to solve the problem of unemployment at the expense of efficiency and freedom. It is certain that the world will not much longer tolerate the unemployment which apart from brief intervals of excitement, is associated – and, in my opinion, inevitably associated – with present-day capitalistic individualism. But it may be possible by a right analysis of the problem to cure the disease whilst preserving efficiency and freedom. (ibid.: 381).

Keynes thus counters that unless some active policy is undertaken, the result most feared by Robbins and Hayek, solution by autocratic means, would nonetheless come about, not from inflation, but from massive unemployment.

The solution Keynes proposed in the *General Theory* was even less acceptable to Robbins and Hayek than his earlier policy of a managed currency. Keynes reduced his emphasis on direct government interference in monetary mechanisms, but now recommended direct government intervention in economic decision-making! Keynes' challenge was related not so much to the question of the merits of government control or economic planning, as to his questioning of the 'law of the market' as a basis for economic adjustment and decision-making. Just as Hayek had challenged price stability as a meaningless objective, Keynes similarly challenged the objective of establishing the law of the market *unless full employment is assured* by means independent of the operation of the market.

As was quickly recognised Keynes' theory implied that economic efficiency was to be judged relative to the level of demand. Robbins had applied the objective law of the market when he referred to the policy of giving relief to 'firms whose position was fundamentally sound' and forcing liquidation on 'firms whose position was fundamentally unsound' (Robbins 1934: 72–3). But the 'soundness' of a firm, as determined by the 'law' of the market, depended on being able to define the normal or natural level of savings which was available to support investment when there were no 'monetary disturbances' if this position was not continually in existence in the market. Sraffa (1932) had already argued that this position could not be given theoretical definition. Keynes went a step further, stating that the level of demand would determine profitability. Once savings were recognised as being determined by income, it was demand that dominated the 'law' of the market. It was necessary to distinguish between an 'unsound' position due to 'malinvestment' and one due to lack of effective demand which would be perfectly 'sound' in conditions of full employment. But this made the law of the market meaningless for policy unless the system was continuously at full employment. In the 1930s it clearly was not. It also eliminated the possibility of an exogenous, automatic arbiter for economic policy. Hayek had advanced his theory on the basis of full employment; he eventually recognised that such a position would not be automatically produced even by the correct operation of the pure gold standard. He continued to search for an *automatic* mechanism that would support the law of the market, preserving individual liberty and minimising the perils of 'undemocratic' social control by central government.

Joan Robinson quickly saw the force of Keynes' argument and analysed the distinction between 'frictional' and involuntary unemployment in the same terms. On the one hand, 'the strength of the frictions largely depends upon the state of effective demand. When the general level of employment is high the frictions are weak .... The man who is "unemployable" in bad times will find, when labour is scarce, that his services are required after all' (Robinson 1937: 40–1). If even the bench-mark of full employment became relative, it became impossible to use market results of profitability as an objective measure for policy.

Townshend (1937) took up Keynes' extension of Sraffa's criticism to emphasise that effective demand would itself affect relative prices and these changes would themselves lead to changes in output and income, or to different rates of growth and saving. Here, all the 'objective' standards of the law of the market – relative prices and profitability – become relative to the rate of expansion of demand. The 'law of motion' replaces the 'law of the market'. Keynes clearly succeeded in 'pointing out that' in Hayek's theory of the law of the market the 'factual assumptions are seldom or never satisfied, with the result that it cannot solve the economic problems of the actual world' (Townshend 1937: 378). In the late 1930s the soup and bread lines attested to Keynes' position, as did the feeling of bankers and businessmen who clearly recognised that their economic failure was due to something other than excessive expansion in the U.S. money supply in the late 1920s or their productive inefficiency as reflected, via the law of the market, in their operating losses. Indeed, it is often bankers who, faced with the charge that they have made excessively risky loans, immediately notice that the general level of activity is something outside individual control and for which they cannot rightly be blamed. Loans that go bad as a result of demand failures are not due to the individual borrower's failure or to the banker's lack of vigilance, and both rightly refuse responsibility for them.

Although Keynes clearly believed that his proposals for government control of investment would be sufficient to produce full employment which would allow the preservation of individual freedom and the law of the market, Hayek clearly did not agree. In his view Keynes' approach would involve the government in every aspect of economic life. The absence of the law of the market would turn the government into the final arbiter of economic relations.

For example, in the traditional theory of the free market inability to repay debt was an indication of the negative judgement of the market on an individual undertaking. But not only was the individual expulsed by the market, he was expulsed from society: 'to fail ... is to commit theft', in the words of Balzac's *Eugénie Grandet*.[3] If one failed on borrowed money in almost all societies, the lender could claim the right to restitution enforced by law. Even before Keynes, bankruptcy laws served to protect bankrupts, but the implication of Keynes' theory was to absolve the bankrupt from personal responsibility, for he could not be held responsible for the failure of the system to produce a level of aggregate demand sufficiently high to permit him to survive profitably in the market. The initial response to the recognition of this fact was the introduction by government of full employment acts, implicitly accepting government responsibility for individual failure. This was eventually extended to the responsibility of government in meeting the losses of individuals (nationalisation is the best example) in order to preserve the 'motion' of the system. Thus something as fundamental to the operation of the law of the market as private debt contracts became subject to government adjudication, and debtors could pass the default claim to the government, which had implicitly defaulted on its guarantee to provide the full employment level of effective demand, to make good individual incomes.

In the hands of Keynesians such as Lerner, who innovated the policy of 'functional finance', Keynesian policy measures to preserve the level of demand did, in fact, enter individual market relationships via the effect of taxation policies on individual effort. It has never been easy for private citizens to understand why in a boom their disposable incomes should fall as a result of government fiscal policy to dampen demand. Here we find the now famous 'supply-siders' wedge', which distorts the market relation between individual effort and real income, as a direct result of the application of aggregate economic policy!

While Keynes believed that government intervention could be limited to securing a sufficient overall level of investment, Hayek was convinced that such a policy would lead to social control, with the government involved in every aspect of economic relations, replacing the law of the market with arbitrary decisions. In the event, the result in Europe was the Welfare State, which combined more individual liberty than Hayek expected, but much more direct government intervention in the form of direct individual income supports than Keynes expected – transfer payments replaced capital expenditure as the expression of the law of motion.

Keynes had already pointed out that the implications of his theory, relative to the then current *socialist* alternatives, were 'Conservative'. Yet his theory was quickly taken up in Labour party circles:

we may ask, if Mr Keynes' aims are fulfilled, what remains of capitalism, except only so much as we on our side are perfectly willing to retain? The central controls of monetary policy will be in public hands; so also will be capital accumulation; the rate of interest will be reduced to next to nothing by the increase in the volume of capital, in the interest of full employment; all this will go in hand with a fully developed policy of social services, aided by redistributive taxation and the public control of investment. What more could any member of the Labour Party, or does the Party in fact, ask for? (Rowse 1936: 36)

Robertson (1936: 91–2) put the relation between Keynes and his opponents starkly: 'Let me try to summarize the opposing view points.... "You are a defeatist!" cries Party A. "You are a Communist", replies Party B, "or if you aren't you should be. For nothing short of a completely authoritarian State could cope with the immense problems of transfer and readjustment, let alone fiscal embarrassment, in which your policy will land if you carry it out to the bitter end."'

The coupling of Keynes' theory with the Labour party and the post-war electoral success of welfare policies put forward by that party certainly laid the basis for the link between Keynes, budget deficits and income maintenance transfers. I have argued elsewhere (Kregel 1983) that this link does not represent Keynes' policy recommendations. It was not, however, this linkage which resolves the paradox suggested by Hicks' statement given above, which is rather to be found in the outbreak of the war.

Keynes' theory is often described as applying to depression conditions. But the explanation of the fact that it was Keynes' *theory* viewed independently of *any* political positions (in contrast to the views of Robbins and Hayek) that predominated discussion can be discovered in the fact that Keynes was able to apply his theory instantly to the conditions of preparation for war – i.e. full employment. It was the complete victory of Keynes' *How to Pay for the War* as the framework of orthodox war planning that produced the post-war conditions in which Hicks could declare himself (as could Harrod, Meade, Hawtrey, etc.) a 'conservative' Keynesian. After the war, Keynes' theory had distanced itself from any particular political connection – it had held sway in the Treasury throughout a Conservative war government.

Here it is important to distinguish Keynes' formal proposals for the war economy, which were not in fact fully adopted, from the link they provided to adapting Keynes' earlier work to the problems of excess demand in war conditions. 'Experts had absorbed his doctrine that inflation was not primarily a matter of the volume of bank deposits, but of the relation between the propensity to save and capital (or war) outlay.... This kind of thinking had begun to permeate official quarters'. (Harrod 1951: 492)

The problems of war finance centre upon the question of inflation. As Keynes remarked he had been cognisant of all the discussion of war-time inflation that took place in Britain during the First World War, and never was it discussed in terms remotely resembling those in which he now presented the problem. Yet now, in 1940, his method of analysis was accepted both by those who were willing and by those who were not willing to support his practical proposals. (ibid.: 190)

It is interesting to note Hayek's recent statement that 'I soon found myself supporting Keynes in his struggle against war-time inflation'. (Hayek 1983:48)

Harrod put the same point with reference to

the question whether easy money was desirable during the war.... In the First War it was regarded as axiomatic that, if the government was to have success in borrowing ... it would have to offer a rate of interest above normal. This was considered to be an axiom flowing from the most elementary theory of supply and demand. Keynes held that it was not an axiom, not even in fact true, but a fallacy. This may well be the most notable case in history in which a new economic doctrine, advanced on purely theoretical grounds, challenged by many, infuriating to some, was proved by a laboratory experiment – war – to be correct. (Harrod 1951: 90–1)

Keynes' final *theoretical* victory can be identified in Hayek's admission that counter-cyclical measures might be needed even under a correctly operated pure gold standard. The position that Hayek and Robbins had taken in the 1930s was that it was not the gold or gold-exchange standard which had caused the Great Depression, but rather the failure to apply it properly. In 1943 Hayek admitted that the *pure* gold standard as then understood undoubtedly had some grave defects 'linked not to errors in operating it', but due to the fact that 'supply adjusted itself only slowly' (Hayek 1943: 176–8). Hayek goes on to recommend a commodity reserve currency which will provide counter-cyclical changes in the demand for raw materials. Hayek continued to insist on the necessity of an exogenous, automatic mechanism, but the point was taken that if there was no natural mechanism by which the system would produce full employment, there was then no basis for a natural 'law of markets'. Keynes' point concerning the necessity of taking measures to assure the maximum output thus emerged as a common theoretical position in Britain of the post-war period. The Welfare State measures of the 1946 Labour government were seen as politically motivated measures, quite separate from Keynesian theory.[4]

Hayek attempted to resurrect the debate on planning and economic freedom in his 1944 *The Road to Serfdom*, but the response was a series of works by 'conservative Keynesians' such as James Meade's *Planning and the Price Mechanism*, which argued that planning could succeed 'in an efficient and free society only if an extensive use is made of the mechanisms of competition, free enterprise and the free market determination of prices and output' (Meade 1948: v–vi).

III

The theme of Roosevelt's campaign against Hoover in the 1932 election can be recalled through the following quotations: 'I accuse the present Administration of being the greatest spending Administration in peace time in all our history. It is an Administration that has piled bureau on bureau, commission on commission, and has failed to anticipate the dire needs and the reduced earning power of the people.' 'I regard reduction in Federal spending as one of the most important issues of this campaign. In my opinion, it is the most direct and effective contribution that government can make to business' (quoted in Lekachman 1966: 113–14). 'Let us have the courage to stop borrowing to meet continuing deficits. Stop the deficits.... Revenues must cover expenditures by one means or another. Any government, like any family, can for a year spend a little more than it earns, but you and I know that a continuation of that habit means the poorhouse' (quoted in Eccles 1951: 96).

One wonders if Ruud Lubbers, as well as Ronald Reagan, have not been studying the New Deal. One of Roosevelt's first acts in office was to cut civil service salaries and fire government employees! The first part of Roosevelt's policy to be abandoned was not that concerning the balanced budget, but that over prices and international finance. The new administration wasted little time in going off the gold standard and devaluing the dollar. This led to an increased inflow of gold into the U.S. (much to the chagrin of those Europeans who viewed the already excessive increase of gold in the U.S. – maldistribution – as one of the basic causes of depression). 'The overvalued gold bloc currencies thus became more overvalued. But Roosevelt's action was not inspired by a 'beggar-my-neighbour' philosophy. Rather he was strongly influenced by the highly dubious theory of George F. Warren, professor of farm management at Cornell University, that raising the gold price would – by a mysterious, unexplored mechanism – raise prices generally. A key element in the early New Deal was to get prices up. Roosevelt's stated aim was the restoration of prosperity 'by reestablishing the purchasing power of half the people, including, of course, the beleaguered farmers' (Rolfe and Burtle 1973:37). It appears that the mentor of this piece of New Deal policy was not Keynes but Irving Fisher, who recommended devaluation strongly to Roosevelt on the basis of 'a surprisingly ready acceptance of the doctrine advanced by George F. Warren and Frank A. Pearson that dollar commodity prices (and output) would move with the dollar gold price' (Allen 1977: 578). 'The President asked Fisher in conversation if he "agreed with Warren and (James Harvey) Rogers that if he (Roosevelt) got the Federal Reserve to buy newly mined gold at say $29 an ounce it would help raise commodity prices", "I said I did"'.[5] 'Warren and Pearson's work seems to me of a very high order. Such a collection and analysis of the facts can find few parallels. I cannot agree with you that his [sic] work is wrong or useless.'[6]

Indeed nearly all of the New Deal 'Alphabetsoup' apparatus initiated in 1933–4 was directed towards creating price floors, and only incidentally affected government spending. The deficits that did result were tolerated as inevitable and never justified by the administration as necessary to employment creation. As Minsky (1982a: 51) has stressed, 'The Rooseveltian policy structure was not aimed at overriding the flaws of capitalism ... by fiscal policy measures.' Lekachman (1966: 123) reports, 'when Roosevelt and Keynes actually talked in 1934, Roosevelt's comment to Miss Perkins (Secretary of Labor) was, "I saw your friend Keynes. He left a whole rigmarole of figures. He must be a mathematician rather than a political economist." For his part Keynes confided to the same Miss Perkins that he had "supposed the President was more literate, economically speaking".'

It was only in 1938 that fiscal policy was actively used to influence the level of activity. The activity of the New Deal was thus just the opposite of that proposed in Britain. Whereas Keynes had insisted on the preservation of the price mechanism, nearly all the policies of the first Roosevelt administration were meant to control or influence the free market mechanism by control of either prices or quantities. In addition they strengthened the bargaining power of certain sectors, e.g. labour unions. Precisely those factors which Hayek feared from Keynes' policy were being implemented in the U.S. by an a-theoretical populist administration committed to a balanced budget and sound finance!

The only similarity was that Roosevelt's measures appeared equally arbitrary in comparison with the operation of the market. Indeed, it did not take much economic acumen to note that an all-round increase in prices would lead only to inflation. Thus the policy was renamed 'reflation' and aimed to achieve price levels prevailing before the crash. This was the main theme of Fisher's policy advice to Roosevelt (and the source of his recommendation to go off gold cited above): 'as the great depression was primarily monetary the remedy must be largely monetary! Massive changes in the money stock – "the chief direct cause of the depression and the recovery" – result in changes in the price level, and both theory and empirical evidence indicate that "deflation reduces employment and reflation restores it"' (Allen 1977: 564).

It has been recognised more recently that such measures also implied redistribution amongst debtors and creditors. As noted by Rolfe and Burtle (1973: 38) Roosevelt's

difference with the gold bloc ... were differences in the trade-offs among social values. Roosevelt wanted to raise American incomes and employment. To do this he was willing to take risks that there would be some losers in the money game. But the whole emphasis of the financial elite in the gold bloc countries (and in the United States where FDR was a 'traitor to his class') was the preservation of capital. Income and employment were secondary values. Results of this perverse trade-off are still evident in sharper class cleavages in post-World War II France and ... the United Kingdom.

Thus although the policy of raising prices was usually represented as a method of supporting incomes, and this was certainly true of the particular agencies, the AAA, the NIRA and the NRA, the Robinson–Patman Act of 1936, the Miller–Tydings Act of 1938, the Social Security Act of 1935, the CCC, PWA and WPA, the actual results of these schemes and the change in the gold parity (which in the U.K. was proposed as a measure to raise *primary producers*' incomes) had no such effect in the U.S. Rather, as Kemmerer (1934: 183) points out, the impact was to lighten the burden of private debt. Commenting in 1934 on a return to the gold parity:

The agitation we have been having over the country for a long time in favor of cheap money to lighten the debt burdens of farmers and others has been dangerously effective. People who advocate a reflation of the currency back to the old gold parity are today looked upon by a large percentage of our population as Wall Street Shylocks demanding their 'pound of flesh', and even the Wall Street saints are today not in good repute in many parts of the country.

'Our administration in Washington since March 4, 1933, has apparently been working for such reflation with the primary object of relieving the debtor classes of the extra burden placed upon them by the great rise in the value of the dollar ... since 1929' (ibid.: 48). Kemmerer notes that there is no difference between this policy and that of expansion of the money supply. Fisher on the other hand limited reflation to the correction of deflation.[7] Fisher's main point was the impact of what he called 'real debt' on activity in deflation, not on distribution.

Thus Roosevelt's policies had exactly the same disturbing effect on the application of economic laws even though they had no Keynesian, or other, theoretical backing. Direct government interference in the market process of price determination also represented government intervention in the distribution of income, and in the relation between social classes. While Keynes fought to re-establish the price mechanism and its role in the distribution of income the 'New Deal' policy of direct intervention clearly enunciated the necessity of abrogating the laws of debt contract upon which the market mechanism was based. In the U.S. this abrogation went all down the line from the failure to honour its international commitments by supporting the gold value of the dollar to the support of the farmer in his debt relation to the private saver via the banks. For Roosevelt, the 'law of motion' was important but appears to have been justified by Fisher's 'debt deflation' theory or populism.

In Fisher's view ... certain conspicuous features of the New Deal – most notably NRA and the AAA – had 'actually retarded recovery'. While not entirely 'out of sympathy' with such programs, he concluded that in general they undesirably obstructed the working of the free market, pegging prices above equilibrium levels, directly and indirectly curtailing production and thus employment, and restricting anticipated profits. (Allen 1977: 581)

For believers in the free market, the puritan ethic based on frugality, and those in the business community faced with such an onslaught on their economic principles there was little choice but support of the Republican party. Although most economic historians now agree that 'Keynesian' policies only took hold in the U.S. administration in 1937 or 1938, such was Keynes' public role in the *post-war* reconstruction that he (rather than Warren or Fisher) was given credit for inspiring the interventionist policies of the New Deal!

In actual fact, Keynes also argued against most of Roosevelt's policy. Keynes comments on the NRA: 'But I agree with the widespread opinion that much of it is objectionable because of its restrictionist philosophy.... In particular it would be advisable to discard most of the provisions to fix prices and to forbid sales below an alleged but undefinable cost basis.'[8] 'I conclude, therefore, that for six months at least, and probably for a year the measure of recovery to be achieved will mainly depend on the degree of the direct stimulus to production deliberately applied by the Administration. Since I have no belief in the efficacy for this purpose of the price and wage raising activities of NRA, this must chiefly mean the pace and volume of the government's emergency expenditure' (Keynes 1982: XXI, 325). Keynes also criticised the ambiguous handling of the 'business classes' by the Roosevelt administration (ibid.: 434–6).

It was this uncertainty of aim which caused Keynes on one occasion to advise the President either to nationalize the public utilities (as Keynes himself wished) or, in default of this clear-cut tactic, simply to leave them alone. Such measures as the Tennessee Valley Authority and the Public Utility Holding Company Act, whatever their merits, nibbled at private ownership and interfered with some of the more fanciful devices favoured by public utility promoters, but they followed neither of Keynes' prescriptions. (Lekachman 1966: 122)

Fisher also urged the President 'to convince the business world ... that you are loyal to the American System of Free Private Enterprise and profits as against statism, whether of the Russian or the German variety'. (Allen 1977: 578)

Thus, while 'Roosevelt himself was unfamiliar with the economics of Keynes' according to Frances Perkins[9] although not those of Fisher, and the policies of the New Deal were in general diametrically opposed to those advanced by Keynes, it was 'Keynesian' economics which was credited with the kind of Big Brother interventionism in the U.S. that Hayek had predicted for the U.K. In the U.K. Hayek's argument was successfully combated in theoretical discourse. The New Deal lacked that discourse, but proved itself indeed.

This point is underscored by a letter from Alvin Hansen to Walter Salant commenting on the contributors to the New Deal economic policy:

Hansen, responding in a letter dated 31 May, 1971, asked – and here I paraphrase – Why Eccles? he had a brilliant and original mind, and he strongly favored public spending in the deep depression but he was by no stretch of the imagination a Keynesian. Ickes with his PWA favored government spending but he also was no Keynesian. Moulton favored a big public works program during the depression but he was anything but a Keynesian. Hansen then quoted a statement (which he attributed to James Conant) that it takes a theory to kill a theory. (Keynes killed neo-classical theory by showing that the economy is not self-sustaining, that unemployment is not just 'lapses' from full employment.... People who in the old days supported public works as offsets to 'lapses' from full employment were not Keynesians.) (Salant 1977: 46–7)

It is thus somewhat ironical that the role of defender of Keynesianism in Roosevelt's administration was the chairman of the Board of Governors of the Federal Reserve System, Marriner Eccles, while sound money was defended in the Treasury by Harry Morgenthau. Eccles was a banker, and his position evolved from his experience during the slump:

In whatever quiet moments were available I began to wonder whether the conduct of bankers like myself in depression times was a wise one. Were we not all contributing our bit to the worsening of matters by the mere act of trying to keep liquid under the economic pressures of deflation? ... In a time of deflation would not the rational policy be one of monetary ease, as against the policy of ease in boom times? But how could we as individual bankers pursue such policies? ... What we did each of us had to do if we wanted to keep our individual banks open. Seeking individual salvation, we were contributing to collective ruin.... As I looked to the business and financial leaders to answer this central question, their stock reply was that a deflation in values, and a scaling down of the debt structure to meet existing price levels, would in time create a self-corrective force.... But under capitalist methods a radical scaling down of debts would clearly prolong the depression. Under capitalism it would require the further liquidation of banks, insurance companies, and all credit institutions. It would increase the hoarding of money, decrease its velocity, freeze credit, and make for endless deflation.... 'Do nothing', some businessmen and financial leaders replied. They argued again that a depression was the scientific operation of economic laws that were God-given and not man-made ... they further explained that we were in the lean years because we had been spendthrifts and wasted in the roaring twenties. We had wasted what we earned instead of saving it.... But was this true? Did economics itself proceed on the basis of God-given laws? My own reaction was that ... the moment the production and distribution of wealth moved beyond a hermit's cave and affected two or more people, economics became artificial in character, in the sense that it was subjected at once to man-made rules and regulations, which were changed constantly in accordance with the needs of a dynamic society. (Eccles 1951: 70–4)

An unbalanced budget, I began to argue, was not an independent condition created by a government decision. It reflected a deep-seated unbalance in the economy, and it was the economy that first had to be balanced, and its governmental bookkeeping effects secondarily. A policy of adequate governmental outlays at a time when private enterprise is curtailing its expenditures does not reflect a preference for an unbalanced budget. (ibid.: 79)

Eccles was eventually appointed to the Fed and remained a lonely voice until 1938. Being a logical man he also noted that once private spending picked up 'the budget can and should be brought into balance to offset the danger of a boom', which again placed him in difficulty when he argued in favour of spending reductions in 1944. He was the driving force behind the famous 'Accord' by which the Fed tried to regain independence from the Treasury – an independence required to apply 'Keynesian' policies!

Hicks thus found in the U.S. a tight identification between Keynesian economics and government intervention and control. Believers in market mechanisms could only be Republican and right-wing pro-business and anti-labour. Indeed, by 1946 the one Keynesian was forced to declare monetary independence from the a-theoretical Treasury. Britain was also to arrive at this position as the Labour party programme became linked to the 'Keynesian' position. Oddly, in the U.S. this was precisely the period in which academic economists were inventing the 'neo-classical' synthesis which was meant to join Keynes' 'macro' theory to traditional price theory. But instead of attempting to unite two economic laws, the 'law of the market' to the 'law of motion', it attempted to link free enterprise and government intervention. This is what eventually became the dominant position in both the U.S. and the U.K. A position based on a misunderstanding of both economic laws, as Hayek continued to insist, and as did a number of Keynes' closer followers and their pupils.

IV

The legacy of Keynes and Hayek was to avoid the worst fears of the other in the post-war period. It also produced an untenable theoretical marriage, which when tested logically and practically proved to be a vacuum devoid of content. It has produced reactionary policy (cf. Parquez 1981), similar to the pre-Keynesian and pre-Hayekian theories. The system has neither the motion required for full employment, nor the full employment required for the operation of the market. The focus of their original debate, the form of international monetary co-operation – automatic or managed – has simply disappeared from active theoretical debate.

On the other hand it is interesting to note that both Marx and Schumpeter embraced the idea of the law of motion, but at the same time preserved their belief in the law of the market. For Marx this is visible through the use of labour value, a reference concept which has no meaning without its confirmation via the law of the market. Schumpeter would have little to do with Keynes' theory. His own law of motion – technical change – was, however, introduced *ad hoc*, but the law of the market was necessary for it to be beneficial.

Neither proved any more successful than Keynes in their attempts to integrate the two. Clearly, Hayek was alone in recognising that Keynes' law of motion, by introducing economic 'relativity', expanded economics from a science of optimisation, to social philosophy. The law of motion and the law of market mark the dividing line between 'value-free' economic science and the relativity of social science once taken outside the hermit's cave. Neither taken alone is sufficient as a basis for economic analysis.

Notes

1 On the problem presented by interest rate policy of the 1920s, see Anderson (1965: 56–8).
2 A good description is given in Beyen (1951: chapter VII).
3 Quoted in Kindleberger (1978: 79n.).
4 The reader is directed to Skidelsky's (1979) analysis for a slightly different, but equally plausible, interpretation.
5 Letter from Fisher to his wife.
6 Letter from Fisher to Viner (Allen 1977: 570–1).
7 Allen (1977) cites a number of letters from Fisher to Kemmerer discussing the size of the desired reflation.
8 From an open letter 'Agenda for the President', published in the *New York Times*, 10 June 1934 (Keynes 1982: XXI, 323).
9 Quoted in Lekachman (1966: 123).

5 Are There Macroeconomic Laws? The 'Law' of the Falling Rate of Profit Reconsidered

DONALD J. HARRIS

I

Are there macroeconomic laws? This is the question which motivates the discussion presented in this paper. To clarify the question, let me first define my terms. By macroeconomic laws I mean, specifically, regularities which operate at the level of the economic system as a whole and which, though deriving from actions of individual agents in the economy, are nevertheless such as to dictate outcomes which discipline, coerce and even contradict the intentions of the individual agents. To constitute a law, moreover, such regularities must be permanent built-in features of the economic process. They cannot be merely transitory, ephemeral elements associated with historically contingent factors.

The presumption that there are such laws derives from the recognition that the economy as a whole is not just the sum of its parts. Hence the motion of the economy cannot simply be deduced from the movement of its individual parts. As such, this presumption entails a profound methodological principle. This principle is, in my view, one of the most important and significant common elements which underpins and unites the analysis of Marx, Schumpeter and Keynes. Here, then, is the point of contact of this discussion with the overall theme of this symposium. If we are concerned to appraise the significance of the works of Marx, Schumpeter and Keynes, it would seem necessary to confront this fundamental presumption that ties together their respective ideas on the nature of the capitalist economic process.

Despite the fact that this presumption occupies such illustrious company, it is nevertheless necessary to pose the question asked above. In particular, it is necessary to ask whether the specific formulation and conception of such macroeconomic laws that have been put forward by these authors in fact constitute a law in the sense defined. Can they be sustained as valid economic laws?

To consider this question in depth I shall examine here in some detail the idea that there exists a necessary tendency (call it FTRP) for the rate of profit to fall in the course of the accumulation process taking place in the capitalist economy. Marx was emphatic in proposing this as a *law*. He considered it to be 'the most important law of modern political economy' (Marx 1973b: 748).[1] He was, of course, following in the tradition of the English Classical Economists in which the same idea had been firmly entrenched, though supported on different grounds. But, interestingly enough, it is also the case that there exists a distinct conception of a FTRP within neoclassical theory.[2] In Keynes, as well, the idea is embodied in his projection of the long-term prospects for capitalism resulting in the 'euthanasia of the rentier' (Keynes 1936: 375–6). In the Schumpeterian system, it occurs in the form of the idea that the profitability of innovations tends inevitably to be eroded so that the economy settles back to the conditions of the 'circular flow' in the absence of new innovations which are not themselves inevitable (Schumpeter 1934). Though it is based in each case on quite different foundations, this conception is one of the most striking and persistent uniformities across different schools of economic thought. Such uniformity deserves further investigation as a significant phenomenon in the history of economic thought, but that task is not undertaken here.[3]

I am interested in focussing here on the analytical structure of the argument which is mounted to sustain the proposition of FTRP. For this purpose, I shall limit the discussion to a consideration of the logic of the Marxian formulation, contrasting it with that of Classical Political Economy. Marx, of course, sought to counterpose his own conception to the Classical analysis. But, in so doing, he had to grapple with the actual content of the analysis developed by his predecessors. It is possible, therefore, to identify the specific features of the Marxian treatment of this problem in contrast with the structure of the Classical analysis. Accordingly, that analysis is the starting point of this discussion.

II

The essential point of the Classical argument that is relevant for present purposes is that accumulation of capital, consisting of the growth of the wage fund with a corresponding increase of employment, drives down the average product on the land so that, consequently, rents increase at the expense of profits and the rate of profit falls. The economic system ultimately reaches a stationary state where the rate of profit falls to zero and the whole product is absorbed by rent plus wages. The system may indifferently be assumed to expand on the extensive or intensive margin of available land. Also, it does not matter for this discussion that there exists any production outside agriculture. It would turn out, in any case, that the overall average rate of profit for the economy as a whole is determined by the agricultural rate of profit or, in the general case, by the conditions of production and profit of 'basic commodities' (Sraffa 1960; Pasinetti 1974 and 1977).

In simple terms, the argument may be expressed symbolically as follows. At any level of employment the rate of profit is

(1.1) $\qquad r = \dfrac{(\phi - w)L}{W} = \dfrac{\phi}{w} - 1; \quad \phi' < 0$

where ϕ is the marginal product of labor-cum-capital, $W = wL$ is the wage fund, L is employment, and w is the wage. For a given level of the wage, the rate of profit falls as employment increases, for the reason that the conditions of agricultural production dictate diminishing returns on the margin of cultivation. Let the capitalists invest a certain proportion α of their total profits. Then the rate of accumulation g is

(1.2) $\qquad g = \alpha r$

which, at a given wage, also corresponds to the growth rate of demand for labor. The supply of labor (its rate of growth l_s) is a function of the wage such that

(1.3) $\qquad l_s = l_s(w); l_s(w^*) = 0, l_s' > 0, w^* > 0$

This relation incorporates the population theory of Malthus. It presupposes a population dynamic governing the labor supply that is uniquely dependent on the level of the wage, where w^* is the 'natural price of labor' or the subsistence wage necessary to sustain a constant population.

Accordingly, there are two sides to the Classical analysis. They come together as integrated features of the Classical theory of accumulation in the manner indicated in Figure 1. On the one side is the productivity of land and its utilization as determined by accumulation in the past. Together with the wage this determines the rate of profit and rate of accumulation from equations (1.1) and (1.2). The higher the wage the lower is the rate of profit and the lower the rate of accumulation. Correspondingly, the demand for labor is a decreasing function of the level of the wage. This relationship is shown as the curve l_d in Figure 1. On the other side is the population dynamic governing the availability of labor. This is shown as the curve l_s. Given these conditions of demand and supply of labor as specified, excess demand for labor drives up the wage which induces expansion of population while reducing profits and thereby cutting down the demand for labor. The wage rises to the point where demand and supply of labor are in balance. A similar process operates in reverse if there exists initially excess supply of labor. In either case, the adjustment takes place through movements in the market wage brought about by excess demand or supply in the labor market. The point of balance occurs at the rate w_0 which exceeds the subsistence level and, at that point, accumulation takes place at the rate g_0. As accumulation continues, however, there is declining productivity in agriculture. This entails that, in the diagram, the l_d curve shifts to the left. There is a corresponding decrease in the overall rate of profit and in the rate of accumulation. The wage rate falls in step. This process continues until, ultimately, the system converges to the stationary state in which (net) accumulation ceases and the wage rate becomes equal to the

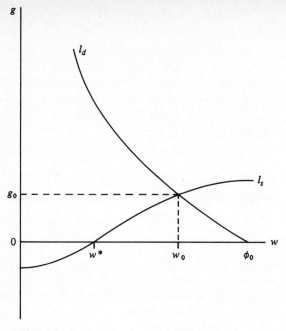

Figure 1

subsistence level. The process as a whole generates not only a falling tendency of the rate of profit but also a falling tendency of the wage. Moreover, it is evident that the wage is not necessarily equal to the subsistence level at all points in the process. In this example, it starts out at a level above subsistence and remains above it as long as accumulation is going on. It is only in the stationary state that the wage is reduced to subsistence. When accumulation is going on, the 'market wage' differs from the subsistence wage; a wedge is driven between them by the rate of accumulation.

We have here the overall dynamic of the accumulation process as conceived within the Classical analysis.[4] In this conception, accumulation of capital runs up against two impenetrable barriers: on the one side the diminishing fertility of the soil, on the other the given condition of availability of labor which is tied to demographic behavioral propensities of the population. These two factors act as a scissors to cut off the possibility of continued expansion and bring the accumulation process to a halt. Thus accumulation is brought to a halt by conditions which are external or 'natural' in the strict sense that they are predetermined or exogenous to the accumulation process itself. At the same time, this consequence is also the product of the capitalists' own actions in relentlessly seeking to expand the size of their capital.

These features of the Classical analysis were explicitly perceived by Marx and subjected to a fundamental critique. In general Marx argued that, while in fact Classical Political Economy is firmly and correctly able to identify that the well-spring of capitalist expansion is profit, it is at the same time incapable of grasping the contradictions *internal* to the accumulation process which cause the pool of profits to dry up. Instead, it sees the barrier or limit to expansion as arising wholly from external causes (Marx 1967: III, 259).

As to one side of the Classical argument, that pertaining to diminishing returns in agriculture, Marx argued that what this fails to grasp is that capitalism, in the course of its expansion, does not take as given the existing production conditions. Rather, capitalists, as a necessary condition of their existence as capitalists, strive to revolutionize the conditions of production and consequently to raise productivity, in agriculture as well as in industry. As capital expands into agriculture, therefore, agricultural productivity would increase due to technical change and any presumed tendency for diminishing returns to exist would be washed out (Marx 1967: I, 504–7; III, 617–19). The basis of that ongoing process of change in productivity throughout the economy, Marx presumed, is an increasing 'organic composition of capital' (ibid.: I, 621–3). So, Marx at once undercuts this side of the Classical argument and puts in its place an alternative basis for conceiving the process of expansion of the economy. At the same time, it is on this new and altered basis that he seeks to construct his own conception of a necessary tendency of the rate of profit to fall (ibid.: III, chapter 13).

A crucial role is played in the Classical analysis by the assumed population dynamic. In particular, the growth of population in response to wages in excess of subsistence is supposed to provide the labor requirements for expansion and thereby hold wages in check. But this is evidently a highly implausible principle on which to base an account of the process of capitalist expansion. If capitalism had to depend for its labor supply entirely upon such a demographic–biological principle, it seems doubtful that sustained high rates of accumulation could continue for long or even that accumulation could ever get started. This is because, first, there must exist a biological upper limit to population expansion. Accumulation at rates above this limit would drive up the wage to such a level as to reduce or perhaps choke off the possibility of continued accumulation. For the Classical labor supply principle to work it must be presumed arbitrarily that this limit is sufficiently far out or, equivalently, that the supply curve is sufficiently elastic over a wide range.

Even if it is granted that population growth is significantly responsive to the level of wages, it is still the case that the adjustment of population is inherently a long-drawn-out process having only a negligible effect on the actual labor supply in any short period of time. In the interim, any sizeable spurt of accumulation must then cause wages to be bid up, eat into profits, and bring accumulation itself to a halt. From the start, therefore, accumulation could never get going in such a system. Even if it did, its continuation would always be in jeopardy because the mechanism of adjustment of labor supply is an inherently unreliable one, fraught with the possibility that at any time wages may rise to eat up the profits that are the well-spring of accumulation.

This feature of Classical analysis was also soundly criticized and completely rejected by Marx (Marx 1967: I, 637–9). In its place, he sought to introduce a principle that was internal to the accumulation process, that would account for the continuing generation of a supply of labor to meet the needs of accumulation from within the accumulation process itself. This was the principle of the reserve army of labor or the 'Law of relative surplus population' (ibid.: I, chapter 25, sections 3 and 4). It is also based on the presumed tendency of the organic composition of capital to rise. The rise in the organic composition of capital results in a 'recycling' of labor through its displacement from existing occupations, due to mechanization of production, into the reserve army where it is held for reemployment elsewhere as the economy expands. In this process, therefore, any presumed external barrier to expansion arising from the size and growth rate of population would be eliminated.

Here, again, Marx undercuts the Classical analysis by reconstituting the accumulation process on a wholly new basis, on the basis of a presumed tendency for the organic composition of capital to rise as the characteristic feature of the process of technical change. Moreover, this step in the argument undercuts both sides of the Classical analysis at one and the same time. For, the very same process of rising organic composition of capital both raises productivity so as to wash out the operation of the law of diminishing returns in agriculture and generates the reserve army of labor so as to eliminate the necessity of the Malthusian Law of Population.

Nevertheless, Marx went on to argue that the process of technical change is itself a contradictory one. Its contradictory feature is that the rise in organic composition of capital would tend to drive down the rate of profit. Thus, in eliminating the basis of the Classical argument, Marx at the same time arrives at a new condition. This is now a condition which is supposed to emerge within the accumulation process itself and is not, therefore, an external condition. It is a condition which is immanent in the capitalist process and derives from the logic of that process. It constitutes an *internal* barrier to capitalist expansion. In this sense, he now claims that 'the *real barrier* of capitalist production is *capital* itself' (Marx 1967: III, 250).

It is thus possible to see here, in the explicit terms of Marx's opposition to and rejection of the Classical analysis, the distinctive features and rationale of the Marxian derivation of the proposed law of FTRP. Both the Classical analysis and the Marxian analysis arrive at the same result, that of FTRP as an inherent feature of the accumulation process. But in each case the specific principles governing the results are fundamentally different. It is now commonly agreed that the twin pillars of the Classical analysis, associated with diminishing returns in agriculture and the Malthusian population theory, are an inadequate and untenable basis on which to constitute a 'law' of the accumulation process or a *macroeconomic law* in the sense defined above.[5] The question to be considered here is: what can be said for the specific case of the Marxian analysis as regards its conception of the law of FTRP? I proceed to examine this question further in the next sections.

III

The argument, in this case, can be considered from the standpoint of the usual definition of the rate of profit which holds on the assumption that wages are advanced, capital goods are purely circulating capital, and the organic composition of capital is uniform across all industries. Thus, the *value* rate of profit (equal, under these conditions, to the *price* of profit) is the ratio of surplus value S (equal to the difference between total labor employed L and the paid labour V) to the total capital (constant capital C and variable capital V). We then have

$$(2.1) \qquad r = \frac{1-v}{q+v}, \quad \text{where} \quad S = L - V, v = V/L, q = C/L$$

Here, v is the value of labor power and q is the organic composition of capital. In this context, the content of the Marxian proposition is the following:

if $v = v^*$, and if q rises indefinitely, then r falls.

But that statement as it stands is tautologically true. It follows from the definition of the rate of profit. For this to constitute a *law* of the accumulation process, a further argument is necessary. In particular, it is necessary to show, first, that there are forces operating within the accumulation process to hold the value of labor power within definite limits. Secondly, it is necessary to give an account of the economic forces which dictate that the organic composition of capital q must inevitably rise as a consequence of the process of technical change which accompanies the accumulation of capital. Moreover, it is necessary to show that these determining forces are permanent, built-in features of the accumulation process which continue to operate despite the existence of counteracting forces, where the counteracting forces themselves are to be regarded as transitory elements entering into the process. Only when these conditions are satisfied could one regard the statement of the law as being fully substantiated.

It is here that one confronts a certain lack of theoretical determinacy or completeness in the existing Marxian analysis of the conditions which are supposed to give rise to the law of FTRP. Put in the simplest algebraic terms, this point may be expressed as follows. For this purpose, note that the value of labor power is to be understood as consisting of the real wage w, representing the magnitude of workers' necessary consumption and λ the magnitude of direct and indirect labor embodied in a unit of consumption. Thus, define

$$(2.2) \qquad v = w\lambda$$

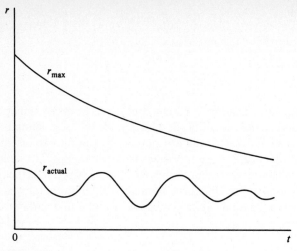

Figure 2

Then, it follows that

$$(2.3) \qquad r = \frac{1 - w\lambda}{q + w\lambda}$$

We therefore have here one equation in the four unknowns: r, w, λ, q. Evidently, for a complete determination of this set of variables, additional information is necessary. In general, what is lacking is an explicitly articulated conception of the accumulation process as a whole that would explain the movement of all these variables.

One approach offered in recent discussions for substantiating the proposition of a FTRP is to express it in terms of the maximum rate of profit (Okishio 1972; Himmelweit 1974; Shaikh 1978). Note, in this connection, that the rate of profit is at maximum when $v = 0$, so that at any level of q

$$r_{\max} = \frac{1}{q}$$

Now, if q rises this evidently entails a decrease in the maximum rate of profit. Since the maximum rate establishes an upper boundary on the actual rate of profit, it is inferred that the actual rate must eventually fall. But it should be evident that the variation in $r_{\max}$ tells us nothing about the movement in the actual rate of profit. The actual rate would lie within the boundary established by $r_{\max}$ but could be rising, falling or constant (see Figure 2). There is no way of saying in which direction it moves without a further analysis. The maximum rate itself could fall indefinitely, for instance asymptotically approaching some positive level, and never hit upon the actual rate. Besides, if the maximum rate were to coincide with the actual rate, this would entail either that the wage had

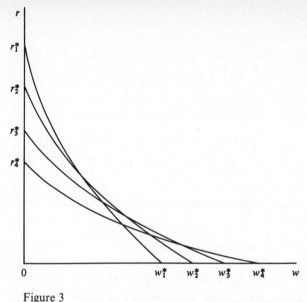

Figure 3

fallen to zero or that $\lambda = 0$. Both of these eventualities are highly implausible outcomes that would have to be ruled out as economically irrelevant. This approach therefore takes us no further than before and amounts simply to a restatement of the condition that the organic composition of capital rises.

It is possible to go further towards an analytical treatment of the argument by giving an explicit specification of the relationships relevant to determination of the rate of profit. For this purpose, a simple model may be constructed which is consistent with the underlying presumptions of the argument.[6] It consists of the following components in addition to equations (2.1) and (2.2).

First is a specification of the production conditions and of technical change. The production conditions are expressed in the magnitudes of the organic composition of capital q and of the labor coefficient λ (or its inverse, the productivity of labor). From equation (2.3), a given technique of production generates a wage–profit curve with intercepts at $w^* = 1/\lambda$ and $r^* = 1/q$, as illustrated in Figure 3. An essential ingredient of Marxian analysis is the presumption that technical change takes the form of an increase in the organic composition of capital which in turn gives rise to an increase in labor productivity. In the diagram this is represented by a sequential lowering and outward shift of the horizontal intercept. This presumption may be written in functional terms as:

$$(2.4) \qquad q = f(t); \quad f' > 0$$

where t is an index of time, and

(2.5) $\lambda = \lambda(q); \quad \lambda' < 0$

Next, assume that the capitalists plow back a given proportion of profits to expand the total capital which in this case is $K = C + V$. Accordingly, the rate of accumulation is given by

(2.6) $g = \alpha r$

Total employment of labor must satisfy $L = C/q = V/v$. This implies

(2.7) $L = \dfrac{K}{q + v}$

and by differentiation of this relation we get

(2.8) $l_d = g - \dfrac{\dot{q} + \dot{v}}{q + v}$

This equation indicates that *net* growth of the demand for labor l_d consists of two components: (1) the 'gross demand' associated with growth of the total capital at the rate g, and (2) the 'displacement demand' associated with increase in the organic composition of capital and in the value of labor power. Here the displacement demand may be considered to represent, in part, the role of the increasing organic composition of capital in recycling the existing labor force through additions to the reserve army of unemployed labor. It is evident that, even if $\dot{v}/v = 0$, there exists some $\dot{q}/q$ which would make $l_d = 0$. If $l_d = 0$, the reserve army is barely replenished. Otherwise, it is either increasing $(l_d < 0)$ or decreasing $(l_d > 0)$. In this respect, the accumulation process could be conceived as Marx does, to regenerate its own labor supply as long as the organic composition of capital increases indefinitely at the appropriate rate. Therefore, there need be no recourse to any additional supply of labor from outside the system.

Finally, to close this model, some specification must be made of the conditions determining movements of the wage. Here, the 'relative power of the combatants' in the struggle between labor and capital is considered by Marx to play a decisive role (Marx and Engels 1968: 226; Marx 1967: I, chapter 25). That, in turn, may be significantly dependent on the state of the labor market as represented by the size of the reserve army. Consistent with this line of reasoning, we may write

(2.9) $\dfrac{\dot{w}}{w} = \Phi(u); \quad \Phi' < 0$

where u is the size of the reserve army as measured by the rate of unemployment. If the size of the available labor force is known, then u is also known.

With these relationships in place, we are now in a position to examine more closely the logic of the presumptions underlying the case for a FTRP. Assume, as in the initial proposition stated above, that $v = v^*$. This implies that $\dot{v}/v = 0$ and hence $\dot{w}/w = -\dot{\lambda}/\lambda$. From (2.9) this entails a specific condition in the labor market. In particular, the rate of unemployment u must remain at a definite level, that level which ensures that the wage rises at the rate required to keep the value of labor power constant. But if $v = v^*$ and q rises, then from (2.1) the rate of profit is falling. Correspondingly, from (2.6) and (2.8), the gross demand for labor must be decreasing and, for a given displacement demand, the net demand for labor must eventually become negative. Hence the rate of unemployment must eventually increase. This development must, in turn, if (2.9) is to continue to hold, exert downward pressure on the wage so as to reduce wage increases below the rate of productivity growth. Therefore, the condition that $v = v^*$ cannot continue to be sustained. Actually, with a continuing rise in the rate of unemployment v must fall. This would serve to counteract the fall in the rate of profit. Note that this result is consistent with a continuing rise in the wage. It requires only that wage increases are less than proportional to productivity growth.

This result indicates that there are systematic forces internal to the accumulation process itself which may serve to counteract or check any tendency for the rate of profit to fall. The counteracting force arises in this case from the built-up unemployment due to operation of the twin factors of declining growth of capital as the rate of profit falls and continuing displacement of labor generated by the increasing organic composition of capital. If there exists a mechanism of wage determination which is sensitive to the state of the labor market, as is commonly presumed in Marxian analysis, then such growing unemployment must be considered to slow down wage increases relative to productivity growth and thereby counteract the fall in the rate of profit.

Generally speaking, what this result suggests is that the rise in the organic composition of capital, presumed to be inevitable, actually constitutes a two-edged sword. On the one side, it increases the mass of capital over which a given rate of surplus value is divided and consequently reduces the rate of profit for all capitalists. On the other side it weakens the bargaining position of workers in relation to capital and thereby pushes up the rate of surplus value from which all capitalists gain a higher rate of profit. Which of these two contradictory effects predominates remains in general indeterminate, and must be considered to depend on particular conjunctures in the accumulation process, such as would correspond, for instance, to different phases of a cycle or 'wave' of accumulation.

IV

From the preceding analysis we are left with the recognition that, at least for this construction of its underlying logic, the FTRP is actually a conjunctural or contingent condition dependent on special circumstances that may exist in some phases of the accumulation process but not in others. In this respect, it cannot be regarded as a general law.

But beyond this finding, the case for FTRP as a law of the accumulation process also runs up against another difficulty.[7] This is that no account is given to support the presumption that the organic composition of capital necessarily rises. The rising tendency of the organic composition is simply posited as a *given condition* of the accumulation process. Precisely this limitation is expressed in equation (2.4) in the model presented in the previous section. If this tendency itself is not to be regarded as an external or natural condition, on the same footing for instance as the Classical law of diminishing returns, then it would require to be given some systematic motivation in terms of the internal logic of the accumulation process. What could conceivably be its underlying rationale?

Some authors have sought to find this rationale in the response of capitalist firms to the pressure of rising wages generated by a shortage of labor (Sweezy 1956: 88–9; Dobb 1940: 102, 127). On this view, the rising organic composition of capital is a form of 'induced bias' in technical change. Others have suggested that this tendency derives from the need of all capitals to control labor in production, which control may be exercised through mechanization of the labor process (Wright 1977). There are other variations on these themes, all of which may be considered to have serious limitations as an account of long-term tendencies in the organic composition.

As a matter of the historical record, however, there is some agreement that a rise in the organic composition of capital (as measured by different empirical indices) may be considered to be a 'stylized fact' of capitalist development in the nineteenth and early twentieth centuries (Blaug 1960; Sweezy 1981: 46–54). Whether any of the above-mentioned approaches could provide a valid explanation of this stylized fact seems doubtful or, at least, remains to be shown. But one significant aspect of this historical record, which has so far been overlooked, deserves to be considered. This aspect is, in fact, suggested by Marx (1968: II, 18–19) when he writes, with reference to Ricardo's argument:

In the manner of the economists, he turns a historical phenomenon into an eternal law. This historical phenomenon is a relatively faster development for manufacture ... as against agriculture. The latter has become more productive but not in the same ratio as industry. Whereas in manufacture productivity has increased tenfold, in agriculture it has, perhaps, doubled. Agriculture has therefore become *relatively* less productive, although absolutely more productive. This only proves the very queer development of bourgeois production and its inherent contradictions. It does not, however, invalidate the proposition that agriculture becomes relatively less productive and hence, compared with the value of the industrial product, the value of the agricultural product rises and with it also rent. That in the course of development of capitalist production, agricultural labour has become relatively less productive than industrial labour only means that the productivity of agriculture has not developed with the same speed and to the same degree.

I wish to propose that there is a potentially powerful inference contained in these comments. Marx is here pointing to a tendency for different sectors of the economy to develop unevenly. He emphasizes, in this passage, the relation between agriculture and manufacturing. Elsewhere, he emphasizes the relation between sectors producing capital goods and consumer goods. In general, we might say that there is in fact a generalized tendency to *uneven development* that is characteristic of the process of capitalist development. Now it may well be that the supposed rise in the organic composition of capital could be explained as the product of a specific dynamic of uneven development taking place within the context of the nineteenth and early twentieth centuries. It would be attributable, in that case, to specific features of the accumulation process in that historical period associated with a relatively more rapid rate of productivity growth in manufactured consumer goods compared to capital goods and raw materials (agricultural and mineral products). Derived changes in relative values and prices of these products, along with a tendency to increased mechanization of production and increased 'through-put', would then show up as a rise in the organic composition of capital appropriately measured.[8]

This is put forward here as a plausible hypothesis that is worth further exploring. Ironically, if shown to be a valid hypothesis, it would then turn out that there is a common 'historical phenomenon' underlying both the Ricardian and Marxian conceptions of FTRP. This historical phenomenon is the tendency to uneven development. But it would then become clear also that the FTRP associated with those specific historical conditions is not an 'eternal law'. This is because those particular historical conditions operating in the nineteenth century had within them the seeds of their own transformation. That transformation would come from the continuing process of accumulation and technical development by which, subsequently, production of certain critical raw materials is revolutionized and the capital goods industry itself becomes fully elaborated and articulated as a self-propelling factor in the process of development.[9]

V

A key feature of the Marxian analysis is the conception of the capitalist economy as a mode of production which is inherently self-limited. Contrary to some vulgar interpretations, this does not imply spontaneous breakdown. Nor does it deny individual will. This self-limited character is supposed to derive from the existence of systematic barriers or internal limits to its movement. Marx set himself the scientific task of discovering those barriers in capital itself. That is, so to say, his 'theoretical project'. It must be taken to mean specifically that the laws of motion of this system cannot be discovered merely from contemplating the behavior of atomistic agents, but rather from analysis of the system-level influences affecting the activities of the individual agents.

The falling tendency of the rate of profit was conceived as one such systematic influence or, in the sense defined in this paper, as a *macroeconomic law*. The essential feature of this law as it is usually proposed is that it expresses the logic of capital in general, which is to say some inner necessity of the system of individual capitals in its totality as a system. In particular, it is argued that each capital acts individually to do the best it can to increase its profits by introducing innovations (or to expand 'relative surplus value'); but when all capitals do, it turns out that there is a reduction in the rate of profit for all of them. However, after all is said and done, the best that can now be said for this supposed 'law' is that it is broadly descriptive of a particular phase in the development of capitalism. Hence it could possibly lay claim to validity only as a contingent historical condition.

In conclusion, I wish to suggest that there is a way forward for continuing the theoretical project. This is to recognize, as suggested in the last section, that there exists a phenomenon of uneven development as a characteristic feature of the development process. What is involved here is a general principle, one might say *the principle of uneven and combined development*. Specifically, it could be argued that the basic impulses which drive the movement and development of the economy emanate from a built-in tendency to uneven development operating at the level of individual sectors of the economy and, at the most microeconomic level, at the level of the individual capitals. This tendency operates always within certain macroeconomic balancing conditions with which it is dialectically interlinked. It is the specific combination and interplay of these macroeconomic conditions with the uneven development of the individual capitals which determines the concrete form of motion of the economy. To put this another way, it is the contradiction between accumulation of individual capitals and the reproduction process of the aggregate capitals which determines the movement of the economy. The exact conditions of operation of this process, as to its mechanisms, interdependencies, determining conditions, and concrete forms, require to be systematically worked out. In this project, it seems clear that the insights of Marx, Keynes and Schumpeter have an important role to play. It is also a many-sided task requiring the efforts of many scholars. Some results of this effort by the present author will be the subject of another work (Harris s.a., s.l.).

Notes

1 The argument for the law itself is given in detail in Marx (1967: vol. III, part III).
2 This conception and its limitations are discussed at length in Harris (1978: chapter 9; and 1981).
3 For a discussion of the long history of the idea of a falling rate of profit see Tucker (1960).
4 In terms of its formal structure, this presentation of the Classical analysis is in

agreement with that of Casarosa (1978). Other renderings are also given by Blaug (1978: chapters 3 and 4), Johansen (1967), Pasinetti (1974) and Samuelson (1978).

5 For an appraisal, see for instance Blaug (1978: chapters 3 and 4).

6 A similar model is presented and analyzed in greater detail in Harris (1983).

7 It also runs up against another theoretical difficulty arising from the underlying logic of competitive behavior among individual capitals. This is discussed in Harris (1983).

8 For some suggestive evidence in this connection, see Lewis (1978), Chandler (1977) and Rostow (1978).

9 The crucial role of the capital goods industry in this respect is emphasized in Rosenberg (1976) and was a factor in Marx's own analysis (Marx 1967: III, chapters 4 and 5).

Comment

JÖRG GLOMBOWSKI

I

A 'macroeconomic law' according to Harris' definition has to pass three criteria. It should be (1) internal, i.e. derived from principles and assumptions being characteristic for a specific mode of production or a certain phase of it, (2) logically consistent, and (3) empirically plausible. My assessment of the state of economic science (including Marxian economics) is rather pessimistic. Therefore, the adoption of these criteria alone seems to me sufficient for a negative answer to Harris' equation: 'Are there macroeconomic laws?' The answer becomes less certain if we restrict our criteria to only one. In this case, concentration on the question of logical consistency seems to me the most obvious candidate, because a test on (3) on the basis of a logically unsound theory is pointless, while a theory passing the second *and* the third criterion will make a good chance to meet the first one, too.

Where Harris tries to draw a sharp distinction between the external laws of classical economics and the internal law of Marx's economics, I would not always agree (and would rather doubt the significance of the criterion of internality). Although Marx made his methodological position quite clear by accusing Ricardo to escape from economics and to resort to organic chemistry,[1] Marx's own account of the productivity lag in the production of raw materials does not seem to avoid Ricardo's 'fault'. As Marx did not develop an endogenous or internal theory on how technical knowledge is developed under capitalism and gives rise to a capital using bias in application, the 'technical progress function' has more or less the same status as the classical law of diminishing returns on land. It does not matter so much to me whether an explanation is external or internal but whether it fits factual developments. With regard to this, I would not overrate the criterion of 'internal' explanation for a 'macroeconomic law'.

II

Harris concludes that the results of the model are 'in general indeterminate, and must be considered to depend on particular conjunctures in the accumulation process' (p. 59). We should distinguish between two kinds of indeterminateness in this context: the first one arising from uncertainty about the relationships governing real economic systems, while the second one refers to results of economic models on the basis of theoretical assumptions. The latter can be overcome by specifying functions and discerning the various possible sets of assumptions and concomitant results. Now Harris does not operate with completely specified functions or time paths for the organic composition of capital and labour productivity, so necessarily he cannot derive determinate results. I think it is worthwhile to work out some specific cases to reduce this kind of indeterminateness – in the sense of demonstrating what will happen under what assumptions.

For this purpose it seems useful to change Harris' wage formation equation. Let us assume that the employment share governs the real wage rate instead of its growth rate, which comes down to ignoring the wage-lag hypothesis contained in Harris' assumption. This modification seems (1) reasonable for a long-period theory and (2) avoids cyclical fluctuations.[2] Moreover, (3) instead of systems of two non-linear, non-autonomous differential equations we will have to deal with the 'simpler' case of only one such equation.

Consider now the following variant of Harris' model:

(1) $\quad r = (1 - v)/(q + v)$

(2) $\quad g = \alpha r,$ $\qquad \alpha = \text{const.} > 0$

(3) $\quad v = \lambda w$

(4) $\quad \hat{L} = g - \dfrac{\dot{q} + \dot{v}}{q + v}$

(5) $\quad \hat{\lambda} = -\varepsilon \hat{q}$ $\qquad \varepsilon = \text{const.} \geqslant 0$

(6) $\quad \hat{w} + \kappa \hat{L}$ $\qquad \kappa = \text{const.} > 0$

(7) $\quad \hat{q} = m$ $\qquad m = \text{const.} \geqslant 0$

The first four equations are used by Harris, too, so they need no further explanation. (5) and (6) give concrete expressions to his general functions, in particular iso-elastic functions are assumed. (6) does not only eliminate the wage-lag – it could be integrated to give w as a function of L – but also switches from the unemployment ratio (u) to employment (L) as independent variable. However, as labour supply is fixed and can be put equal to one by an appropriate choice of units, L is at the same time the employment ratio and can easily be retranslated into Harris' variable u.

In terms of Kaldor's conception of a technical progress function (TPF) what is involved by our assumptions is a linear TPF through the origin lying under the 45°-line, so that every technical change will imply a rising capital coefficient.[3] Moreover, by assuming (7), one point on this TPF is fixed.

The model can be reduced to a single differential equation, e.g. in the labour share v. After some manipulations,[4] we obtain

(8) $\quad \hat{v} = \dfrac{\alpha\kappa - (\alpha\kappa + \varepsilon m)v - m(\kappa + \varepsilon)q}{q + v + \kappa v}$

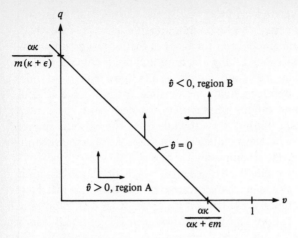

Figure 4

Obviously, its denominator is positive, therefore its sign is determined by and identical with the sign of its nominator. There exists a falling straight line in the v,q-plane which contains all combinations of v and q giving rise to $v = 0$, and which divides the plane into a region where $v > 0$ and a region where $v < 0$. This line is given by

(9) $$q \gtreqless \frac{\alpha\kappa}{m(\kappa + \varepsilon)} - \frac{\alpha\kappa + \varepsilon m}{m(\kappa + \varepsilon)} \Longleftarrow\Longrightarrow \hat{v} \lesseqgtr 0$$

and shown in Figure 4. An initial point lying in B will stay in this region but will move in north-west direction because v falls according to (9) while q rises according to (7). An initial point lying in A is bound to move north-eastwards and to cross the border after which no return is possible. This implies that the value of labour power is bound to fall, either from the start or after a finite period of time, depending on initial conditions. Note that the directions in which points (v,q) will move can be calculated from its coordinates by

(10) $$\frac{dq}{dv} = \frac{\dot{q}}{\dot{v}} = \frac{\hat{q}q}{\hat{v}v} = \frac{mq}{\hat{v}v}$$

where (8) has to be inserted for $\hat{v}$.

What will happen to the other variables? With respect to employment almost the same procedure can be followed. Solve the two equations in note 4 for L to obtain

(11) $$\hat{L} = \frac{\alpha(1 - v) - mq + \varepsilon mv}{q + v + \kappa v}$$

This gives rise to a straight-line locus for $\hat{L} = 0$ in the v,q-plane, i.e.

(12) $$q = \frac{\alpha}{m} - \frac{\alpha - \varepsilon m}{m}v$$

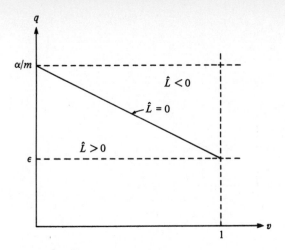

Figure 5

which falls under the reasonable parameter restriction

(13) $\alpha/m > \varepsilon$

and divides the plane into a field above it with falling employment and a region below it with rising employment, cf. Figure 5. Comparison of $\hat{L} = 0$ with $\hat{v} = 0$ shows that the former lies above the latter in the interval $v = [0,1]$.[5] Making use of (10) one can show that along the line given by (12) the trajectories will have slopes

(14) $\dot{q}/\dot{v} = -\dfrac{\alpha - (\alpha - \varepsilon m)v}{\varepsilon m v}$

The slope will be -1 for $v = 1$ and will continuously fall (rise in absolute terms) with a decline in v and finally approach $-\infty$ for $v \to 0$. There exists a critical value of v, call it v^*,

(15) $v^* = \dfrac{\varepsilon}{(1 + \varepsilon)(\alpha - \varepsilon m)}$

for which the slope of $\hat{L} = 0$ is identical with the slope of the trajectory in (v^*, q^*). Points on $\hat{L} = 0$ left of v^* will go to the region above $\hat{L} = 0$, which means that employment will fall. As the same type of argument can be applied for other $\hat{L}$-loci, fixing $\hat{L}$ at different constant values, one arrives at the conclusion that not only the value of labour power but also employment have to fall, at least in the long run. Note that because of (6) this result implies a falling real wage rate in the long run, too.[6]

Finally, let us consider the rate of profit. From (1) we can conclude in the old-fashioned way that if $v \to 0$ and $q \to \infty$, then the rate of profit will approach zero as time goes to infinity. The same result can be derived by means of our

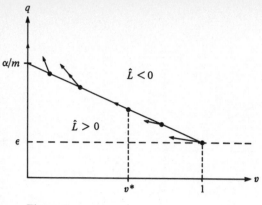

Figure 6

simple graphical framework. Let $\bar{r}$ be a certain positive value of the rate of profit. Then from (1) the locus of all points (v,q) which give rise to this particular $\bar{r}$ is calculated as

$$(16) \qquad q = 1/\bar{r} - v(1 + \bar{r})/\bar{r}$$

This, again, is a falling straight line which rotates clockwise around the pivot $v = 1, q = -1$ when $\bar{r}$ takes on ever smaller (positive) values, cf. Figure 7. Once again one can compare the slope of the trajectories along such an isoquant with the slope of the isoquant itself. And once again one will find that on any isoquant there is a point left of which points will move to the region above the isoquant, i.e. to lower profit rates. By repeating the argument one can show that no positive rate of profit can be preserved forever.

The model-exercise has shown that definite conclusions about the course not only of the profit rate but of employment and distribution can be derived if one chooses concrete assumptions on technical progress. Moreover, the results fit common Marxist assertions of an increasing reserve army of labour and an immiserisation of the proletariat alongside rising productivity and a falling rate of profit. This is also the way in which Schumpeter (1950b) has discussed the results of Marx's economics. A spectrum of interconnected laws – call it the law of long-run capitalist development – is obtained instead of merely a law of the FTRP if Harris' postulate is followed and 'appropriate' assumptions are used.

III

One could argue that the results of section II are founded on rather special assumptions and I would not object to this qualification. Nevertheless, the model can be used somewhat more flexibly. For instance, one is not forced to stick to certain values of $\hat{q}$ and $\hat{\lambda}$ forever.

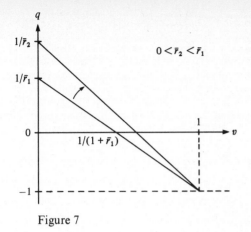

Figure 7

What happens, for instance, if $\hat{q} = 0$? This would be the case of neutral technical progress (or of no technical progress at all if at the same time $-\hat{\lambda} = 0$ were assumed). In this particular case the loci for $\hat{L} = 0$ and $\hat{v} = 0$ would both stand vertically in $v = 1$ and $v = 1$ would be a stable equilibrium value. As this vertical line is at the same time the locus for $\bar{r} = 0$, the profit rate will vanish in this situation as well. But this example of a FTRP-theory is very different from Marx's and has different – less gloomy – implications in terms of employment and distribution, at least for the working class.

In order to develop a macroeconomic law along Marxian lines, one should continue to develop models with non-neutral or rather Marxian technical progress. Of course, restrictions imposed by the constancy of growth rates and/or elasticities should be overcome. A particularly appealing case for investigation seems to me

$$(7)' \qquad \hat{q} = at, \qquad a = \text{const.} > 0$$

with the rest of the model. We would then have $q = a = \text{const.}$, $\lim\limits_{t \to \infty} q = \infty$ and a movement along the 'Marxian' technical progress function into the origin.

Beyond the 'logical consistency' issue there is the 'internal' quality of the law which should be improved by making technical progress endogenous via the profit-maximisation principle and/or other typical capitalistic motives or pressures. The empirical content of the Marxian law of long-run capitalist development will – according to my opinion – raise the greatest doubts. I think that it is precisely this difficulty which lies behind Harris' restriction of Marx's law to 'different phases of a cycle or "wave" of accumulation' (p. 59). If Marx's law does not work at any time, why shouldn't it work sometimes? But can a law restricted like that seriously claim the status of a 'macroeconomic law'?

Notes

1 Cf. Marx 1953: 639.
2 Cyclical fluctuations arise in Goodwin's growth cycle model as a consequence of the same assumption which Harris uses. As Goodwin's model is a special case of Harris', to be obtained by taking $m = 0$, $\alpha = 1$ and $-\hat{\lambda} = \text{const.} > 0$, cycles are liable to occur around the trend in Harris model, too. A short comment on that will follow below. Cf. Goodwin 1972.
3 Let k and y be capital intensity in the normal sense and labour productivity, respectively. Kaldor's TPF gives a relationship between $\hat{y}$ and $\hat{k}$. These variables are related to Harris' as follows:

(i) $k = q/\lambda;$ $\hat{k} = \hat{q} - \hat{\lambda}$

(ii) $y = 1/\lambda;$ $\hat{y} = -\hat{\lambda}$

From (i) and (5) we get

(iii) $\hat{k} = (1 + \varepsilon)\hat{q} = -[(1 + \varepsilon)/\varepsilon]\hat{\lambda}$

Therefore, there exists a TPF

(iv) $\hat{y} = [\varepsilon/(1 + \varepsilon)]\hat{k}$

with the properties described in the text.
4 Rewrite (3) in growth rates, i.e. $\hat{v} = \hat{\lambda} + \hat{w}$, and substitute (5)–(7) into it to obtain

(i) $\hat{v} = \kappa\hat{L} + \varepsilon m$

Next, substitute (2) and (1) into (4) and make use of (7) to get

(ii) $\hat{L} = \dfrac{\alpha(1 - v)}{q + v} - \dfrac{mq + v\hat{v}}{q + v}$

(8) follows if one substitutes (ii) for $\hat{L}$ and solves for $\hat{v}$.
5 It can be seen from equations of the model that $\hat{v} = 0$ is at the same time the locus for $\hat{L} = \varepsilon m/\kappa > 0$.
6 The latter result would not necessarily be true under the alternative assumption

(6)' $\hat{w} = \kappa\hat{L} - \gamma\hat{\lambda},$ $0 < \gamma = \text{const.} < 1;$

i.e. when real wage rises are also linked to productivity gains.

6 Economic Dynamics and Innovation: Ricardo, Marx and Schumpeter on Technological Change and Unemployment

PETER KALMBACH AND HEINZ D. KURZ

> We are being afflicted with a new disease of which some readers may not yet have heard the name, but of which they will hear a great deal in the years to come – namely technological unemployment. (Keynes 1930)

I

In the Preface to the first edition of the first volume of *Capital*, Marx (1977:20) wrote: 'It is the ultimate aim of this work, to lay bare the economic law of motion of modern society.' Schumpeter, in the Preface to the Japanese edition of *The Theory of Economic Development*, conceded frankly that his idea and intention were exactly the same as Marx's. Hence a comparison of the theories of economic dynamics of the two celebrated economists does not need to be justified.

Yet not only the general idea and intention of Schumpeter is the same as that of Marx, there are quite remarkable similarities in both theories. This is particularly true with regard to the theory of innovation. Although it would be most interesting to analyse in detail the two authors' approaches to this problem, this is too big a task for the present paper. In what follows only one, albeit important, aspect of this problem will be discussed. It is the question whether or not and under what conditions technological change will lead to persistent unemployment.

As is well known, this problem had been raised for the first time in respectable economic literature by Ricardo in the chapter 'On Machinery' in the third edition of the *Principles*. With this contribution, Ricardo triggered off a sometimes heated debate about the pros and cons of the possibility of what is frequently called 'technological unemployment'. Scrutiny shows that both Marx and Schumpeter in their own discussion of the problem under consideration started from Ricardo's analysis. In short, whereas Marx concentrated on an elaboration of Ricardo's arguments pro displacement, Schumpeter concentrated on those pro compensation. Hence they arrived at completely different conclusions as to the effect of technological change on employment.

The composition of the paper is as follows: in part II Ricardo's treatment of the machinery question will be expounded. Parts III and IV are basically devoted to a test of Marx and Schumpeter as historians of economic thought, i.e. the question is examined whether their representation of Ricardo is correct. In parts V and VI Marx's and Schumpeter's own views about innovation and economic dynamics with particular emphasis on the problem of employment will be discussed.

II

According to Sraffa (1951: lvii) the new chapter 'On Machinery' 'was the most revolutionary change' in the third edition of the *Principles*, published in 1821. In it Ricardo retracted his former opinion on the subject, according to which 'the application of machinery to any branch of production, as should have the effect of saving labour, was a *general good* accompanied only with that portion of inconvenience which in most cases attends the removal of capital and labour from one employment to another' (Ricardo 1951–73: I, 386).[1] The essence of Ricardo's original opinion can be summarized as follows: Technological progress of necessity reduces the quantity of labour that is needed (directly and indirectly) to produce one unit of the commodity, in whose production the technological change occurred; it reduces 'the sacrifices of labour' (ibid.: IV, 397). If the demand for the sectoral output does not grow in proportion to the increase in labour productivity, some workers would be discharged. However, 'as the capital which employed them was still in being ... it would be employed in the production of some other commodity, useful to the society, for which there could not fail to be a demand' (ibid.: I, 387). This is of course Say's Law. In Ricardo's formulation the latter states 'that there is no amount of capital which may not be employed in a country, because demand is only limited by production' (ibid.: 290). The tendency towards labour displacement due to the labour-saving character of technical progress is thus effectually counteracted by Say's Law and the assumption of the continued existence and mobility of the social capital. The problem of (additional) persistent unemployment could not arise, 'because the capitalist would have the power of demanding and employing the *same* quantity of labour as before, although he might be under the necessity of employing it in the production of a *new*, or at any rate of a different commodity' (ibid.: 387).

The third edition of the *Principles* came as a surprise to both friend and foe because of Ricardo's confession that he now thought his former views erroneous.[2] He no longer took it for granted that the working of Say's Law could, under any circumstances whatsoever, prevent the displacement of labour: 'I am convinced, that the *substitution* of machinery for human labour, is often *very injurious* to the interests of the class of labourers' (ibid.: 388). Ricardo's famous reasoning reads:

My mistake arose from the supposition, that whenever the net income [profits and rents] of a society increases, its gross income [profits, rents and wages] would also increase; I now, however, see reason to be satisfied that the one fund, from which landlords and capitalists derive their revenue, may increase, while the other, that upon which the labouring class mainly depend, may *diminish*, and therefore it follows ... that the same cause which may increase the net revenue of the country, may at the same time render the *population redundant*, and deteriorate the condition of the labourer. (ibid.: 388)

The argument can be put as follows: The newly invented machine will be introduced, i.e. the invention will become an innovation, if it raises the rate of profit, first of the entrepreneurial 'pioneer', then, for a given and constant real wage rate, of the economy as a whole. In fact, initially the capitalist, 'who made the discovery of the machine, or who first usefully applied it' (ibid.: 387), would pocket extra profits. Competition will then bring about a fall in prices to costs of production and thus establish the new *normal* rate of profit (r_1), which will be either equal to or higher than the previous rate (r_0).[3] Hence, with a *given* value of social capital $\bar{K}$, the technique that produces and uses the machine will be adopted, if

$$r_i = \frac{Y_i - W_i}{\bar{K}} \geqslant \frac{Y_0 - W_0}{\bar{K}} = r_0$$

where r_i ($i = 0,1$) is the rate of profit associated with technique i, Y_0 is the corresponding 'gross revenue', consisting of profits and wages (for simplicity rents are ignored), and W_i is the sum total of wages. Obviously, a fall in the value of the gross product ($Y_1 < Y_0$) does not of necessity prevent the introduction of the machine, since wages may also fall ($W_1 < W_0$). If they fell by more than the 'gross revenue', i.e.

$$W_0 - W_1 > Y_0 - Y_1,$$

then there are 'motives enough ... to substitute the fixed for the circulating capital' (Ricardo 1951–73: VIII, 389), i.e. the machine for labour. Clearly, capitalists are interested in 'net income' or profits and not in 'gross income' and thus employment. This is repeatedly stressed by Ricardo (see e.g. ibid.: I, 389).

The only type of technological innovation which according to Ricardo may cause serious (temporary) problems can be described in terms of the wage–profit frontier. In Figure 8 the profit rate r is measured on the horizontal axis and the real wage rate w and labour productivity y on the vertical axis. T_0 represents the wage–profit frontier of the technique that does not employ the machine whereas T_1 represents the frontier of the technique that does.[4] It is a characteristic feature of the type of innovation discussed by Ricardo that labour productivity (in physical terms) rises from y_0 to y_1, whilst the maximum rate of profits (associated with a hypothetical wage rate of zero) falls from r_0 to r_1. Clearly, whether or not the machine will be introduced depends on the level of the real wage rate. For $\bar{w}$ larger than the switchpoint wage rate

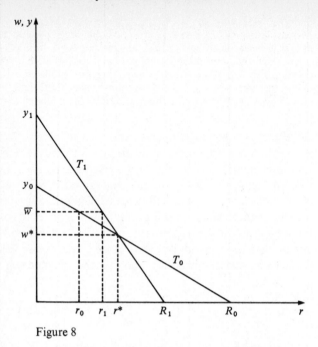

Figure 8

w^*, technique T_1 is superior to T_0, since it yields the higher (normal) rate of profit: $r_1 > r_0$. However, if $\bar{w}$ happens to be smaller than w^* the machine will not be adopted, because technique T_1 is less profitable than the received technique T_0.

Let us briefly turn to the case where the machine cannot be introduced *immediately* upon its invention because at the ruling real wage rate it is not profitable to do so. Does this mean that at *this* level of the *real* wage rate the invention will never become an innovation? This question, i.e. the problem of 'induced changes in process', is dealt with by Ricardo subsequent to his discussion of 'autonomous changes in process'.[5] Ricardo stresses: 'Machinery and labour are in constant competition and the former can frequently not be employed *until labour rises*' (ibid.: 395). This passage is typically interpreted in the manner suggested by Ferguson (1973: 6): 'In this passage one must interpret "labour rises" as meaning an increase in the *real* wage rate.' Now, although Ricardo left no doubt that with a rapid accumulation of capital and the ensuing tendency towards an excess demand for labour the real wage rate could rise and this for a considerable period of time, his above proposition does *not* imply a rising *real* wage, rather it presupposes a rising *money* wage. Ricardo's reasoning runs as follows: In the course of the accumulation of capital and the growth in population less and less fertile land has to be taken into cultivation and/or given land has to be cultivated more intensively in order to provide (on the no-rent land) per unit of output increases, which in

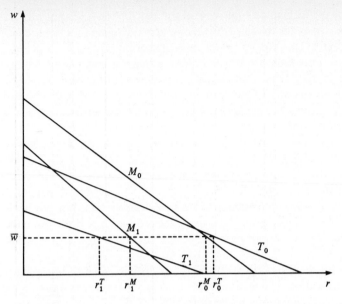

Figure 9

turn leads to an increase in the price of food and necessaries relative to the price of manufactured goods. In order to keep *real* wages at their previous (possibly subsistence) level, *money* wages have to rise to compensate for the increase in food prices. Hence, whereas in Ricardo's view agriculture is subject to diminishing returns, manufacture exhibits approximately constant returns, i.e. constant 'real' costs of production. It follows:[6] 'The *same* cause that raises labour [money wages], does *not* raise the value of machines, and, therefore, with every augmentation of capital, a greater proportion of it is employed on machinery' (Ricardo 1951–73: I, 395). Ricardo's considerations can again be expounded by means of the wage–profit frontier (see Figure 9). In the purely hypothetical case in which the accumulation is carried out without any improvements in the methods of production,[7] the wage–profit frontier would gradually shift towards the origin due to diminishing returns in agriculture and the related rise in the rent of land (see Kurz 1978). In Figure 9, for example, two wage–profit frontiers relate to this hypothetical course of events. Whereas T_0 refers to an 'early' stage of economic development, T_1 refers to a later one on the premise that no (improved) machinery has been introduced. Clearly, with a given and constant real wage w the profit rate would fall from r_0^T to r_1^T; the money wage would of course have to rise in order to counterbalance the associated rise in the price of wage commodities.

Now, Ricardo presupposes that in period 0 inventions exist already, which would allow the construction and application of a (new) machine. These methods of production can be thought of as collected in a sort of 'book of blue-prints'. The question arises, if, and when, these inventions become *innovations*. In order to answer it we have to investigate the consequences the introduction of machinery would have in periods 0 and 1 respectively. In accordance with Ricardo we shall assume that the machine is of the gross produce reducing type. Consequently the wage–profit frontiers shift in the characteristic way from T_0 to M_0 and from T_1 to M_1 (see Figure 9). Ricardo's idea that 'machinery can frequently not be employed until labor rises' is now clearly perceivable in terms of our diagram. In period 0, which is characterized by a relatively low money wage rate, the introduction of the machine would not be profitable at the given real wage rate $\bar{w}$, since $r_0^M < r_0^T$. In period 1, however, with its higher money wage rate, the introduction would be advantageous to the capitalists, since M_1 yields a higher rate of profit than T_1, i.e. $r_1^M > r_1^T$. The falling tendency of the rate of profit can thus be checked by means of a switch to the machine-using technology. Yet this is prejudicial to the interests of the labouring class, which suffers from the displacement of labour.

Despite his demonstration of the labour-displacing effect of the particular type of innovation which diminishes the gross produce, Ricardo did not advocate any policy measures to slow down or even stop the introduction of cost-reducing technological innovations: 'The statements which I have made will not, I hope, lead to the inference that machinery should not be encouraged' (Ricardo 1951–73: I, 395; see also ibid.: V, 303). He was convinced that such a policy was bound to fail. Indeed, it would be counterproductive, because it would aggravate the employment problem. Capital would be carried abroad, 'and this must be a much more serious discouragement to the demand for labour, than the most extensive employment of machinery' (ibid.: I, 396). In addition to this short-run effect such a policy would deteriorate the country's competitive position in the world market, i.e. lead to 'disadvantageous exchange' (ibid.: 397). Moreover, technological innovations generally increase profits and thus tend to stimulate accumulation and eliminate the damage they initially may have caused. To sum up: Ricardo relied on 'animal spirits' that propel the system's economic expansion and lead to a quick reabsorption of displaced workers. In other words, Ricardo was convinced that the 'principles' he had developed before the third edition of his *Principles* were still valid and were able to check and balance the new 'principle' presented in the third edition.[8]

After having set up the (exemplary) testing ground for Marx and Schumpeter as historians of economic thought let us now turn to the two celebrated scholars themselves and see how they came to grips with Ricardo's treatment of the machinery question.

III

The sincerity with which Ricardo recanted his former opinion made Marx praise his 'scientific impartiality and love of truth' (1954: 412), his '*honesty* which so essentially distinguish him from the vulgar economists' (1968:555; Marx's emphasis). However, there appears to be an additional and indeed deeper reason for Marx's approval of Ricardo's change of front on the matter. As Schumpeter (1954: 682n.) pointed out:

In this chapter, Ricardo comes nearer than he does anywhere else to the profit analysis that Marx was to make his own. Nowhere else is their relation so clearly the relation of *Professor Ricardo and tutee Marx* – though, as may be the case sometimes, neither would have been completely pleased with the other's performance.

So let us have a closer look at Marx's discussion of Ricardo's contribution to the theory of technological change, income distribution and employment.

Marx on the one hand welcomed Ricardo's attack on the naive theory of 'automatic compensation' and on the other hand accused the latter's analysis of being based on a number of 'false assumptions'.

He gave credit to Ricardo because 'redundant population or over-population is presented here as the *result of the process of enrichment itself,* and of the development of productive forces which conditions this process' (Marx 1968: 565). He criticized Ricardo's notion of accumulation as effectively providing for the reabsorption of all displaced workers: 'But in fact, it is capitalistic accumulation itself that *constantly* produces, and produces in the direct ratio of its own energy and extent, a relatively redundant population of labourers ... and therefore a surplus-population' (Marx 1954: 590): *the industrial reserve army of the unemployed.*

It is worth mentioning that Marx fully adopted Ricardo's idea that machinery will be introduced if (and only if) it reduces the quantity of labour necessary to produce one unit of the respective product. Indeed, Marx (ibid.: 417) considered this an 'infallible law' (*absolutes Gesetz*). However, as the debate on the choice of technique in linear models of production has shown, the 'law' Marx speaks of is far from infallible. As a matter of fact cost-minimizing systems of production need not be labour-minimizing (see e.g. Kurz 1979).

Moreover, Marx proposed very much in the same way as Ricardo (see e.g. Ricardo 1951–73: VI, 294) to ascertain the *hypothetical* (as opposed to the effective) displacement of labour on the basis of a *given* amount of the commodity in the production of which the technological improvement occurs. Hence, in order to determine the hypothetical employment effect of the introduction of machinery in one sector of the economy, one's attention must not be restricted to the change in the amount of labour *directly* employed in that sector; rather, the changes in employment in *all* sectors, i.e. in the *vertically integrated industry,* have to be taken into account. As Marx (1954: 417) pointed out:

Although machinery necessarily throws men out of work in those industries into which it is introduced, yet it may, notwithstanding this, bring about an increase of employment in other industries. This effect, however, *has nothing in common with the so-called theory of compensation.*

Secondly, Marx accepted the fundamental premise on which Ricardo's analysis rests. Accordingly each capitalist is seen as aiming at an increase of the rate of profit he can get and as being not at all concerned with the task of maximizing the total quantity of labour employed. (In this context it deserves mentioning that the neoclassical notion of 'full employment of labour' plays no role in Classical political economy.) In Marx's view machinery 'is a means for producing surplus-value' (ibid.: 351); its introduction is a purposeful act to raise the sum and rate of profits.

Marx, like Ricardo, stressed the importance of the extraordinary profits the introduction of machinery helps to provide: 'These profits not only form a source of *accelerated* accumulation, but also attract into the favoured sphere of production a large part of the additional social capital that is being constantly created, and is ever on the look-out for new investment' (ibid.: 424). And he was convinced that the dynamic forces inherent in the capitalist economy would lead to a long-run increase in the number of people employed in the industrial sector and possibly in the total amount of employment despite the postulated rise in the organic composition of capital, i.e. an increase in the demand for labour that is less than proportionate to the increase in social capital. Indeed, 'a relative decrease in the number of hands is consistent with an actual increase' (ibid.: 423; see also 1968: 560). Finally Marx also confirmed Ricardo's finding that machinery can often not be employed until wages rise (cf. ibid.: 370–2, 405).

So much as to Marx's agreement with Ricardo. Let us now turn to the more interesting question of his discrepancies from Ricardo's analysis. In this context it is worth mentioning that in contrast to Ricardo (and Schumpeter) Marx did not advocate the view that the first innovator reaps the large rewards. There are basically two reasons why those who first apply new technologies often go bankrupt, and only those who later enter the stage make money out of it. First, there are rapid improvements in the design of an innovation in its early stages, which lead to a quick 'moral depreciation' of its premature variants. This process of continual improvements, 'which lower the use-value, and therefore the value, of existing machinery ... has a particularly dire effect during the first period of newly introduced machinery, before it attains a certain stage of maturity, when it continually becomes antiquated before it has time to reproduce its own value' (Marx 1977: 113). Secondly, there are improvements in techniques for producing the machines which sharply reduce their cost of production and facilitate their application: 'When machinery is first introduced into an industry, new methods of reproducing it more cheaply follow blow upon blow' (Marx 1954: 380). Therefore, it is often sensible not to adopt the first vintage of a technological innovation but to wait until it has matured. In this context Marx points out that the capitalist's fear of 'moral depreciation' of his capital stock provides a special incentive to the prolongation of the working day.

The politically most remarkable difference consists of course in Marx's claim that it is not the use of machinery, but its *capitalistic* use, that causes all the problems: 'It is an *undoubted fact* that machinery, as such, is not responsible for "setting free" the workman from the means of subsistence .... The contradictions and antagonisms are *inseparable from the capitalist employment of machinery*' (ibid.: 415–16). In another passage it is contended that 'in a communistic society there would be a very different scope for the employment of machinery than there can be in bourgeois society' (ibid.: 371). Yet no satisfactory explanation of this view is provided.

Marx considered Ricardo's optimism as to the capitalist system's ability to reabsorb all the displaced workers 'nonsense' (Marx 1968: 561) and referred to it as the 'apologetic bourgeois presentation of machinery' (ibid.: 571). Rather it is 'the *constant* artificial production of a surplus population, which disappears only in times of feverish prosperity, which is one of the *necessary* conditions of production of modern industry' (ibid.: 560). This creation of a permanent reserve army of workers 'greatly increases the power of capital' (ibid.: 554); it keeps wages low and facilitates the extension of the working day and the intensification of labour. Yet how is the *permanence* of the reserve army explained by Marx? Since we shall come back to this problem in section V of this chapter a few remarks must suffice.

One reasoning is that even if the effects of each distinct act of mechanization were of a temporary nature, it is the continuous occurrence of such distinct acts that contributes to the explanation of persistent unemployment. In Marx's (1954: 407) words: 'since machinery is *continually* seizing upon new fields of production, its temporary effect is really *permanent*'.[9] A parallel can perhaps be drawn between this type of argument and Marx's rejection of Say's Law on the grounds that crises in single markets do always exist and that therefore there will never be a situation of full equilibrium. Furthermore Marx argued that single market crises may trigger off cumulative effects and result in 'a more or less general (*relative*) over-production.... On the one hand there is a superabundance of all the means of reproduction and a superabundance of all kinds of unsold commodities on the market. On the other hand bankrupt capitalists and destitute, starving workers' (1968: 523; Marx's emphasis). Thus in both cases, with respect to machinery and to Say's Law, Marx was concerned with a radicalization and generalization of the received (Ricardian) doctrine.

Let us dwell a little more on Marx's criticism of Say's Law, because it is in fact the starting point of a further argument put forward by Marx to explain the persistence of unemployment. The reader may have noticed the 'Keynesian flavour' of the passage quoted last. Indeed, it can be argued that Marx came very close to formulating the principle of *effective demand*, according to which aggregate demand may be insufficient to absorb the output produced from normal utilization of the existing productive capacity.[10] It will be remembered that in Ricardo's opinion 'demand is only limited by production'. Hence, if consequent upon the introduction of machinery the production of food and necessaries falls, the demand for these commodities and *thus* the demand for labour must also fall. Marx (1968: 579–80) objects to this reasoning: 'This relative diminution in the reproduction of variable capital, however, is not the reason for the relative decrease in the demand for labour, but on the contrary, its effect.'

Consequently, we need a theory of *demand for labour* rather than of *supply of commodities in the support of labour*. Moreover, Ricardo's assertion that there can be 'no amount of capital that does not find employment' contradicts the facts. To provide an example, Marx referred to 'the plight of the Lancashire unemployed labourers' on the one hand and '"the difficulty of finding employment for money" on the London money market' on the other. In Ricardo's theory such a coexistence of unemployment and idle capital is not allowed for. Indeed, according to Ricardo 'some new field of employment ought to have been opened up, for on the one hand there is capital in London, and on the other, unemployed workers in Manchester' (Marx 1968: 580–1; see also p. 560).

Closely connected with Marx's criticism of Say's Law is another important departure from Ricardo's analysis. It consists in Marx's emphasis on the *cyclical* pattern of the accumulation process. Once the modern industrial system has been established, once the factory system has gained 'a certain breadth of footing and a definite degree of maturity' and 'machinery is generally produced by means of machinery', 'this mode of production acquires an *elasticity*, a capacity for sudden extension by leaps and bounds that find no hindrance except in the supply of raw material and in the *disposal of the produce* [*Absatzmarkt*]' (Marx 1954: 424). Hence:

The life of modern industry becomes a series of periods of moderate activity, prosperity, over-production, crisis and stagnation. The uncertainty and instability to which machinery *subjects* employment, and consequently the conditions of existence, of the operatives become normal, owing to these periodic changes of the *industrial cycle*. (ibid.: 427)

A further objection of Marx's was directed against Ricardo's neglect of the elements of circulating capital other than wages, such as raw and auxiliary materials, etc. (see e.g. Marx 1968: 564–5).[11] Moreover, Marx criticized Ricardo for having left out of consideration the '*moral depreciation*' of parts of the received capital stock. The phenomenon Marx referred to owes its existence to the fact that 'competition compels the replacement of the old instruments of labour by new ones before the expiration of their natural life, especially when decisive changes occur' (Marx 1972: 174). Consequently: 'In this case, not only is the labourer displaced, but his instrument of production too ceases to be capital' (Marx 1968: 556). This in turn reduces the volume of employment opportunities in the system as a whole.

Finally, Marx radicalized the proposition that the machine is a means to prevent a rise of wages and drew an important conclusion. Insofar as the increase in the reserve army of the unemployed entailed by technological changes tends to decrease the (real) wage rate, capitalists in certain branches may find the employment of machinery no longer profitable and switch back to 'labour intensive' methods of production (see Marx 1954: 371).

Schumpeter in his assessment of Marx's contribution to the analysis of technological change and employment arrives at the somewhat harsh judgement: 'Marx ... accepted Ricardo's analysis, adding nothing essential but minimizing the Ricardian qualifications, beating out the slender result to its thinnest leaf' (Schumpeter 1954: 685). So in Schumpeter's view Marx failed. Did Schumpeter succeed?

IV

Schumpeter introduces the section 'Distributive Shares and Technological Advance' in the *History of Economic Analysis* with the provocative contention: 'The study of the nineteenth-century literature on this topic is a tedious task. The economists of that period were *unable to see the general problem at all*' (1954: 679–80). If they did not, who did?

According to Schumpeter 'the controversy that went on throughout the nineteenth century and beyond, mainly in the form of argument pro and con "compensation", is dead and buried:...it vanished from the scene as a better technique filtered into general use which left *nothing to disagree about*' (ibid.: 684). The better technique was well expounded, he suggested, in Hicks' *Theory of Wages* (1932). Schumpeter was mistaken. Ironically, it was Hicks himself who disproved Schumpeter's bold assertion. In particular, Hicks considered Ricardo's discussion of machinery a most useful guide to the understanding of the early phase of industrialization. In his *A Theory of Economic History* (1969) Hicks used Ricardo's argument to explain why the rise in the real wages was so long delayed during the process of mechanization in England.[12] Hence Hicks, like Ricardo, changed the front on the matter, i.e. adopted the view that the introduction of machinery may be injurious to the interests of the workers. Hicks (1969: 151) praised Ricardo's 'candour and courage; he followed his reasoning where it led him, not just where he (or his friends) wanted it to go'.[13] May we not praise Hicks for having followed his reasoning where it led him, not just where Schumpeter (and others) wanted it to go?

Schumpeter was mistaken a second time. He regarded the Ricardian approach as a 'detour' that 'falls out of the historical line of economists' endeavours'. More specifically, he accused Ricardo of having 'failed to see the explanatory principle offered by the valuation aspect' to the problem of distribution (Schumpeter 1954: 568). Now, it is true that Ricardo did not determine the division of the product in terms of the 'opposing forces' of the demand for and the supply of given 'factors of production'. Instead, his determination of wages are centred around the notion of a historically and biologically explained level of subsistence, whereas profits were considered as a social surplus distributed in proportion to the capital advanced in each industry. It is also true that Ricardo's analysis of the problem of value and distribution contained several shortcomings. Yet to conclude, as Schumpeter did, that *in principle* no coherent solution can be provided along the Classical line of thought is a *non-sequitur*. Moreover, what Schumpeter thought impossible was accomplished by the late Piero Sraffa whose *Production of Commodities by Means of Commodities* (Sraffa 1960) laid the foundations for a revival of the Classical approach and critique of the marginalist theory of value and distribution.

In his discussion of Ricardo's analysis of machinery Schumpeter stressed that two cases of technological change must be carefully distinguished. First, there is the case of innovations that revolutionize the 'technological horizons' of producers. According to Schumpeter (1954: 679–80n.) the Classical writers, with the exception of Barton, 'thought exclusively or almost exclusively of this case'. They hardly ever realized that there is a second case, 'a change in the combination of factors within unchanging production functions'.

This criticism of the Classical authors in general and Ricardo in particular is closely related to Schumpeter's contention that the failure of the Classical economists derives from their inability 'to understand substitution (both of factors and of products) in its full importance' (ibid.: 68n.). Indeed, the fact that these authors 'were not in possession of [the principle of substitution] ... constitutes one of the most serious shortcomings of their analytic apparatus' (ibid.: 590).

Now it is of course *not* true that Ricardo failed to see the second case of technological change Schumpeter referred to. After having dealt with the case in which improved machinery is suddenly discovered and extensively used, he turned to the case in which consequent upon a change in income distribution the introduction of machinery that is already known becomes profitable. As we have seen in section II it is precisely this latter case that is addressed in Ricardo's famous dictum that 'machinery and labour are in constant competition, and the former can frequently not be employed until labour [i.e. the money wage] rises'.

By the same token it cannot be maintained that Ricardo had no concept whatsoever of 'substitution'. Indeed chapter XXXI is expressly devoted to a discussion of the 'substitution of machinery for human labour' (Ricardo 1951–73: I, 388). But Schumpeter is correct in stressing that in Ricardo we find neither the marginalist notion of substitutability of 'factors of production' along given 'production functions' nor the marginalist notion of substitutability in consumption between goods. Ricardo's case refers explicitly to *changes in the methods of production*, i.e. 'process changes', that bring with it qualitative changes in the means of production which are produced and used. Due to the specificity of the means of production and the various kinds of labour associated with different techniques this case of 'substitution' generally lacks smoothness. This was demonstrated by Ricardo, whose investigation of the introduction, i.e. the construction and utilization, of (improved) machinery can be regarded as an 'early and rude' *traverse* analysis. Moreover, in the light of the recent controversy in the theory of capital Ricardo's failure 'to understand substitution in its full importance' does not seem to be that serious. For it has been shown that in heterogeneous capital goods models the traditional marginalist concept of substitution breaks down, since the direction of change of the input proportions cannot be related unambiguously to the changes of 'factor prices'. This is a crucial point. Generations of neoclassically trained economists had been accustomed to think that a change in a specific direction of the input proportions is of necessity associated with a change in the opposite direction of the corresponding relative 'factor prices'. This traditional belief, which is given so much prominence in Schumpeter's critique of Ricardo, is false.

Schumpeter then goes on to discuss Ricardo's argument.[14] He emphasized the increase in the organic composition of capital entailed by the process of mechanization. Yet strangely enough he concludes that 'the manufacturers' wage fund will be *permanently* decreased'; he adds that this 'is what Ricardo set out to prove' (Schumpeter 1954: 682–3). Subsequently, however, he correctly points out that according to Ricardo additional accumulations will fill up the depleted 'wage fund' and lead to an increase in the level of employment. Schumpeter's main concern is with what happens to the displaced workers in the short run. He contends that 'they cannot remain unemployed unless we are prepared to violate the assumption that perfect competition and *unlimited flexibility of wages* prevail' (ibid.: 683). Of course, this assumption is not to be found in Ricardo's theory, in which a fall in the real wage is considered neither a necessary consequence of nor an effective remedy to the displacement of workers. Rather it is the standard assumption underlying the marginalist theories of employment. In contrast to Schumpeter Ricardo did not base his argument on the familiar 'factor price–factor quantity' mechanism, i.e. did not ascertain the level of employment in terms of a demand and supply analysis of the labour market. But even if in Ricardo's system a fall in real wages consequent upon a rise in unemployment had been allowed for, this would not necessarily have implied the reabsorption of all displaced workers. For, as was mentioned earlier, Ricardo did not presuppose the possibility of producing any commodity with different proportions of the same factors. Moreover, in Ricardo's view there existed at any rate a lower-bound to the fall in the real wage rate given by the minimum level of subsistence.

V

While Ricardo was convinced that the emergence of a considerable displacement of labour which cannot be reabsorbed in the short run is tied to the case where improved machinery (of the output-reducing type) is *suddenly* discovered, and extensively used, Marx tried to show that the long-run consequences of technical change *and* accumulation of necessity consist in an increasing industrial reserve army of the unemployed. In what follows we shall investigate how he arrived at this radicalization of Ricardo's view, i.e. why what in Ricardo's system was a possibility of limited empirical importance became the *general law of capitalistic accumulation* in Marx's.

Many interpreters of Marx's theory seem to think that the answer is simply this: The secular rise in the industrial reserve army is due to the secular rise in the organic composition of capital. Several objections are here in order. First, the concept of the organic composition of capital is a dubious one. Marx defines the organic composition of capital as the value composition of capital insofar as it is determined by the technical composition of capital. Even if there is only homogeneous labour, and a constant basket of wage goods, the technical composition of capital can only be expressed as a ratio of two vectors and even when most of the elements in the numerator increase some elements normally will fall. However, if there is a fall in just one it is no longer possible to speak of a rising technical composition in an unambiguous way. So the Marxian hypothesis only makes sense if it is formulated as follows: The value composition of capital rises, even if there is some capital-saving technical progress (some elements in the vector fall, a case which Marx surely was aware of (Marx 1977: 79)) and even if the labour values of some or all elements of constant capital fall. Consequently there is only one concept of the composition of capital that is important economically: the value composition.

Secondly Marx was not able to provide a convincing argument why that form of technical progress which leads to a rising value composition of capital necessarily dominates the capitalist development. This is, of course, an important objection to Marx's reasoning, but it is not an objection to the view that a rise in the value composition of capital entails a rising industrial reserve army. Therefore the latter problem can be analysed separately.

So let us assume that the value composition of capital rises. Marx's analysis was not unambiguous and sometimes it was even contradictory as to its implications for the reserve army. On the one hand he wrote: 'Since the demand for labour is determined not by the amount of capital as a whole, but by its variable constituent alone, that demand falls progressively with the increase of the total capital' (Marx 1954: 590). But this was obviously meant in a relative sense, because he also wrote: 'With the growth of the total capital, its variable constituent or the labour incorporated in it, also does increase, but in a constantly diminishing proportion' (ibid.: 590). Consequently, the rising value composition cannot be used without additional qualifications as an argument in support of a decline in total labour demand.

So the question arises whether the rate of growth of variable capital can be permanently positive or whether this assumption contradicts other elements of Marx's theory. To go a little deeper into this question we use some very simple arithmetics.

The growth rate of capital in the Marxian system (g) is a weighted average of the rates of growth of variable and constant capital.

(1) $$g = \frac{\dot{c}}{c}\frac{c}{c+v} + \frac{\dot{v}}{v}\frac{v}{c+v} = \frac{1}{\frac{c}{v}+1}\left(\frac{\dot{c}}{c}\frac{c}{v} + \frac{\dot{v}}{v}\right)$$

A rising value composition of capital is, of course, equivalent to $\dot{c}/c > \dot{v}/v$. It is not completely clear whether Marx argued in terms of first- or second-order derivatives, i.e. whether the difference between the two growth rates itself rises or is constant. Let us assume it is constant (an assumption which abstracts from the fact that in Marx's view the accumulation process exhibits vast discontinuities and cyclical behaviour, a view shared by Schumpeter; in what follows we shall disregard this complication):

(2) $$\frac{\dot{c}}{c} - \frac{\dot{v}}{v} = \bar{d}, \quad \bar{d} > 0$$

From (1) and (2) we get

(3) $$g = \frac{\dot{c}}{c} - \frac{\bar{d}}{1 + \frac{c}{v}}$$

As can be seen, a rising organic composition makes the differences between g and $\dot{c}/c$ smaller and smaller in the course of time. On the other hand the difference between g and $\dot{v}/v$ approaches $\bar{d}$.

(4) $$\frac{\dot{v}}{v} = g - \frac{\bar{d}}{1 + \frac{v}{c}}$$

If both $\dot{c}/c$ and $\dot{v}/v$ are constant rates of growth (which is a special case of (2)), g, $\dot{v}/v < g < \dot{c}/c$ must rise and approach asymptotically $\dot{c}/c$.

Now let us assume g is constant ($\bar{g}$). If we retain the assumption expressed in (2) this is only possible if $\dot{c}/c$ and $\dot{v}/v$ fall, as can be seen from (3) and (4) with $g = \bar{g}$ which gives us two differential equations

(3a) $$\dot{c} = \bar{g}c + \frac{\bar{d}c}{1 + \frac{c}{v}}$$

(4a) $$\dot{v} = \bar{g}v - \frac{\bar{d}v}{1 + \frac{v}{c}}$$

The assumption of constancy of g implies a fall in $\dot{v}/v$. What is more, $\dot{v}/v$ must become negative sooner or later, provided that $\bar{d} > \bar{g}$. As can be seen from (4a) there is a value of the composition of capital at which $\dot{v}/v = 0$, i.e.

(5) $$\frac{c}{v} = \frac{\bar{g}}{\dfrac{\dot{c}}{c} - \bar{g}}$$

$\dot{c}/c$ is, of course, equal to $\bar{d}$ if $\dot{v}/v = 0$, as we already know from (4), $\dot{v}/v$ can only become negative if $\bar{d} > \bar{g}$. The value of c/v defined in (5) is the line of demarcation between positive and negative rates of growth of v.

According to Morishima (1973: chapter 10) the Marxian rate of accumulation is not identical with the rate of growth of capital, rather it is defined in the following way:

(6) $$q = \frac{\dot{c} + \dot{v}}{m}$$

where m is the surplus value. If e is the rate of exploitation (m/v), we can write

(7) $$q = \frac{1}{e}\left(\frac{\dot{c}}{c}\frac{c}{v} + \frac{\dot{v}}{v}\right)$$

Comparing q and g we see that

(8) $$g = q\frac{e}{\dfrac{c}{v} + 1}, \quad \text{or}$$

(9) $$g = qr,$$

where r is the Marxian (value) rate of profit.

Occasionally it is assumed that q is a constant in the Marxian system. However, in contrast to the propensity to save out of profits in the Cambridge growth model q cannot be considered a simple behavioural parameter. For it is derived from magnitudes which are conceptualized in terms of labour values that are not observable and therefore cannot be regarded as guiding the behaviour of economic agents. Yet if this assumption should underlie the Marxian system and if in addition the law of the falling rate of profit should hold, it follows that g must decline.[15] With d constant or even rising the line of demarcation between positive and negative rates of growth of v must indeed sooner or later be reached.

We cannot be sure that a declining growth rate of capital is the adequate representation of the Marxian idea about capitalist development. The 'Faustian conflict' between accumulation and consumption may be solved in a way which results in a rising rate of accumulation. The increase in the rate of accumulation[16] can result in a constant or increasing g, even if the rate of profit falls. Therefore it is not possible to give a definite answer as to the direction of change in variable capital (v). It is possible that the variable capital sooner or later declines but this is not a necessity which follows from the rising value composition of capital. Obviously it is necessary to study the relationship between the different variables of the Marxian system and to specify certain technological and behavioural assumptions before anything definite can be said.

But even if we know the development of variable capital (v) we do not know yet how the demand for *labour* develops. The expression v stands for a value magnitude which is defined in the following way:

$$v = (\Lambda \cdot \omega) \cdot L$$

where Λ is the vector of direct and indirect labour embodied in the various commodities, ω the real wage bundle per unit of labour (e.g. hour) and L total labour (hours). Now it makes no sense to assume that technical progress does not affect the production of wage goods. However, if at least one element in Λ decreases and this is not completely neutralized by an appropriate change in the vector ω there is obviously no proportionality between v and L. Therefore, in general we cannot rule out the possibility that L increases even if v decreases.

Our provisional result is that the assumption of a rising organic composition of capital *per se* is not sufficient to establish a theory of decreasing demand for labour. Much less still can the theory of an increasing industrial reserve army be deduced from this assumption because the rate of unemployment is determined not only by labour demand but also by labour supply. Evidently Marx's theory of the industrial reserve army in addition needs a theory of the supply of labour.

There is ample evidence that Marx did not assume the labour force to grow at a constant and exogenously given rate. He stated quite explicitly: 'Capital works on both sides at the same time' (Marx 1954: 599). This expresses his view that accumulation is not only a process the result of which is an increase in the demand for labour. In his opinion the process of accumulation at the same time generates the labour force it needs – and this in various ways. To mention but three: First, in the non-capitalistic sector of the economy there is hidden unemployment which provides additional work-force available to the industrial sector. (This argument bears some relationship to the one put forward by Lewis.) Second, capitalistic production will invade the non-capitalistic sector and as a consequence there will be an absolute decline in the demand for labour in that sector, which in turn increases the labour supply in other sectors. Third, the process of centralization and concentration has the consequence that persons who formerly had been capitalists will become members of the working class.

We do not want to discuss here how realistic the different assumptions are or have been for certain periods in history. What is of interest in our context is that the Marxian theory of a rising industrial reserve army obviously does not rest on one pillar only, i.e. the tendency of the composition of capital to rise, but in addition at least on a second one, i.e. a theory of the supply of labour which stresses the latter's dependence on the accumulation process itself. So, even if the demand for labour should not decline in the process of accumulation there are still arguments in support of a rising industrial reserve army in the Marxian system.

What Marx tried to show is that there are cyclical variations in the volume of the industrial reserve army, but that it will not disappear even in the boom. If this could be shown to be an adequate description of the process of capitalistic development there would never be any labour-constraint to the process of accumulation. And this is, of course, a central idea of Marx: In his view neither the growth in population nor the scarcity of land are binding constraints to the capitalistic development: 'the *real barrier* of capitalist production is *capital itself*' (Marx 1977: 250; Marx's emphasis).

But a third pillar on which Marx's theory rests can be identified. It is the principle of effective demand which is clearly present, at least in an embryonic form, in Marx's work.

In Ricardo's approach to the problem of technological change, Say's Law was not challenged: 'Productions are always bought by productions, or by services; money is only the medium by which the exchange is effected' (Ricardo 1951–73: I, 291–2). Marx launches a severe attack on this view. According to Ricardo 'no man produces, but with a view to consume or sell, and he never sells but with an intention to purchase some other commodity.... By producing, then, he necessarily becomes either the consumer of his own goods, or the purchaser and consumer of the goods of some other person' (ibid.: 290). In Marx's view this is a completely deceptive conception of capitalist production. Even in simple commodity production there are two phases of the circuit, sale (M–C) and purchase (C–M). Money is not just the medium by which the exchange is effected: 'In *commodity production* the conversion of the product into money, the sale, is a *conditio sine qua non*' (Marx 1968: 509; Marx's emphasis). The *possibility* of crisis 'arises from the fact that the commodity must be turned into money but the money need not be immediately turned into commodity, and therefore *sale* and *purchase* can be separated' (ibid.: 509; Marx's emphasis).

Capitalist production is different from simple commodity production. The production cycle begins and ends with capital in the monetary form and the circuit of capital comprises three stages, as it is expressed in the famous formula M–C ... P ... C'–M' (Marx 1972: 103). This formula forms the basis of Marx's critique of Ricardo. To the latter's statement that nobody sells but with an intention to purchase Marx objects: 'Everyone *sells* first of all in order to sell, that is to say in order to transform commodities into money'; and: 'The immediate purpose of capitalist production is not the possession of other goods, but the appropriation of value, of money, of abstract wealth' (Marx 1968: 503; Marx's emphasis).

Clearly, for Marx the *possibility of crisis* derives from the separation of sale and purchase. However, this separation does not constitute in itself a theory of the *necessity* of crisis, even though in places Marx gives the impression that this is the case at least with regard to capitalist production: 'it appears that capital may provide a much more concrete basis for turning this possibility into reality' (ibid.: 511). We cannot go deeper into this question. Instead in what follows we shall briefly trace the implications of Marx's 'classical theory deprived of Say's Law' for his theory of unemployment.

In his discussion of the compensation theory it becomes clear that he takes into consideration the leakage in demand which occurs when improved machinery displaces labourers. He writes: 'The circumstance that they were "freed" by the machinery, from the means of purchase, changed them from buyers into non-buyers' (Marx 1954: 414). But this is not the end of the story: The declining demand for wage goods entails a displacement of workers in the production of these goods, which in turn leads to a displacement of workers in the production of the means of production, and so on.

The important conclusion drawn by Marx reads: 'machinery throws workmen on the street, not only in that branch of production in which it is introduced, but also in those branches in which it is not introduced' (ibid.: 415). Marx is well aware of the fact that this is only the case if there is not an injection of additional demand that steps in place. This is, of course, an important theme in Keynesian and Post-Keynesian theory. The injection which is necessary has to come (in the closed economy without government expenditures) from (additional) investment, but if an accelerator principle is involved the declining consumption or even a decline in consumption growth has negative effects on investment and hence the required injection does not come about.

Given the structure of Marx's theory of the industrial reserve army it cannot simply be qualified as a theory of *technological* unemployment (see Schumpeter 1954: 685). The rising value composition is but one, albeit important, element in his theory. In addition, the dependence of the supply of labour on the process of accumulation itself and the rejection of Say's Law play important roles in his reasoning. Especially in his critique of Say's Law it becomes clear that cyclical and technological aspects of unemployment have to be considered a unity. Marx certainly did not have the 'habit of distinguishing between, and contrasting, cyclical and technological unemployment' (Schumpeter 1939: 515). On the other hand Marx would presumably not have subscribed to the view 'that basically cyclical unemployment *is* technological unemployment' (ibid.: 515).

VI

If the essence of Marx's approach to the problem can be seen in a radicalization of Ricardo's theory about the effect of new machinery, Schumpeter's can be seen as an attempt to show that Ricardo's theory foundered because of the shortcomings of the analytical apparatus at his disposal.

As we have seen in section IV Schumpeter saw a superior technique contained in Hicks' *Theory of Wages*. However, nine years after the publication of Schumpeter's *History* Hicks wrote in the Preface to the second edition of his book: 'I let it go out of print because my own views upon its subject had changed so much that I no longer desired to be represented by it' (Hicks 1963: p. v). This is particularly true with regard to the chapter mentioned by Schumpeter, chapter VI on 'Distribution and Economic Progress'. Since then Hicks frequently stressed that he considers the methodology used in his *Theory of Wages* especially unsatisfactory for the analysis of technical change. In *Capital and Time* (Hicks 1973) he used a neo-Austrian approach which is completely different from his approach in *Theory of Wages*. In the former, technological change is seen as a process which can be understood only if the so-called traverse, i.e. the transition between steady-states, is analysed. Such a process needs time and is normally connected with a restructuring of capital as has been shown by A. Lowe (1976), another pioneer in the analysis of the traverse.

It is in the first instance the neglect of time which Hicks now thinks to be inadequate in his old approach. With regard to his famous distinction between autonomous and induced inventions (also contained in chapter VI of *Theory of Wages*) his present view is as follows: 'It is a static distinction, quite out of time, though it concerns a matter where some time-preference is essential. When one puts it back *into time*, it looks quite different' (Hicks 1982: 295).

But let us turn to the arguments which Schumpeter offers himself pro compensation. Already in his *Theory of Economic Development* he entered into a brief discussion of this question. After having stated that mechanization must have the result that a given product is produced with less labour, he pointed out:

This ... spells great and painful, but in the main only transitory, difficulties. For the total real demand for labour cannot in general permanently fall, because, neglecting all compensating and all secondary elements, the expenditure of that part of entrepreneurial profit which is not annihilated by the fall in prices necessarily more than prevents any lasting shrinkage. Even if it were expended solely on consumption it must be resolved into wages .... When, and to the extent that, it is invested an increase in the real demand for labour takes place. (Schumpeter 1934: 250f.)

This is not just Say's Law in its purest form, it is the theory of automatic compensation which is basically identical with the one put forward by McCulloch (cf. Blaug 1958).

In the *History of Economic Analysis* another argument is put forward. Referring to Ricardo's example he remarked that 'we are not told what happens to the workmen who have lost their jobs' and stresses that they cannot remain unemployed unless we are prepared to violate the assumption of unlimited flexibility of wages (cf. Schumpeter 1954: 683). This argument is exactly the same as Wicksell's, who argued that 'as soon as a number of labourers have been made superfluous by these changes, and wages have accordingly fallen, as Ricardo failed to see, more labour intensive methods of production ... will become more profitable ... and absorb the surplus of idle labourers' (Schumpeter 1934: 137). The only problem which may arise is that the full-employment wage rate may be smaller than the subsistence level. Schumpeter did not discuss this possibility, whereas Wicksell did. Even in this case Wicksell did not advocate trying to set some lower bound to the fall in the wage rate. Instead, he suggested that workers should be supported by the government to the extent of the differences between the subsistence level and the going wage rate.

In Hicks' book, to which Schumpeter referred, this problem was discussed too. Hicks conceded that such inventions which reduce labour's marginal product are possible, but: 'there are simultaneously at work other forces, derived from the increase of capital and the expansion of autonomous invention, tending to increase the marginal product of labour. There can be no doubt that these latter forces are usually far more important' (Hicks 1963: 129). But immediately thereafter Hicks provided an argument which should have alarmed Schumpeter:

it may be suggested, very tentatively, that a fall in the general level of wages is really likely to occur as the result of invention only on those rare occasions when invention breaks into a new extensive field of industry that has long been conservative in its methods. Such economic revolutions always cause maladjustment; but it may be useful to point out that in such times the malaise may go deeper. A fall in the equilibrium level of wages is here a real possibility. (ibid.: 129)

However, Hicks adds: 'Our continuous "industrial revolution" protects us from the discontinuous revolutions of the past' (ibid.: 129).

Now, in Schumpeter's view discontinuity is certainly not a matter of the past, it is the essence of capitalist development and moreover the boom, caused by discontinuous innovations, is characterized by rising wages (Schumpeter 1934: 248). Evidently there is a contradiction between Hicks' and Schumpeter's views.

Some conclusions can be drawn now. As is well known, not only innovations are of central importance to the Schumpeterian system but also the discontinuity of innovations. 'Clustering' of innovations is a central argument in Schumpeter's theory. It is precisely this case which economists as different as Ricardo and Hicks thought most dangerous for the working class, Ricardo emphasizing the possibility of unemployment, Hicks of falling wage rates. Schumpeter gives no satisfactory answers in this respect. Instead, he repeats the traditional arguments of the received compensation theory. The impression is well-nigh unavoidable that he wanted to escape a discussion of the different effects which different types of 'new combinations', in particular new products as opposed to new methods of production, may have on the economic system. Yet it is exactly this question which is again on the agenda.

Notes

1 If not otherwise stated emphases are ours.
2 For a detailed discussion of Ricardo's views on machinery, see Jeck and Kurz (1983).
3 Whereas in the *Essay on Profits* Ricardo (1951–73: IV, 25–6) thought that the introduction of machinery could not affect the *normal* rate of profit, later he changed his opinion; see, for example, his correspondence with McCulloch in June 1821 (in particular, ibid.: VIII, 389).
4 Following Ricardo's lead we set aside the influence of the rate of profit on relative prices and plot the wage–profit frontiers as straight lines.
5 The terminology is Hollander's (1979: 351, 355).
6 Ricardo did not properly take into account the impact of increasing costs of raw materials on the prices of industrial products.
7 Ricardo referred to this case as the 'natural progress' of society.
8 The criticism put forward by several authors (see e.g.: Malthus' letter to Ricardo of July 1821, Ricardo 1951–73: IX, 18–19; Blaug 1958: 69–70; and Clair 1965: 251, according to which Ricardo's new view on machinery is incompatible with the rest of his analysis) appears thus to be unfounded. For a detailed discussion of this issue see Jeck and Kurz (1983: part III).
9 Apparently, Schumpeter missed this argument in Marx. Otherwise he could not have written that precisely this argument 'would have supplied Marx with a theory of permanent unemployment that would have been much less untenable than was his own' (Schumpeter 1954: 681n.).
10 This has been convincingly argued by Garegnani (1978).
11 This criticism of Ricardo's analysis is already to be found in Mill (1965: 97).
12 See also the controversy between Beach (1971) and Hicks (1971).
13 As is well known, McCulloch who in 1820 became a convert to Ricardo's former view fiercely protested against Ricardo's new one published in the third edition of the *Principles* (see, especially: Ricardo 1951–73: VIII, 382).
14 Apparently, he tends to overestimate Barton's influence on Ricardo's change of mind on the subject of machinery; for a more balanced view of this see Hollander (1979: 349–57).
15 Without giving an exact proof we can state that a declining growth rate of capital and a growing difference between the rates of growth of the two parts of capital will lead to this result all the more.
16 For the difference of growth rate of capital and rate of accumulation see Morishima (1973).

7 Schumpeter as a Walrasian Austrian and Keynes as a Classical Marshallian[1]

BERTRAM SCHEFOLD

I

'Schumpeter and Keynes were two outstanding economists of their time. Neither felt that there was much room for the other.' I am grateful to J.K. Galbraith for this characterization of the two persons whom we celebrate; in fact, their theories seem to exclude each other as much as the policies they advocated. Keynesianism represented a provocative challenge for the more traditional – though in his own way also unorthodox – Schumpeter. In order to learn as much as possible from the opposition, it seems appropriate to take the less well-known Schumpeterian view and his system as our our point of departure.

In his research, Schumpeter consistently aspired to elevate economic theory to the ranks of a 'pure' science. He believed in a core of economic theory which was applicable to primitive, medieval, capitalist as well as socialist economies. It was his essentially Walrasian formal theory of the static state.[2] As everybody knows, he had on the other hand an astounding historical knowledge which he displayed not only in his many writings about the history of economic doctrines (Schumpeter 1914 and 1954) but also in his works on economic history and his sociological essays such as his *Imperialism, Social Classes* (Schumpeter 1955). As a Doctor utriusque iuris by formation, an amateur of mathematics and a founder of econometrics he certainly did not have a one-sided 'economistic' view of the world. But he attempted to keep the different perspectives methodologically separated – that of law, of history, of economics – and united only in application. We may today be inclined to view Schumpeter's intellectual development as a 'life-long struggle to escape from Marx' (Robinson) – among other things because of the prominent place of his critique of Marx in his most popular book, *Capitalism, Socialism and Democracy* (Schumpeter 1950a), because of his discussions with socialist authors and because of his political attempts to attenuate socialism in practice when some of the students whom he had met in Böhm-Bawerk's seminar at the University of Vienna (Otto Bauer, Rudolf Hilferding) became, like himself, ministers of socialist governments in Austria and Germany. But even the most casual reading of Schumpeter's early economic work reveals what was most natural, given his originality: Schumpeter had quarrels on all fronts. He just as much was engaged in a struggle with the historical school, and with a special variant, Knapp's *Staatliche Theorie des Geldes*, which sought the foundation of economic categories (in particular of money) in legal institutions. Schumpeter's aim was not to ignore the historical and institutionalist perspective but to combine it with the theory – in his case a variant of Walrasianism – not in order to modify the theory according to historical circumstances but in order to analyse specific developments simultaneously from different points of view.

The outstanding example of his approach is, of course, given by his *Business Cycles* (Schumpeter 1939). The sociology of the entrepreneur (who is not an exclusively capitalist phenomenon but who appears in specifically capitalist disguises and who uses the specifically capitalist institution of credit) provides one important bridge between historical and analytical considerations.

Schumpeter was thus opposed to a one-sided approach to economic phenomena which would rely exclusively on either analytical or historical considerations, but he was just as strongly opposed to *ad hoc* theorizing which elevates models adapted to special circumstances to the rank of abstract general theories.[3] In methodology Ricardo was his arch enemy who 'piled one simplifying assumption upon another until, having really settled everything by these assumptions, he was left with only a few aggregative variables between which, given these assumptions, he set up simple one-way relations so that, in the end, the desired results emerged almost as tautologies. For example, ... profits "depend upon" the price of wheat'. This reproach is what Schumpeter called the 'Ricardian Vice', and he levelled it primarily against Keynes who was – among other things – accused of having illegitimately proclaimed as a 'General Theory' a dangerous and inconsistent model of 'England's aging capitalism' (Schumpeter 1954: 42; and 1951a).

It is arguable that Schumpeter neither grasped the significance of the classical method behind Ricardo's 'assumptions' nor the logic of the theory of effective demand. But his endeavour to apply each scientific discipline according to its merits and to avoid facile generalizations reflected without doubt the fundamental personal principles of a universal mind aspiring to find objective standards.

This does not mean that Schumpeter was incapable of partisan action in deed and in writing. To get hold of what he stood for it suffices to open any of his books anywhere. On the other hand, very interesting material about Schumpeter's practical political ambitions have recently been brought to light by Christian Seidl (1982). Seidl has traced some letters and three secret memoranda written by Schumpeter during the First World War while he was professor in Graz. It is clear from this that Schumpeter took an active part in attempts to formulate a policy for the Austro-Hungarian Empire to obtain greater independence from Germany, if necessary by means of a separate peace. In view of Schumpeter's postwar activities it is to be stressed that he primarily aimed at the maintenance of the monarchy and the empire, that he sought an equitable solution for the aspiration of the different nationalities within the empire and that it was to be a new conservative party, to be led by the upper nobility, which was to realize the programme. The spirit of the whole is illustrated by proposals such as that of a crowning of the King in Prague.

This is to be contrasted with Schumpeter's postwar activities. The first was his participation in the *Sozialisierungskommission* in Berlin for the nationalization of key industries which he later defended, saying that if someone wanted to commit suicide it was useful if a physician was present. The second was holding office as the Minister of Finance in Renner's socialist government of Austria with the politically impossible task of stabilizing the currency, of subsidizing the consumption of the poor, and of solving the problem of war debts. 'We have only one ambition, which must be served by financial policy, too: to obtain bread for the people' (speech of April 2, 1919). He proposed a capital levy in his memorandum *Die Grundlinien für die Finanzpolitik der nächsten drei Jahre* (Schumpeter 1919). But in the end he had to resign to inflationary financing of the deficit.

Seidl is right to suggest that the socialists might have found Schumpeter's activity as an expert unacceptable if they had known about his confidential war-time pamphlets.

Schumpeter, unable to return to the University, attempted a career as a banker after his retreat from the government, failed, was rescued by an offer of a chair in the University of Bonn and became there and later at Harvard the celebrated academic with the – as Leontief (1950: 103) says in his memorial – 'often expressed conviction that science and politics, the urge to understand and the drive to act, far from being complementary, are actually incompatible'. We might add the hypothesis that the sadness about the demise of the monarchy as well as the experience of the intrigues in which Schumpeter was involved as a politician (Haberler 1951: 34) are the background to his cynical though not untruthful theory of representative democracy in his nowadays most popular book, i.e. *Capitalism, Socialism and Democracy*.

It has been said that Schumpeter felt Keynes to be so much superior to him that he could not bear it: The continuity in Keynes' political and cultural environment, his art of expression, his skilful combination of theory and practice in economics and politics, the seemingly effortless transition from the formulation of hypotheses to their application, were beyond Schumpeter's reach. The details do not need retelling.

Yet these gifts, in which Keynes excelled in his time as much as Ricardo and Marshall in their own, were in part turned into a reproach when Schumpeter spoke of the 'Ricardian Vice'. I quote at some length from Schumpeter's review of the *General Theory* (Schumpeter 1951a: 153):

The unfavourable reviews in a sense but testify to the reality of that success, and I for one, being about to write another of those unfavourable reviews, heartily rejoice in this implication and wish it to be understood that what I am going to say is, in its own unconventional way, a tribute to one of the most brilliant men who ever bent their energies to economic problems . . . .

Speaking to us from the vantage ground of Cambridge and from its author's unique personal position, defended by a group of ardent and able disciples, the book will undoubtedly dominate talk and thought for some time . . . .

It is, however, vital to renounce communion with any attempt to revive the Ricardian practice of offering, in the garb of general scientific truth, advice which – whether good or bad – carries meaning only with references to the practical exigencies of the unique historical situation of a given time and country. This sublimates practical issues into scientific ones, divides economists – as in fact we can see already from any discussion about this book – according to lines of political preference, produces popular successes at the moment, and reaction after – witness the fate of Ricardian economics – neither of which have anything to do with science. Economics will never have or merit any authority until that unholy alliance is dissolved.

And later, in the *History of Economic Analysis* (Schumpeter 1954: 1171), we read:

But he was Ricardo's peer also in that his work is a striking example of what we have called above the Ricardian Vice, namely, the habit of piling the heavy load of practical conclusions upon a tenuous groundwork, which was unequal to it, yet seemed in its simplicity not only attractive but also convincing.

This was, first of all, an objection concerning a method of reasoning, as we have seen above. Second, there was a political motive. Schumpeter had by will and by destiny been exposed to more varied cultural influences and social tensions, he had broader historical outlook and a greater disposition to study authors outside the main stream.

Schumpeter's historical outlook did not make it impossible for him to recognize the Keynesian vision as a viable and lasting system of political economy as was the case with some conservative economists. But according to Schumpeter's *political* interpretation it was going to be 'Labourism' not capitalism (characterized as 'the civilization of inequality and of the family fortune' – Schumpeter 1950b: 419). Accordingly, his *theory* caused him to believe that the result would be stagnation.

With this, we come to the third and main objection which will alone concern us in what follows: while most neoclassical economists eventually came round and accepted the possibility of an underemployment equilibrium, Schumpeter never did. The possibility of a coexistence of a welfare state with capitalist enterprise did not mean that Keynes' theory was true. There was one curious agreement: 'I wish, however, to welcome his purely monetary theory of interest which is, as far as I can see, the first to follow upon my own' (Schumpeter 1951a: 156). Otherwise, there seems to have been something in Schumpeter's conception of economics which made it impossible for him to swallow the concept of effective demand. What was it?

II

The dichotomy between micro- and macroeconomics is modern and can by no means be regarded as a traditional division of labour among economic theorists. The microtheorists postulate that the explanation of economic laws must be explained in terms of decisions of individual agents. The theory for them is therefore to be based on units for which decision rules can meaningfully be defined. A theory based on aggregates such as 'the workers', 'the consumers' can according to this concept of the social sciences not yield an explanation since aggregates are not capable of action (this was emphasized already by Menger in his opposition to Schmoller). Aggregates are admissible if they are obtained by summing up as the results of individual decisions. Such aggregates do not yield information beyond what we know about individual units.

This method had been practised already by Walras, Menger, Pareto and others, but Schumpeter helped to elevate it to the status of a principle and coined its name: it is the 'Methodological Individualism' which he treated in the sixth chapter of *Wesen und Hauptinhalt* (Schumpeter 1908). But in the first methodological dispute between the historical and the Austrian school the 'historians' objected to the 'atomism' of the 'Austrians'. Today, his reductionist programme has become increasingly popular; it might be called the 'Walrasian illusion'.

Schumpeter's analysis is based on a static system in which the rate of interest is zero. This starting point he regarded – and indeed it is – as absolutely essential in his system. Production proceeds by means of land, labour and produced means of production. Competition eliminates profits which are the source of interest. All costs are thus reduced to those of land and labour. Time preference is admitted as a possible cause of interest even in a static state but regarded as inessential and therefore excluded by means of a simplifying assumption. From a modern point of view Schumpeter's account of how the satisfaction simultaneously is assured in a static system corresponds to a standard neoclassical model (despite his sceptical rejection of the importance of time preference) but it is interwoven with most interesting and challenging considerations about the relationship between pure economic theorizing according to the school of methodological individualism and historical factors. This aspect cannot be treated here but it may be important to stress again that Schumpeter is not only trying to convince the theoretical economist but also – perhaps primarily – the adherent of the historical school.

Schumpeter recognizes the importance of exogenous historical factors but points out that there is an endogenous force of economic development – the ideal is explicitly borrowed from Marx (Schumpeter 1934: 60) – which takes place in the productive sector and is not primarily induced by changes of preferences. It is, of course, technical progress which is represented as the adoption of 'new combinations' by 'entrepreneurs'. Here Schumpeter, speaking of Marx, admits that 'my structure covers only a small part of his ground' (ibid.). In fact, in Marx technical progress results from *various* internal contradictions (if one prefers, tensions) in the system. For instance: given the length of the working day (that is, given a limit to the production of absolute surplus value), surplus value can only be increased by means of changing the work processes, by intensifying cooperation between workers, by organizing a better division of labour and by substituting machines for workers. That is, total profits are to be raised by means of a labour-saving technical change (Schefold 1976). Another form of technical progress (the saving of raw materials) is discussed by Marx in the context of movements of capital to increase individual rates of profit.

Schumpeter was right against Marx in emphasizing that the rate of profit to be earned at given prices is the sole theoretically relevant criterion for the adoption of new methods, although his theory of the cycle might have gained if he had developed the Marxian phenomenology of different forms.

Schumpeter's key variable for the discussion of change was the entrepreneur who had played only a subordinate role in Marx. One reason was that Marx was looking for a materialistic, 'objective' explanation of entrepreneurship; hence his stress of the macroeconomic determinants of technical progress – the *necessity* to produce relative surplus value. Another reason was, perhaps, that any stress of the creative function of entrepreneurs as individuals under capitalism would have led to the question of how the dynamic, innovative, therefore unique, but also destructive aspects of entrepreneurial activities could be accommodated in a more or less egalitarian socialist society.

In Schumpeter's system, on the other hand, the entrepreneurs (independent businessmen or administrators) realize productive inventions by drawing produced means of production from old to new uses. We cannot enter into the discussion of the sociology of Schumpeter's entrepreneur – he is *not* thought to be motivated exclusively by rationalist principles – but we must point out that for Schumpeter the change in the methods of production is characteristically financed by means of credit in a capitalist society. Interest flows from the repayment of the surplus profits made by means of the adoption of new methods of production at prices of the old stationary equilibrium. Interest is therefore essentially a phenomenon of capitalist production; a planner in a socialist society could have new combinations ordered to be undertaken through a direct reallocation of the means of production so that credit would not have to intervene and interest was not necessary. It is this type of interest on productive loans which rules the roost according to Schumpeter and not the interest on consumptive loans (where time-preference may play a role). Interest is therefore a monetary phenomenon arising in the context of the disequilibrium engendered by waves of innovations. According to Schumpeter the profit (we should say quasi-rent of extra-profit) due to innovative investment exists also in a communist society even if it does not appear in monetary form in a fully planned economy, but interest on production would be meaningless where money-markets do not exist and time-preference is absent.

Schumpeter retained many of Marx's basic insights, but, of course, without adopting the classical theory of value. In his theory of development the abstract principle of the production of 'Relative Surplus Value' is replaced by the endeavour of entrepreneurs to reap profits by underselling their competitors. The theory of exploitation is negated because there is no fixed standard for the real wage so that, in the absence of rents, prices are lowered until the purchasing power of the workers absorbs the whole product in the static state. There is no surplus in the static system (or the 'circular flow') because there is no monopoly which would allow the capitalists owning the means of production to prevent the wage from rising to the level determined by the balance between the disutility of work and consumption (Schumpeter 1934: 22). And indeed, if there is no time-preference and free competition unimpeded by increasing returns to scale and indivisibilities of capitalist enterprise, it is difficult to see how profits could be positive in an economy which is not growing. Schumpeter's proof of his contention that profits are zero in the static society consists in an effective and comprehensive survey of existing theories of profit which all lead to the conclusion that profits must be zero under the assumptions which he has chosen. The many arguments raised against this idea (first by Böhm-Bawerk) were answered in his 'Eine "dynamische" Theorie des Kapitalzinses', and Samuelson's authority confirms that Schumpeter's argument is impeccable from the *neoclassical* point of view (Samuelson 1943, 1951).

But then profits do arise when capitalists obtain credits to finance new methods of production ('combinations'). After the introduction of the new methods, real wages and rents rise as soon as competition lowers prices in accordance with the gains in productivity so that factor incomes absorb the temporary profits (to the extent that they cannot be converted themselves into permanent new rents because of a natural or artificial monopoly); profits persist only for a while and supply the money-market with interest as repayments of credit.

Interest is therefore determined by supply and demand for credit on the investment market. There is a listing of possible new combinations, each with its perspective rate of return, and they will be realized to the point where the marginal investment project yields a return just above the rate of interest. Schumpeter's dislike of the concept notwithstanding (1954: 1176), this is an investment function with a marginal efficiency of capital – even though Schumpeter was, of course, absolutely right in emphasizing that his determination of the level of investment, given the rate of interest, referred to underlying causes of the investment process and not simply to 'expectations,' about which he had this to say in his Keynes review (Schumpeter 1951a: 154b):

The emphasis on *expected* as against *actual* values is in line with modern tendencies. But expectations are not linked by Mr Keynes to the cyclical situations that give rise to them and hence become independent variables and ultimate determinants of economic action. Such analysis can at best yield purely formal results and never go below the surface. An expectation acquires explanatory value only if we are made to understand *why* people expect *what* they expect. Otherwise expectation is a mere *deus ex machina* that conceals problems instead of solving them.

Schumpeter's own account of the investment process in his *Business Cycles* is to be assessed below. The disagreement is more apparent than real insofar as Keynes accepted the Schumpeterian view of investment in chapter 27 of his *Treatise* (Keynes 1971–83:VI).

The supply of funds is provided by the credit system – in Schumpeter's view by the banks. If we express Schumpeter's early concepts in terms of the national income accounting concepts, we find that the savings equal to the investment to be made are 'forced' savings, since time-preference is ruled out. The static state is, as a matter of fact, one of full employment. The demand generated by the investors, the 'New Men with New Ideas', is financed by the banks. The increase in purchasing power leads to a rise of the prices of goods produced by means of 'old methods' relative to factor incomes so that consumers are compelled to buy less in real terms than in the static state.[4] The underutilized factors can now be used for the introduction of the new methods. (It is therefore bank credit which permits a reallocation which might be commanded under socialism.) The new methods of production, through being more productive (this term Schumpeter held to be more general than roundaboutness, but it is the 'Austrian' aspect of his doctrine), result partly in a cheapening of the goods which were already on the market, partly in the replacement of those goods. Prices can fall again.

But prices are not lowered at once. The differences between 'old' costs of production and new ones yield quasi-rents – in Schumpeter's words simply 'profits' which must first be used to repay the debts to the banks. After that (provided we have only one wave of innovations), prices are lowered; and in this deflation, the rate of interest tends back to its zero level as the system settles down to a new static equilibrium; the revolution of methods of production, of habits and tastes, and of social strata has run its course.

We can thus draw the diagram in Figure 10 for saving and investment in Schumpeter, where saving is not necessarily voluntary, and where it is essential that the savings schedule goes through the origin (*i*-interest). How long is the long run when the rate of profit is uniform because profits are zero? This is a question which will be asked later. Meanwhile we have, as in a Keynesian short period, only quasi-rents.

All difficulties with the concept of a uniform positive rate of profit disappear because Schumpeter simply denies the existence of such a rate. It cannot exist because there is no permanent equilibrium of a uniform positive rate and also because a factor 'entrepreneurship' which might justify a positive equilibrium rate of profit as a factor income is not measurable. This is his crucial contention. Schumpeter's point can be illustrated by applying his arguments to the classical model. To this end, we assume the static system to be stationary. If we adopt the classical point of view, in an economy in a stationary state there must be a uniform rate of profit and – if labour is homogeneous – a uniform rate of wages. If real wages are not fixed and competition prevails, the rate of profit can be positive only if there is something which prevents prices from

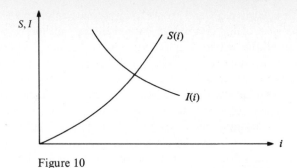

Figure 10

falling relative to money wages under conditions of full employment. So far, Schumpeter and any of his opponents must agree. In Marxian theory it is the monopoly of the means of production, based on the indivisibility of plants and equipment – hence increasing returns – which prevents the workers from becoming capitalists and forces them into the unequal bargain in which they have to sell their labour power at a fixed price which cannot rise permanently because *un*employment is the normal state of affairs. Barring such monopoly, it might be the level of demand which determines the margin between prices and costs (including depreciation), given the money-wage and a mark-up on direct costs. However, the operation of the Anglo-Italian theory of income distribution of the Kaldor–Pasinetti type is not plausible in the stationary state since the level of effective demand cannot explain the variation in capacity utilization in the stationary state with full employment as it may do in a growing economy which is demand-constrained, where investment is going on and where adequate savings are not forthcoming otherwise. At any rate, zero net investment implies zero net profits, and a Kaleckian variant of this theory would be based on a 'degree of monopoly', hence again on imperfect competition. One might fall back on Sraffa's hint according to which the monetary rates of interest regulate the general rate of profit. If firms are indebted to the banks, their receipts must cover the costs of interest payments. The rate of profit cannot be lower than this rate of interest. But Schumpeter seems to believe that there is a tendency towards an excess supply of credit in the stationary state because of the 'elasticity' of the banking system which is there to supply credit even if there is, in the absence of investment, no new demand. Hence the rate of interest itself cannot be kept up above zero. Moreover, it is not plausible in the stationary state that firms finance the purchase of produced means of production through banks when the costs are covered period after period by receipts.

Schumpeter's assumptions concerning the static state appear therefore to be consistent even outside marginalism, if we insert them (as far as that is possible) into a classical and/or Keynesian framework. The ugliest and least realistic aspect of this intellectual exercise seems to be the abstraction from increasing returns and indivisibilities. But if we ask not for *some* but for *perfect* competition, the result is fairly clear and seems to imply that Schumpeter is immune against a critique of his concept of capital along the line of the Cambridge debate about the production function and Walras' model of capital formation and credit; the relevant concepts of the rate of profit and of capital simply are not there. On closer look, one observes that the problems of capitals do not even reappear with an attempt to arrive at a consistent formulization of the investment process, since all accounting is done in terms of prices of the new or the old stationary state, therefore at the same (zero) rate of profit.

The dreadful loss of realism involved in this heroic abstraction is not my concern yet. Schumpeter elaborated his basic idea mainly in two directions. One, that of business-cycle theory, is well known in the Anglo-Saxon world. There is Schumpeter's own publication in English (his *Business Cycles*) as well as a useful survey (Clemence and Doody 1950). I will comment upon it later. But Schumpeter developed the monetary side with equal intensity. Money and finance were the chief objects of his teaching in Bonn. It has been said by his biographer and pupil, Erich Schneider, that his book on *Das Wesen des Geldes* could not be published in 1930 because Keynes had anticipated all his essential ideas in the *Treatise on Money* (Schneider 1970: 56). It would require more space to check the truth of this conjecture. I, for one, am sceptical, since *Das Wesen des Geldes* (which has been published posthumously in 1970) is based on a manuscript which, unlike earlier sketches,[5] stops short of the presentation of Schumpeter's monetary theory of interest which he had regarded as one of his main achievements before 1914, when everybody else – Keynes included – believed in a determination of the rate of interest by the 'real' system. The question of priority was thus settled and *Das Wesen des Geldes* might yet have been completed to include his monetary theory of interest. It enlarges the important earlier articles mainly in regard to banking.[6]

For the benefit of readers who do not have access to the German texts the following extremely brief indication may be given. Schumpeter's work roughly covers the ground of books I, II, IV and V of Keynes' *Treatise*, but the monetary theory, too, is Walrasian. For Schumpeter money is a title – any title – for goods in a social accounting system such as might also be used in a socialist society where services rendered entitle to obtain goods. It is possible that money exists only in the abstract form of the accounts themselves although Schumpeter does not regard this as the historical origin of money, which he thought was in the use of the precious metals.[7] What mattered for Schumpeter was not the historical origin of money but its economic logic, and in this he was decidedly antimetalist (money is *not* the most liquid commodity) and nominalist. But he was, to the dismay of some contemporaries, also resolutely antilegalist. A commodity currency or state money were 'only' institutions to 'secure' the accounting system. He also argued against the use of supply and demand concepts in monetary theory – the purchasing power of money must already be given when people demand it (Schumpeter 1970: 233).

Money includes not only gold, notes and deposits but also bills, even government bonds if they are used for making payments (Schumpeter 1952a: 62). The quantity equation holds but the quantity of money is not exogenously supplied. Whether prices rise with an increase in credit or of newly discovered gold depends not on the level of employment – the starting point is always an equilibrium situation – but on how the quantity of money rises, in particular on whether the additional purchasing power is used for consumption (which is inflationary) or for investment (which is also inflationary at first but which leads, through the process of 'forced saving' and the financing of 'new combinations', to a rise of productivity and eventually to a symmetrical deflation). Competing banks are able to lower interest, to enlarge credit and to create purchasing power – in principle, without limit. It was therefore not Schumpeter's monetary theory but his concept of equilibrium between real forces which led him to take a sceptical view of monetary policy for the purpose of raising effective demand. To stabilize the price level, he withdrew his theoretical nominalism for practical purposes. In 'Die goldene Bremse an der Kreditmaschine' (Schumpeter 1952a) he argued that the gold standard was, after all and despite its atavistic shortcomings, useful for the prevention of inflation. What an anticlimax to his revolutionary and mercantilist monetary theory of interest!

Schumpeter's tools of economic analysis come into their own when they are combined for the explanation of the business cycle. This is the best-known aspect of his work. New combinations appear in the form of waves of innovations which engender a business cycle during which profits rise and become the cause of secondary innovations and eventually of profits accruing even to firms using backward methods of production because of the general rise in the level of prices in the boom. The boom comes to an end with a deflation, when credits have to be paid back and a general fall in economic activity, if not a crisis, sets in. The point is that only this depression leads to a new equilibrium in which prices are reduced to the level corresponding to the new methods of production. Old methods are eradicated. The depression is therefore indispensable in order to lead back to a healthy state of affairs in which new entrepreneurs will be enabled, on the basis of 'correct' prices, to assess their changes for the adoption of new combinations in the next wave of innovations. Financial panics do not cause the crisis; they are more or less inevitable by-products of a necessary process of adjustment (Schumpeter 1952a: 98).

One of the first objections (raised by Lowe in the twenties) against Schumpeter's theory of the business cycle was that the length of the cycle could not be determined. Schumpeter's later work on business cycles gave a differentiated answer. He had first tried to use five, later he adopted the well-known three-cycle hypothesis. When it turned out that the equilibrium was to be attained at the end of a Kondratieff-cycle stretching over some 55 years, it seemed that the concept had been strained.

Yet it ought to be pointed out that Schumpeter's *Business Cycles* gave a very detailed explanation of the crisis of 1929 and the subsequent evolution of the Depression. Malignant readers may surmise that Schumpeter calculated the periods of his three cycles from the first Kondratieff (beginning 1786) to the last so as to get his dramatic superposition of a downward Kondratieff, Juglar and Kitchin in 1929, and the weakness of the New Deal in the thirties, but it should then also be observed that a prolongation of the scheme leads, with a little benevolence, to surprisingly good predictions of postwar developments. At the time of writing *Business Cycles*, Schumpeter wanted to reduce the three-wave pattern to one common cause, the cycles of innovation, but he later thought about different explanations for the Kitchin and one may toy with the idea that the length of a Kondratieff corresponds to two generations, inviting sociological explanations, the Juglar corresponds to the old trade cycle which must have something to do with fixed capital, and the multiplier–accelerator remains for the Kitchins.

In better moods I abhor such speculation. What I regard as least satisfactory in the Schumpeterian system – granted all his assumptions – is the curious contrast between the exclusive use of equilibrium concepts in theoretical analysis for all purposes and the 'empirical' finding that the wave lasts 55 years, hence the (implicit!) conclusion that the economy is anywhere near equilibrium only twice in a century. This was probably not foreseen in 1911 when Schumpeter made no explicit reference to the length of the cycle that apparently meant the old trade cycle.[8]

III

When Keynes proclaimed a theory based on the IS-relationship, in which unemployment was a state which could be attained in an equilibrium and was not associated with a temporary deviation from an equilibrium, he caught the attention of the economists. Both in view of the modern evolution of general equilibrium theory and in view of the fact that the Walrasian Schumpeter represented the investment process as a *departure* from equilibrium, it is remarkable that Walras himself attempted to formulate an equilibrium for any given phase in the process of accumulation.

Walras treated the process of investment and saving in his model of capital formation and credit (Walras 1954, formalized by Morishima 1964 and Diewert 1978). There are fixed coefficients of production. Stocks of factors (including inherited capital goods) are used to produce consumption goods and new capital goods. Prices must cover direct costs plus depreciation plus interest according to a uniform rate. It follows that there are two methods to determine prices of capital goods: on the one hand, there is the supply price deriving from the scarcity of the capital goods relative to the requirements for production which arise from the demand for consumption goods. On the other hand, the prices of new capital goods must correspond to the hire-prices of stocks of the same capital goods which are already there.

The rate of interest is such that savings in terms of the numéraire-commodity are adequate to finance the purchase of new capital goods, i.e. investment.

This model leads to a famous difficulty which was first pointed out critically by Garegnani (1960) – though it had been noticed earlier – and which may be illustrated as follows: suppose that a certain quantity of bread is to be produced by means of flour and ovens. Flour is in short supply, there is an excess of ovens. Walras was only dimly aware that under such circumstances there is no room for the production of new ovens; yet all capital goods must be reproduced. The contradiction shows the discrepancy between the hire-price of the stock of ovens (which tends to zero with an excess supply) and the price of production of new ovens. Morishima (1964) gave a proof of existence of an equilibrium for the Walrasian model of capital formation and credit by using inequalities instead of equalities. As John Eatwell (1975) has pointed out, the proof of existence is valid but it means that only those capital goods will be produced which are in short supply so that, in the example under consideration, ovens would not be reproduced. In general, the rate of profit could trivially be uniform in such a model because only *one* capital good, namely that which limits production by being in short supply, will be reproduced. Alternatively, if equalities were to be used, one would have to assume that capital is malleable and that ovens could be transformed (be substituted for) flour. (The critical argument must be modified – but continues to hold – if there are variable instead of the fixed coefficients of production as suggested by the example.)

It ought to be clear that, from the point of view of long-period equilibrium in which market prices and prices of production are supposed to coincide, the stocks of capital goods to be used up in production should be counted among the unknowns. The long period is defined as a state in which the supplies of means of production are just adequate for the requirements of production. In each line of production, the same rate of profit is earned and, in neoclassical terms, the capitalization of the incomes determined by demand and supply for the stock of each capital good per period defines a set of relative prices which is equal to that derived from the structure of cost of production, taking account of depreciation, and using a positive rate of interest for capitalization. (This concept of long-period equilibrium is also applicable to classical theory, although it is in this case preferable to speak of a 'long-period position' in which the rate of return is the same in all lines of production, with input prices being equal to output prices, but in which there is not necessarily full employment.)

It is well known that the concept of long-period equilibrium was replaced by the temporary equilibrium method developed by Hicks and others. I have not been able to determine whether Schumpeter departed from the Walrasian method of long-period equilibrium because he was aware of the inconsistency in the Walrasian model of accumulation. He made it clear in *History of Economic Analysis* that he disagreed with the Walrasian theory of interest and, therefore, also with Walras' model of capital formation and credit.

But Schumpeter certainly did remain faithful to Walras in so far as he retained the Walrasian concept of the supply of stocks with its consequent rejection of a Marshallian supply curve based on the flow of 'expenses of production'. In a Walrasian model the quantities of each primary factor are given. The owners decide according to their preferences the prices of factors and of consumption goods how much they wish to offer. It is characteristic for this construction that the technology influences the determination of factor prices only indirectly. The demand for each factor derives from the demand for consumption goods. As Wicksteed had shown, the offer of the factor consists in the difference between the available stock and the demand of the owner himself. In a sense, there is therefore no supply curve at all but only a demand for each factor as a fixed stock comprising the demand by the owner as well as the derived demand from others: 'We have found that we are compelled to consider the schedule of supply as a value curve. There are therefore *two demand curves* which intersect and not a demand curve and a supply curve which would be essentially different' (Schumpeter 1908: 235; my translation).

In his *History of Economic Analysis* (and similarly in 'The Instability of Capitalism') Schumpeter consequently denies the relevance of returns to scale for the determination of cost curves for 'we have derived, from the marginal utility principle, a new "law of decreasing returns", which is independent of any physical law of decrease, and which will assert itself even in the face of a physical law of increasing returns' (Schumpeter 1954: 917).

This seems to be entirely logical from the point of view of a subjective theory of value. All factor incomes have the character of scarcity rents; there is no interest on a factor 'capital'. Tools and machines used in known processes are valued at factor costs (of land and labour) because they are not scarce. The owner of a tool cannot expect to gain by withholding it from the process of production, because more tools can be produced and time-preference is zero. The tendency to an increasing supply price of increasing returns to scale must therefore derive from the competing derived demands for labour and land.

One should in this context not be confused by the fact that the 'circular flow' in Schumpeter is said by him not to be 'stationary' but 'static' (cf. Schumpeter 1908: 397). His 'static' system must have the properties of a stationary state; it is called 'static' only in order to indicate that there are endogenous forces which cause it to depart on a dynamic path. Schumpeter prefers not to call it 'stationary', on the other hand, because the stationary state implies a perennial replacement of worn-out equipment with new equipment *of the same kind*, while he held that replacement usually involves some innovation. His 'static' system therefore represents an economy which maintains its stocks and temporarily lacks the impetus to create new means of production. The static system is a stationary state only in the sense of a standstill of indefinite (but probably brief) duration. It is clear that a real economy could only approximate this state of affairs (cf. ibid.: 421).

Schumpeter's approach seems to avoid the known difficulties of the theory of capital which stem from the consideration of production, but at the expense of sacrificing the theory of the production of new capital goods (and there may be other pitfalls in the reasoning, relating to the stability of his circular flow). Equilibrium becomes the initial and the terminal state which the economy reaches after long waves of repercussions of innovations. Schumpeter knew that the logic of his arguments requires the fundamental data of the equilibrium (preferences and endowments) to alter during the process of adaptation. It is, for instance, essential that entrepreneurs are able to influence preferences when they introduce new goods. But if the process of reaching the equilibrium determines the terminal state, it is difficult to see what use such a concept of equilibrium can have, as Joan Robinson (1974) has emphasized. Moreover, Schumpeter's claims to have found a new dynamic theory is questionable; he really compares static systems, and the details of how the transition from one static system to the other affects the outcome dynamically are never worked out with analytic precision. Schumpeter promises to show how the stream of profits is converted into interest but a rigorous analysis of the corresponding *process* is never given since his monetary theory is also based on general equilibrium.

IV

By claiming that the very state of unemployment could be analysed in terms of an equilibrium of a specific type, Keynes made his theory much more attractive for economists who seek to analyse the real world by means of stringent concepts. The first approach to the Keynesian determination of employment is based on his principle of effective demand as stated in chapter 3 of the *General Theory*. The aggregate demand curve reflects 'the proceeds which entrepreneurs expect to receive from the employment of N men' while the supply curve shows 'the aggregate supply price of the output from employing N men'. A. Asimakopulos (1982) has questioned this construction by pointing out that the entrepreneurs cannot be expected to know their proceeds; they determine output (that maximizes expected profits) acting on *expected* prices, which are independent of their individual rates of output.

In the derivation of the supply curve the problem of aggregation is also crucial. At any level of total employment, the supply of individual industries will vary depending on the proportion of employment allotted to it. The levels of employment of individual industries may be derived, for instance, on the basis of an assumption regarding the relative prices at which each industry can be expected to sell a given quantity of its product. Kregel (1980), Asimakopulos (1982), Parinello (1983) and others have discussed the theory of effective demand in terms of the intersection of such aggregate supply and demand functions, with expectations about prices playing a decisive role, for without expectations, the aggregation could only be based on a prior analysis of simultaneous general equilibrium, and employment and proceeds could not be related.

Yet the difference between this approach and that of the French equilibrium school does not seem to me to be all that important. The role of price expectations is taken up by the assumptions about fixed (administered) prices; they prevent the attainment of a full employment equilibrium. One can then show how a state of unemployment even with increasing returns to scale obtains if prices are such that the real wage is too low at the given level of investment to exhaust the total product (Schefold 1983).

But neither representation of Keynes' principle of effective demand (along a Marshallian construction of his aggregate demand and supply curves or the modern crude – if instructive – 'dis'-equilibrium version) shed much light on the difference in the concept of equilibrium used by Schumpeter and Keynes which we set out to investigate. The appropriate concept of equilibrium has to be defined at a more disaggregated level. We had seen that there was a conflict between the analysis of exchange in terms of stocks of capital goods and in terms of flows of produced investment goods in the Walrasian model, and that Schumpeter avoided the problem by taking the static system as his point of departure.

A similar difficulty exists in Marshall's short period. Capital in the short period is here a stock by definition. Marshall therefore treats fixed capital like land: it does not yield profit according to uniform rates but a rent, the quasi-rent. Circulating capital goods are produced and are therefore inputs as well as outputs. There is a uniform rate of interest included in the cost of the production of circulating capital goods in the short period, but the income derived from fixed capital goods depends on the use which can be made of them within the period under consideration. This contrast is most characteristic of Marshallian analysis and appeals to applied economists. The task of reproducing the stock in the long period induced Marshall to visualize the long period ultimately as a true stationary state. Since it was not possible to transform the capital stock into a flow, the capital stock was in this tradition later made an endogenous variable which had to be determined (cf. Pigou 1943).

It may be remarked at this point that our theoretical outlook today is completely different since Sraffa has taught us to transform fixed capital into a flow by means of the joint production approach. A tractor is no more a stock than seedcorn, for both seedcorn and tractor are transformed within the period under consideration into corn, straw and a tractor which is one year older. This trick, together with the device of distinguishing market prices from prices of production, replaces the evasive concept of equilibrium by that of a state of self-replacement. At any one time the structure of production (at normal conditions of capacity utilization) defines, together with a distributive variable such as a given rate of profit, a set of prices of production. Market prices may be different from prices of production but the latter are important nevertheless as centres of gravitation. A long-period position is a state of self-replacement in which this gravitation is operating and, to this extent, it is a long-period equilibrium.

Deficiencies in the old form of the classical theory of value as well as the need to take account of the principle of utility had induced Marshall to abandon part of the classical approach. It was out of the question to analyse the supply of 'factors' in terms of a labour theory of value and nobody seemed to be aware that the supply of 'factors' leading to the production of consumption goods is really the 'production of commodities by means of commodities' where the phrase 'demand and supply' is misleading when we are dealing with basics. Marshall proceeded sequentially. The quantities of factors are not considered as given (except the stocks of land and fixed capital) but, given factor prices, cost functions can be derived for each produced mean of production under *ceteris paribus* conditions. Functions for the supply price are derived from these cost functions which are to reflect the costs of production within a theory of demand and supply (the supply price is here a function of quantity produced, while a supply curve shows vice versa the quantity supplied as a function of the price). It should be clear that the existence of returns to scale must become an important consideration in the Marshallian context while they play only a subordinate role within a Walrasian approach.

The prices of the factors in fixed supply are thus residually determined by capitalization of the quasi-rents which they happen to earn. The prices of factors which are produced within the period are cost-determined. In his model of capital formation and credit Walras had attempted to reconcile both aspects and had failed. In a Walrasian model without production of capital goods or in an Austrian model the prices of factors only depend on the uses which can be made of them, or, in Austrian formulation: the prices of goods of higher order (factors) are determined by the prices of goods of lower order (consumption goods).

The point is that these residual incomes (quasi-rents) play a crucial role in the theory of effective demand.

V

Let the stocks of fixed capital (which earn quasi-rents) and of labour be offered in fixed quantities in our Marshallian model of the short run. The expenditure on consumer goods will cover their direct costs and therefore yield the income of wage earners which will be spent on consumer goods. If workers do not save and capitalists do not spend, the demand for investment goods will generate the quasi-rents accruing to the capitalists. This idea is discernible in Keynes' *Treatise*.[9] Marshall himself did not quite put matters in the Kaleckian fashion. As Volker Caspari will show in his forthcoming dissertation, there is a propensity to save implicit in Marshall which depends on the rate of interest. Entrepreneurs hold expectations about the level of their quasi-rents. The quasi-rents, discounted at the ruling rate of interest, determine the value of investment which is equal to savings at that rate of interest. Marshall *assumes* full employment, to be realized because prices, wage rates and the rate of interest are flexible. A given labour force is employed because wages are flexible downwards. Consumption out of wages and quasi-rents corresponds to what remains, at the given level of employment, when the level of investment has been determined which is made equal to savings by the rate of interest. The similarity between this and the determination of the rate of interest in Schumpeter (e.g. 1934: 192) is due to the fact that Schumpeter's *departure* from equilibrium replaces the Marshallian short run.

Now we can see the changes which Keynes introduced in order to explain unemployment. First of all, he simply dropped the full-employment assumption. Second, the rate of investment was made to depend on expectations concerning quasi-rents which are volatile. This component of demand could be regarded as a datum for some purposes; it then determined, together with the consumption function, a level of employment, as can be shown by means of the standard multiplier formula or the more sophisticated schedules for aggregate demand and supply referred to above. The change here concerned the savings function (propensity to consume). Third, the level of employment followed from that of national income and determined the real wage (marginal product); the money wage was conventional. But, since the full-employment condition had been dropped, an equation was missing and this was provided by the new monetary theory of the rate of interest which closed the system. This conclusion is not in the least new and does not therefore require further elaboration.

Keynes' theory became an effective challenge to traditional economic teaching because unemployment was represented as an equilibrium and because the equations defining this equilibrium were still in terms of demand and supply and not all that different from the well-known Marshallian apparatus. Apart from the consumption function, the main change was introduced in the money market with the introduction of liquidity preference. Yet the implications were the opposite of those derived from traditional theory. It was precisely this seemingly cheap transformation of received doctrine for radical purposes which offended Schumpeter as a historically conscious purist of economic theory. Where Schumpeter had anticipated the fury of modern neoclassicism by trying to isolate the core of economic theory, Walrasian general equilibrium, and had made the most daring constructions to deduce the theory of money and the business cycle, starting from the static conditions in order to reveal the logical coherence of the whole, Keynes had patched together bits and pieces from the Marshallian short period (in itself not the most rigorous model) and added what seemed to Schumpeter *ad hoc* definitions. Was that a 'General Theory'? And were not liquidity preference, propensity to consume, inducement to invest, all concepts themselves in need of theoretical foundations?

In a sense, from his point of view, Schumpeter was right in his assessment, but we have been led to conclusions which are opposed to those which he wanted. We have learned a great deal about the limitations of the General Theory (Kaldor 1983), hence about limits to its generality. Kalecki's work has allowed us to replace the propensity to consume by the classical assumption about savings so that the effective demand links investment and profits. An endogenous determination of the supply of money had turned out to be more important than variations in the velocity for the criticism of the quantity theory. It is true that Keynes introduced a new way of thinking and cleared the way for these and other subsequent developments. He was and still is far the greater economist. If it is Schumpeter's objection that these are all partial amendments of the received Marshallian and Keynesian doctrine, two conclusions (or a compromise) remain possible for those who do not share the Walrasian illusion: Either we admit that economic reality is not to be explained on the basis of one coherent theory; there are many models which are somehow complementary; their appropriate combination is – as far as theory is concerned – a question of art rather than of systematic method. Or there is another foundation of the theory of value. Perhaps the classical theory of value is useful in combination with some other models; this is my own working hypothesis. But the confinement of pure theory to general equilibrium with full employment as in Schumpeter, regarding everything else as a departure, has been discredited and the project of integrating Keynesian ideas with a neoclassical microeconomic equilibrium foundation so as to obtain one General Theory is not what Schumpeter expected to happen. The converse operation, the introduction of Schumpeterian ideas about the investment process in the Keynesian framework, has proved more fruitful.

Notes

1 I should like to thank V. Caspari for valuable suggestions in form of both a preparatory paper and discussions. I am also greateful for discussions with Dr R. Dickler and with participants of the Marx–Keynes–Schumpeter Symposium.
2 Cf. 'Eine "dynamische" Theorie des Kapitalzinses', originally published in 1913, reprinted in Schumpeter 1952a: 427.
3 Cf. also Leontief's 'On Implicit Theorizing' (Leontief 1966: I, 58).
4 This is called 'forced saving' in 'Zinsfuss und Geldverfassung', originally published in 1913 (Schumpeter 1952a: 23); see also 'Das Sozialprodukt und die Rechenpfennige', originally published in 1917/18 (Schumpeter 1952a: 108).
5 Mentioned in note 4.
6 For a summary of Schumpeter's later work on money see Marget (1951).
7 Laum's book on primitive money *Heiliges Geld* and the work on transactions in the oriental empires, collected later by Polanyi, appeared only after 'Das Sozialprodukt und die Rechenpfennige' (Schumpeter 1952a), i.e. after the First World War.
8 That is the Juglar, see the Preface to the English edition of *Theory of Economic Development* (Schumpeter 1934).
9 It was even more explicit in Rüstow's dissertation of 1926 – see Kaldor (1983) – whereas investment causes profits in Schumpeter, too, but the profits are used to pay interest and savings are forced.

HYMAN P. MINSKY

This year marks the hundredth anniversary of the birth of Keynes and Schumpeter. It is also the fiftieth year of the collapse of the American and the capitalist world's financial and monetary structure. Thus in 'mid-career' – from 1929 to 1933 – when Keynes and Schumpeter were approaching their fiftieth year, a traumatic event and a startling piece of evidence about the possible behaviour of capitalist economies was unfolding: it seemingly was clear that it is possible for capitalism to collapse.

Keynes' response to this trauma of the economy was his magnificent performance: *The General Theory of Employment, Interest and Money* (Keynes 1936). According to Paul Samuelson, Schumpeter's response to the appearance of *The General Theory* was to abandon his long-promised and in-process book on money. In 1939 Schumpeter's *Business Cycles* appeared (Schumpeter 1939). It was a minor performance when measured against either Keynes' *General Theory* or Schumpeter's 1911/1934 *Theory of Economic Development* (Schumpeter 1934). As far as Schumpeter's analysis of money, it can be argued that there was no advance beyond the vision of Chapter III, 'Credit and Capital', in the *Theory of Economic Development*. The crisis of capitalism evoked a magnificent theoretical performance from Keynes; Schumpeter's response was banal.

For well nigh 35 years after 1933 (until the second half of the sixties) no serious threat of a repetition of a 1929–33 type crisis occurred. In more recent years – and quite currently – there have been episodes that the world's financial markets and leading central banks interpreted as threatening another crisis. The central banks – particularly the Federal Reserve System in the United States – reacted to these threats by refinancing endangered organizations and by a 'generalized' infusion of bank reserves. We know that in spite of the obvious fragility of the financial structure no interactive collapse has taken place.

Understanding the causes and consequences of financial turmoil is an important current issue in economic theory and policy. I want to examine in part how Keynes and Schumpeter reacted to the crisis of 1929–33 in terms of their pre- and post-crisis theorizing. My view is that Schumpeter really did not react to the crisis, whereas, as I have argued elsewhere, Keynes' *General Theory* and the theoretical writing he did after *The General Theory*, can be best understood by assuming that the causes and consequences of financial crisis are central to the concerns that prompted *The General Theory* (Minsky 1975). While Schumpeter may be the source of great insights into the capitalist process, he did not leave a useful theoretical framework for the analysis of capitalism. On the other hand further progress in understanding capitalism may very well depend upon integrating Schumpeter's insights with regard to the dynamics of a capitalist process and the role of the innovative entrepreneurs into an analytical framework that in its essential properties is Keynesian. Capitalism has exhibited both fragility and resiliency over the century since the death of Marx and the birth of Keynes and Schumpeter. Keynes' analytical structure enables us to understand and even cope with the fragility of capitalism. Schumpeter's vision of entrepreneurship helps us understand the resilience of capitalism and in particular how policy reactions to slumps that reflect Keynesian insights lead to resilience and add new dimensions to the fragility of financial structures.

In my view Keynes over the period of the great collapse (1929–33) recognized that the economics of his *Tract* and *Treatise* was a dead end with respect to how our economy worked and the impact of money in our economy.[1] Not being an Austrian and not writing with 'Marx' as the hidden subject, Keynes naturally fell into treating money within a framework of the Marshallian Short Runs and Long Run. If we take the old-fashioned partial equilibrium textbook models as the basis for discussing prices and production, then Keynes' short-run expectations of profits are 'embodied' in the short-run equilibrium of production with given facilities, whereas the long-run expectations of profits are related to a short-run disequilibrium (determined by the relation between price and average out-of-pocket cost) that either triggers movement along a long-run set of cost curves or entry of new firms with unchanged cost curves (Lerner 1937; Viner 1952). The 'book of blueprints' and the 'set of demand curves' confronting those whose expectations are relevant are not changing in Keynes but are 'new' and 'radically different' in much of Schumpeter. In Keynes' formal structure the high-uncertainty, high-potential-pay-off entrepreneurial/innovation investment decision is not central. In Keynes' structure great depressions – or even ordinary recessions – reflect an integrated view of capitalizing expected profits, supply prices of investment output and financing conditions: thus in Keynes the collapse of investment and a breakdown of the financing structure is a result due to the mechanisms of capitalism as such, whereas to Schumpeter such events are due to either the innovative reactions or secondary waves. Keynes interpreted the Great Depression as evidence that a paradynamic shift in economic theory was necessary whereas to Schumpeter the old vision was retained and embedded in a set of Ptolemaic cycles.

The inability of Schumpeter to assimilate the Great Depression into his thinking is somewhat surprising in the light of his early views. He noted that 'The money market is always, as it were, the headquarters of the capitalist system' (Schumpeter 1934: 126). This seemingly implies that the sequence of events that can be said to have been triggered by the break in stock market prices in October 1929 – that led to the complete closure of the banking system in March of 1933 – was not peripheral but rather was central to the functioning of a capitalist economy. This is so because 'the main function of the money or capital market is trading in credit for the purpose of financing development' (ibid.: 126, 127); i.e. money and the institutions of the money market – mainly banks – provide the means by which the rupturing of the stationary circular flow is effected. Not only development – which may really mean accumulation – but also profit, interest and the very spirit of capitalism depend upon the existence of a financial mechanism by which resources can be 'abstracted' from the circular flow and put at the behest of the dynamic entrepreneur. Therefore one would expect that a clear reading of Schumpeter would lead to views as to what conditions must be satisfied if the financial system is to continue to function as a handmaiden to entrepreneurship. Schumpeter may write of financial catastrophe, but he nowhere explains catastrophe. The significance of liability structures and the importance of business profits to banks as holders of business liabilities are only peripheral concerns in Schumpeter's analysis of both *The Theory of Economic Development* and *Business Cycles*.

One of the peculiarities in any discussion of money and crises in the thought of Schumpeter and Keynes is that Schumpeter's early vision, as stated in his *The Theory of Economic Development*, is more compatible with a view of money that leads to an understanding of financial crisis than was true of Keynes' early vision. The difference in the import of Keynes and Schumpeter over the 50 years since the culmination of the crisis in the collapse of 1933 is that Keynes quite clearly interpreted what happened in 1933 as a source for repudiating prior theory whereas Schumpeter interpreted the events as reinforcing the basic validity of his earlier views. Schumpeter's *Business Cycles* of 1939 is if anything a retrogression from his 1912 *Theory of Economic Development*. The three cycles – Kitchin, Juglar and Kondratieff – of Schumpeter's business-cycle theory are mechanical and the vast presentation of data is numbing rather than enlightening.

In the light of the problems of performance of the capitalist economies over the past several years interest in the ideas of our predecessors must be conditioned by the problems we face and whether they have any message for us. For both Schumpeter and Keynes the question is whether their insights help us build a monetary theory that is useful to our times. Perhaps because Schumpeter's career was largely spent in 'exile' whereas Keynes was always 'at home', Schumpeter on policy and economic structure is abstract whereas Keynes is concrete. One could not expect Schumpeter to have been a hard negotiator in an institution-building effort such as led up to the Fund and the

Bank, whereas Keynes threw himself fully into such projects. As Schumpeter remarked in his comment on Keynes, Keynes was always a patriot involved in projects for the betterment of the world; Schumpeter was not involved.

Keynes' essential contribution to an understanding of capitalist processes and why capitalism is different from the abstract 'socialisms' of Marshall and Walras lies in identifying the two-price-system nature of capitalism: in a capitalist economy there is a price system for capital assets as well as the price system of current output. Furthermore these two price systems are based upon quite different considerations. The price system for current output is based upon consumer preferences, consumer income, and costs, prime and overhead, of business. The price system of assets – capital and financial – is based upon expected profits (cash flows), expected financing costs, the need to make payments on contracts and the insurance that assets embody because they can yield cash by being sold as well as income by being held or used.

The theory of the determination of the prices of capital assets is what Keynes called liquidity preference. This interpretation of liquidity preference as the determinant of the price system for capital assets is present in *The General Theory* but really is much clearer in the two expository exercises of late 1936 – the contribution to the Fisher *Festschrift* and the rebuttal to Viner (Keynes 1973: XIV, 101–8 and 109–23).

The argument in the Fisher *Festschrift* runs in terms of six propositions, four of which are held by both the orthodox theorists of his day and Keynes, and two of which differ. The like propositions are:

1. Interest on money is the premium obtainable on current cash over future cash (i.e. interest is what is observed on financial contracts).
2. All assets have a marginal efficiency in terms of themselves and in a world with complex financial structure these marginal efficiencies break down into the utility gained from income and liquidity and lost through carrying costs.
3. Assets will exchange at values proportionate to their marginal efficiencies.
4. Prices of assets in excess of the supply prices of investment output will induce investment.

The two propositions that differ, in the form that Keynes (1973: XIV, 104) states as his version, are:[2]

5*. The marginal efficiency of money in terms of itself is, in general, a function of its quantity (though not of its quantity alone), just as in the case of other capital assets.
6*. Aggregate investment may reach its equilibrium rate under proposition (4) above, before the elasticity of supply of output as a whole has fallen to zero.

As Keynes made clear in chapter 17 of *The General Theory*, the marginal efficiency of money in terms of itself reflects the only utility that money yields: the utility value or efficiency on the margin of liquidity. If money increases as other things don't change then the utility of the liquidity embodied per unit of money decreases; this implies that the money value of other assets rises. Furthermore, if the payment commitment on liabilities rises relative to the cash flows assets are expected to yield, then the marginal valuation of liquidity increases and the price of assets that are valued for the profits or interest they yield decreases. Liquidity preference, as affected by the quantity of money, financial commitments and the expected flow of profits (in the Kalecki sense) yield a price system of assets. And it is this price system resulting from the relationship between the marginal efficiencies of different capital assets including money, measured in terms of a common unit, which determines the aggregate rate of investment (Keynes 1973: XIV, 102). Proposition 6* states that investment as determined by the prices of capital assets and the supply prices of investment output can fall short of the amount necessary to yield full employment.

Unfortunately, Keynes' emphasis upon the price system of assets was lost in the controversy with Ohlin and Robertson over the loanable funds versus the liquidity-preference theory of interest and the formalisms of Hicks etc.

The basic proposition of this two-price-system view is straightforward: assets will trade at prices such that on the margin each asset yields the same utility per dollar of asset value. The utility embodied in holding a unit of money is derived from the utility of being protected against emergencies and being able to fulfil contracts without having to unload price-sensitive assets. Underlying the view that holding money to fulfil contracts yields utility is the 'fact' that there are payment commitments on account of prior engagements to banks and other holders of debts. In fact money in its most common form, as the liabilities of banks, is the outgrowth of financing contracts. In an abstract world, where government is virtually nonexistent and foreign entanglements are minimal, the commitments to pay money because of debts to banks exceed the amount of money in existence. All the monetarist propositions, which so clutter up the discourse, assume that the rate of payments by business and households to banks and the rate at which banks extend loans to finance business and households are always such that the path of bank liabilities in the form of money can be kept on track.

Whereas 'money' mainly yields 'utility' by these liquidity and insurance attributes, other assets have income, liquidity and insurance inputs to the 'utility' they yield their owners. Any shift in the income, liquidity or insurance that an asset is expected to yield will change its value in dollars. Furthermore any change in preferences or expectations with respect to the future that increase the utility schedule for holding money will change the relative prices of assets as well as the dollar prices of non-money assets. Even before he published the *General Theory* Keynes (1972: IX, 151)[3] wrote:

There is a multitude of real assets in the world which constitute our capital wealth-buildings, stocks of commodities, goods in course of manufacture and of transport, and so forth. The nominal owners of these assets, however, have not infrequently borrowed money in order to become possessed of them. To a corresponding extent the actual owners of wealth have claims, not on real assets, but on money. A considerable part of this 'financing' takes place through the banking system which interposes its guarantee between its depositors who lend it money, and its borrowing customers to whom it loans money wherewith to finance the purchase of real assets. The interposition of this veil of money between the real asset and the wealth owner is a specially marked characteristic of the modern world.

Money is the product of banking processes. I do not want to do more than recommend the work of Steiger and Heinsohn (s.a.) on the origins of money, in which they contend that money had its origin in banking: I do not want to enter over my head in discussing usages and institutions of three and four thousand years ago. I do want to assert though that whatever the validity of the Steiger/Heinsohn hypothesis of the origins of money, the proposition about money today for a capitalist economy is *no money without banking* and *no banking without payment commitments in money to banks that at every moment exceed the amount of money in existence.* This is the essence of the Keynesian veil of money – it is a financing veil.

Profit-maximizing bankers create money in exchanges with businessmen; this money is used by business to finance both positions in capital assets and investment. When the expected profitability from using capital assets is high, for given states of the utility of holding the protections embodied in money the price of capital will be high, the pace of investment will be high and profit-maximizing bankers will be eagerly seeking to expand their financing. Of course the Schumpeter–Kalecki insights make us recognize that profits are high because in the simple case investment is high.

The price level of investment output is determined by money wage rates, the interest rate on financing, and the protection, in the form of an expected excess of prices over labour, material and interest costs that profitseeking and risk-aware bankers and businessmen 'negotiate'. Once the relation between the money supply and the price of capital and the relation between the price level of capital, the price level of investment and the rate of investments are introduced then there is an essential nominal aspect to the operations of the economy. More about this later.

Therefore Keynes (and Schumpeter) hold that money itself is not an outside asset but is introduced into the economy in a financing transaction which, in the abstract case of no government and household debts, is a transaction that finances investment output and ownership of capital assets. By these financing transactions a portion of the cash flows earned by business are committed to the payments to banks that are the 'second part' of the financing contract. But the cash flows or profits to business are, as Schumpeter had it, determined by investment spending.

Of course the Kalecki way of putting the basic accounting identities in terms of profits rather than G.N.P. makes the investment–profits relation much more precise than they ever were in Schumpeter (Kalecki 1971: chapter 7).[4] Furthermore the Kalecki way of putting these relations makes it clear that

Gross Profits are related to Gross Investment – Schumpeter's insistence that zero investment yields zero profits is, in special cases, valid for net investment and net profits – and that government deficits may lead to net profits even in the absence of net investment.[5]

One of the basic characteristics of orthodox Walrasian theory is the 'axiom of reals'. As Hahn (1983: 34) puts it:

> the objective of agents that determine their actions and plans do not depend on any nominal magnitudes. Agents care only about 'real' things, such as good (properly dated and distinguished by states of nature), leisure and effort. We know this as the axiom of the absence of money illusion, which it seems impossible to abandon in any sensible analysis.

But once the need to explain the price level of capital assets is put forth as a central problem of economic theory and once this price level is explained in terms of the relative utility of money and other assets then an essential nominal core is introduced into economic theory. As Keynes (1973: XIV, 103) put it:

> the orthodox theory maintains that the forces which determine the common value of the marginal efficiency of various assets are independent of money, which has, so to speak, no autonomous influence, and that prices move until the marginal efficiency of money, i.e. the rate of interest, falls into line with the common value of the marginal efficiency of other assets as determined by other forces. My theory, on the other hand, maintains that this is a special case and that over a wide range of possible cases almost the opposite is true, namely, that the marginal efficiency of money is determined by forces partly appropriate to itself, and that prices move until the marginal efficiency of other assets falls into line with the rate of interest.

That is, Keynes denies the validity of the axiom of reals. The essential capital asset pricing model and the view of banking by which the cash flows that validate contracts destroy money even as new financing creates money, implies that nominal values matter to agents that own, finance and create capital assets. One cannot legitimately use production functions and preference systems over real variables to determine anything of significance in a capitalist economy with a modern banking system.

A further implication of the denial of the axiom of reals is that Walras and Keynes are like oil and water; they don't mix. Formal theory has to abandon the axiom of reals if formal theory is to be relevant to a modern economy. The axiom of reals is analogous to the axiom of parallels at an earlier stage in mathematical analysis; only by abandoning the axiom of parallels did particular significant problems become tractable.

As was mentioned earlier, Schumpeter's 1939 *Business Cycles* is a retrogression from his 1911 *The Theory of Economic Development*. By the time he wrote the 1939 book Schumpeter was emphasizing Walras and Walrasian insights. But the development of Walrasian doctrines that was proceeding at that time (Hicks' *Value and Capital*, 1939; Samuelson's *Foundations of Economic Analysis*, 1947) was enshrining the 'axiom of reals'. This implied that Schumpeter's insights about the 'supply conditions for money loans' and the notion of money capital as the result of a capital asset valuation process that are so evident in *The Theory of Economic Development* were not only no longer central but barely relevant in the *Business Cycles* book. The 'circular flow' tendency was identified with the Walrasian equilibrium. Whereas Keynes made a substantial breakthrough in response to the critical experiment of the Great Depression, Schumpeter reacted to the crisis by pushing a mechanical 'three cycle' explanation of capital development.

Given that money supply directly influences the price of capital assets, it cannot directly affect the price of current output. The price level of current output, however, is linked to the price level of capital assets through aggregate demand and supply. Given a price level of capital assets, the supply price of investment output and the financing conditions for investment, the level of investment and, with the level of investment, aggregate demand as well as the derived demand for labour are determined. The state of aggregate demand and supply of labour at existing wage rates determines whether there will be upward or downward pressure on wage rates.

If the price of capital relative to the supply function of labour is such that investment and the demand for labour are high then money wages will rise, 'pulling' the supply function for investment towards the demand price for capital. Similarly the supply price of investment output will be raised when interest rates rise. The price level of current output is not determined by the quantity of money in any simple sense as the quantity theory puts. The path from money prices is by way of asset prices, investment financing and the reaction of money wages to excess demand or supply in labour markets. As is well known the response of wages to excess labour supply or demand is strongly conditioned by institutional relations. It is also apparent from the above that inflation affects the economy by affecting the price of output relative to the price of capital assets. The argument of the post-Friedman monetarists postulating neutrality of the behaviour of output and relative prices with respect to inflation is not sustainable once the axiom of reals is abandoned.[6]

Once money is linked to banks via a debt creation–debt payment process in calendar time the question needs to be addressed as to what determines whether debt payment commitments will be met and what are the consequences of such commitments not being met. Keynes carried the argument up to but not through this point. In his chapter on the trade cycle in *The General Theory* (chapter 22) the primary cause of the crisis – which he identifies with the transition from expansion to contraction – is a collapse of the marginal efficiency of capital. But the gross profits of business depend not upon the 'productivity' of capital in any technical sense, but upon the amount of investment. The profitability of existing capital – and profit expectations from investment – can only decline if investment and expected investment decline. Thus we have to look elsewhere – to arguments other than those derived from assumed properties of production functions and hand waves with regard to over-investment – to explain why the marginal efficiency of investment falls. The natural place to look within the Schumpeter – Keynes – Kalecki vision is in the impact of financing relations – relations which involve both the financing of positions in the stock of assets and of investments.

We have data from the Flow of Funds which enable us to draw inferences upon the aggregate liability structure of business. It is clear that over the post-war period the ratio of business indebtedness to the total estimated value of business assets and the ratio of payment commitments on debts to total gross capital income have increased dramatically.[7] Once these ratios – and other balance sheet ratios like the ratio of private debts to total assets in the banking system – increase, rather small changes in expected profitability of business or in the carrying costs of debts can lead to significant changes in the value of being liquid. The greater the private indebtedness the greater the possibility of a collapse in asset value. In Keynes' structure, which integrates asset values with the value of the insurance and liquidity of money, investments to the relation between asset values and current prices, profits to investments, and debt validations to profits, financial collapses are possible. Financial collapses being possible does not mean that the economy is always on the brink of disaster, for the actual structure of relations determine whether a crisis is possible, likely or a clear and present danger. Keynes' structure also allows for policy if inept to make things worse and if apt to ameliorate dangerous situations.

Why does the economy become financially fragile? Why does the transition to fragility – so clearly shown by the data and experience – take place? We have mentioned profit-seeking banking. In 1983 it is not necessary to do more than mention innovation in finance, whether it takes the form of an increase in the diversity in the menu of assets available for households or the form of an increase in the alternative ways of financing available to business. The Schumpeterian vision of the experimenting entrepreneur who innovates need but be extended to financial firms and their clients to explain why portfolios migrate to a brink at which a shortfall of cash flows or a rise in financing terms may lead to a marked revision of asset values and therefore of investment programmes.

Early on we raised the question of today's financial fragility and why we have gone to the brink of crises but always succeeded in containing the damage in the years of increasing turbulence since the mid-1960s. The answer is that the big government of the welfare and military state is an effective stabilizer of profits. When in the course of events a rise in liquidity preference (a fall in asset prices) takes place so that investment decreases the impact on profits of this decline is offset by the impact on profits of the deficit. If a capitalist economy is to avoid the pitfalls of a Great Depression then profits must be sustained so that almost all of the outstanding debt contracts are fulfilled. With almost all debt contracts being fulfilled and with profits sustained by deficits the fall in asset prices when liquidity becomes more valuable is contained. The deficit as it accumulates increases the liquidity of the private economy. As a result the capitalization rate on the sustained profits does not collapse. Once the financial structure of a modern economy with big government and an interventionist central bank is made integral to the processes of the economy, the explanation of the contained recessions since the mid-1960s becomes apparrent. Furthermore the fact that crises have been contained to date in the post-war period does not guarantee that fully developed crises cannot occur if the financial structure evolves towards even greater fragility and policy interventions are inept.

Schumpeter had a vision of the capitalist process in which instability was a normal outgrowth of a combination of entrepreneurial activity and accumulation. The entrepreneurial activity led to the sustaining of profits even as accumulation led to the using up of profit opportunities. He also recognized that a banking system, i.e. a set of institutions that were not dependent upon prior savings in order to finance investment, was necessary. In Schumpeter's early vision banking was a full partner in the development process. He did not do more with his dynamic vision than state it. Even though aggregate profits reflected aggregate externally financed spending, he never was able to tie it down to broader relations in which banks' financing of government yielded profits to business. Furthermore Schumpeter got enmeshed in a Walrasian trap that assumed only real things matter, whereas in his original vision money mattered.

Fortunately for the development of economics, Keynes never was a Walrasian. His Marshallian roots were too strong. However he never did state his theory in fully intertemporal manner; his reliance on functional relations that could be forced into the simultaneous equilibrium among a number of markets led to the loss of insights. Only as problems of comprehensive debt validation arose in the mid-1960s did it become evident that the simultaneous market-clearing approach had missed the most significant dimensions of Keynes' theory.

The task confronting economics today may be characterized as a need to integrate Schumpeter's vision of a resilient intertemporal capitalist process with Keynes' hard insights into the fragility introduced into the capitalist accumulation process by some inescapable properties of capitalist financial structures. The 'fact' that intervention has prevented the fragility of finance from leading to a great depression in recent years may point the way to an integrated market economy in which the development of fragile financial structures is contained by an organization of industry that emphasizes competitive private enterprises for the mass of small and modest industries and firms alongside a comprehensive socialization of the liability structures of those firms and industries that use exceptionally expensive large-scale capital assets. Perhaps a lesson that the practical men and scholars can learn from the teaching of Keynes and Schumpeter is that a mixed economy, which has socialized sectors side by side with the aggressive private firms, works better in terms of stability and growth than either a comprehensive socialism or a laissez-faire capitalism.

Notes

1 In a letter to R.H. Brand of 29 November 1934 Keynes (1982: XXI, 344) wrote: 'I am afraid there is nothing which I can yet refer you to which deals with the problem of demand along my lines. I am working hard at my new book, but it may be nearly another twelve months before it comes out. When it appears, it will be on extremely academic lines; since I feel, rather definitely, that my object must first of all be to try and convince my economic colleagues. I have, indeed, succeeded in convincing those at Cambridge whom I have seriously tack[l]ed with them so far. If I prove right, a good many fundamental matters of theory will be seen in rather a new light.'

2 The orthodox propositions 5 and 6 according to Keynes (1973: XIV, 103–4) are:
  5. The marginal efficiency of money in terms of itself is independent of its quantity. This according to Keynes is a 'consequence of the quantity theory of money' and of the assumption – as became clear in later discussions with Robertson et al. – of the orthodox theory that productivity and profit (i.e. 'real world concerns') determine money interest rates.
  6. 'The scale of investment will not reach its equilibrium level until the point is reached at which the elasticity of supply of output as a whole has fallen to zero.'

3 It is to be noted that the version printed in the Collected Works first appeared in the magazine *Vanity Fair* in January 1932.

4 Incidentally this essay by Kalecki first appeared in 1942.

5 The full statement of the Kalecki profit relations allows for savings out of wages, consumption out of profits, foreign trade and government budget surpluses or deficits. This provides a framework for an effective understanding of how a capitalist economy whose behaviour depends upon realized and expected profits operates. See Minsky 1982a: chapter 5; and Minsky 1983.

6 Although Frank Hahn is a theorist who sees no way to abandon the 'axiom of reals' his remarks on neutrality of inflation are germane. See Hahn 1983: chapter III.

7 As this paper was being processed three items that integrate financial relations with behaviour and decisions arrived in the mail. These are: McKeon and Blitz (1983), Giordano (1983) and Bernstein (1983). Post-Keynesian analysis is alive and well among perceptive commentators on Wall Street, although the Wall Street commentators are not necessarily Post-Keynesians in their theory!

9 Financing Industrial Enterprise in Great Britain and Germany in the Nineteenth Century: Testing Grounds for Marxist and Schumpeterian Theories?

RICHARD TILLY

This chapter attempts to present a rough comparative summary of historical experience in the financing of industrial enterprise in Great Britain and Germany in the nineteenth century and to link that summary in an even rougher way to ideas of Karl Marx and Joseph Schumpeter on the role of finance in capitalist economic development. After some introductory remarks on the origins of Marx's and Schumpeter's views on the role of finance the chapter moves into a comparative discussion of the history of industrial finance in the two countries, dividing that history into two periods: from the Industrial Revolution to around 1870 and then from 1870 to World War One. Since Marx did not live long enough to experience the contrasting development in the financial histories of Britain and Germany in the latter period, the work of Rudolf Hilferding is taken and discussed as an extension of his thought. The paper ends by attempting to draw some conclusions from the comparative British–German experience about (1) the role of financial institutions in the economic development of those two countries and (2) the relevance of Marx–Hilferding and Schumpeter to understanding that and similar experience.

I

The difference between Marx and Schumpeter on the role of finance is naturally related to the economic history they experienced. Marx was powerfully influenced by the British developments of the first two-thirds of the nineteenth century, Schumpeter by Continental economic development at the beginning of the twentieth. Although a full doctrinal analysis would require much more differentiation, I believe one may associate Marx with the view that financial and credit problems in capitalism are basically epiphenomenal and derived from the 'real' problems of production, whereas Schumpeter's work is inseparable from the thesis that finance – in his terminology, credit creation – is the very engine of capitalist development.[1]

Marx recognized the great quantitative dimensions attained by banking activities and credit in the British economy in this period but he saw them as essentially passive adjustments to real forces:

In fact, what is happening is that through the system of commercial credit, one producer lends to another the money he needs to maintain reproduction. However, this takes the form of transactions in which bankers, to whom producers have lent the money, appear as lenders – and hence benefactors – to other producers; at the same time, command over this flow of funds passes into the hands of the intermediary, the banker. (Marx 1964: III, 522; author's translation)

Marx seems to be saying here that money payments made by or in favor of producers have somehow remained socially invisible, although in this view all money capital derives from production. Marx's position would certainly seem to understate the positive role of intermediation.

By and large, banks were seen to respond to needs of trade, and for this reason Marx tended to favor the 'banking school' interpretation of bank notes over that of the 'currency school'.[2] British industrial development during the first half of the nineteenth century, I suggest, made such views seem reasonable. In this age of British industrial supremacy, enterprise growth in the leading sectors – mainly textiles, coal and iron – could be financed very largely out of profits and short-term, revolving trade credits. In this context, bank credits were not qualitatively different from trade credits, and, moreover, tended to center around the same financial instrument, the bill of exchange.[3] To be sure, Marx recognized that credit expansion could drive capitalist production to higher levels, but this he saw as temporary and generally as a prelude to crises of overproduction (Marx 1964: III, 420ff., 523–4). It is striking that the first great railway boom of the 1840s appears in Marx's eyes as the product of a surplus of money capital with problems of finding an adequate rate of return for surplus funds figuring as a major factor: although the Industrial Revolution represented an unprecedented wave of investment,

Not all of the newly constructed factories, steam engines, spinning machines and weaving looms were adequate to the task of absorbing the massive flow of Lancashire profits. The job of building railways was now taken on with the same energy with which production had been increased; industrialists and merchants at last found an object capable of satisfying their speculative compulsions, especially since about the Summer of 1844. They subscribed as many shares as possible. (Marx 1964: III, 421; author's translation)

That is a striking statement, because more recent historical analysis of this chapter in British financial history does in fact confirm the ease with which railroad capital was mobilized (Broadbridge 1970). Moreover, the historical sequel to this chapter in economic history which covers the period up to the 1870s also stresses the problem of surplus funds and relates them in a causal way to the growing use of joint-stock companies with limited liability (Jeffreys 1938; Cottrell 1980: chapter 3). In brief, Marx's views on the role of finance in capitalist development were formed against the historical background of an economy experiencing rapid growth powered largely by the self-financed investment of family firms, growth which was unstable and frequently interrupted by crises triggered off by banking and credit collapse, and which in a more fundamental, long-run sense was continually re-threatened by the accumulating surpluses of money capital and shrinking rates of return.

In Schumpeter's theory, economic development is defined as innovation, or the 'carrying out of new combinations of productive resources', and these depend upon credit creation which transfers control over existing resources from old combinations to new. Credit is thus the means by which 'one who wishes to carry out new combinations outbids the producers in the circular flow in the market for the required means of production'. Bankers are typically the source of such credit. The banker is, in Schumpeter's words, 'the capitalist par excellence. He stands between those who wish to form new combinations and the possessors of productive means .... He is the ephor of the exchange economy' (Schumpeter 1961: especially p. 74).[4]

A case can be made for the thesis that Schumpeter's *Theory of Economic Development* derived some of its most crucial propositions directly from the experience of the Austrian economy in the 1900s (März 1964). Industrial growth in the Cisleithian Monarchy was very rapid in the 1895 to 1912–13 period and was characterized by a movement toward larger, more concentrated producers' units fostered by the unusually vigorous expansion of the large Viennese banks. Historians are uncertain about the precise contribution made by the promotional banks to Austrian growth (März 1964; März 1968; Mosser 1980; and Rudolph 1972) but there can be no doubt about (1) the emergence to prominence of those banks in the Austrian economy at this time or (2) the parallel between this emergence and the somewhat earlier development of 'industrial banking' by large banks in Wilhelminian Germany. But another related factor also played a role here: a growing concern with socialist thought and in particular with Marxist interpretations of capitalism. It was at this time, after all, that Schumpeter's contemporary and fellow student of Böhm-Bawerk, Rudolf Hilferding, developed his study of *Finance Capital*, a Marxist analysis (drawing heavily on recent German experience) in which banks and finance assume an importance far beyond that envisioned by Marx and which really amounted to significant modification of Marx's basic interpretation.[5] That Schumpeter integrated the same institutions into his model of economic development – in a different way from Hilferding, to be sure – paid testimony to Schumpeter's concern with Marxist theory. In any case, the great German banks were the model, as Schumpeter later made clear in *Business Cycles*, for the combined provision of current-account banking (with overdraft facilities) and underwriting and security issue services became the hallmark of these banks. Their novelty, in Schumpeter's words,

consisted only in the directness with which the problem of financing innovation was faced and the energy with which regular banking business was made ancillary to it. While elsewhere this use of short-term credit, created ad hoc, led to a situation in which it was up to the entrepreneur to look (unless receipts were coming in very quickly) for some method of funding and thus consolidating their position, these 'industrial' or 'promoting' banks provided machinery to do this themselves. They took care of necessary issues of stocks and bonds, thus helping the enterprise to redeem its short debt and providing it with additional means. In order to effect this they were ready to take those stocks or bonds for their own account, not only if they were unable to place them, but in the ordinary course of their business routine. (Schumpeter 1939: I, 348–9)

Although recent historical work shows that self-financing dominated in the development of most German industrial enterprises for which continuous records exist, those enterprises and sectors marked by especially rapid growth and innovation owed much to the financial and organizational assistance of the banks. Thus the continuous link between current banking business and the raising of long-term capital was a fact clearly distinguishing German from British institutional arrangements (Feldenkirchen 1982a; Rettig 1978). This means that Marx and Schumpeter were really 'modelling' different slices of historical experience, and that their work can only serve as imperfectly comparable guides to the financial history of British and German industrial development. That fact must be borne in mind in the following sections.

II

We traverse the ground of early-nineteenth-century financial history with seven-league boots, for the variety of details defies easy summary and this paper is no place for the details.[6] Cottrell's impressive survey of the Industrial Revolution from the point of view of the financial needs of industrial enterprise tends to support earlier work emphasizing the importance of working, relative to fixed, capital, the related importance of short-term credits raised via bills of exchange either from other manufacturing firms or through the banks (or both), and the predominance in most industries and development phases of self-financing by plowing back of profits. It is well to remember, however, that the average lives of business firms were short in this period and their mortality rates high (Cottrell cites a figure for the 1830s and 1840s suggesting a turnover of firms in industries of close to 50 per cent within a decade), with the evidence on longer-run financial behavior confined to a relatively small number of unusually successful firms (Cottrell 1980: 35). That is, there is a hint here that finance in the early stages of an enterprise's history may have been extremely scarce. As Cottrell writes:

Generally in the early years of any enterprise profits were low, if they were generated at all, and conversely fixed assets loomed large in any balance sheet struck. In this situation finance was required for both stocks and plant and consequently the firm was highly susceptible to any tightening of monetary conditions. Entry into an industry may have been encouraged by the lure of high profits during a boom and assisted by a bank willing to discount any type of paper presented in order to obtain customers. The crucial factor was whether a firm could survive its first four or five years, which usually would have spanned the upper turning point of the trade cycle and some form of credit crisis. (Cottrell 1980: 35; see also Chapman 1979)

A look at the contemporary development of the banking sector reveals a rather fragile structure subject to high failure rates in times of financial stringency, failures which both reflected and exacerbated the difficulties of industrial firms just mentioned. Moreover, Cottrell cites evidence to the effect that banks were 'overlent' in industrial areas in this period (by which he means the relationship between deposits and advances plus discounts) and other authors have also suggested that liberal bankers' support of industry was not untypical (Cottrell 1980: 32; Hudson 1981: 379–402). Nevertheless, even if it were shown that many firms failed when their bankers failed or refused them credits, the question of the net effects of finance on long-run enterprise growth as a whole would remain. In short, the evidence of British manufacturing industry during the Industrial Revolution does not suffice to support generalizations about the importance or unimportance of finance for the growth of industrial enterprise.

However, industrialization involved not only the development of manufacturing, but also the growth and modernization of what one may term the infrastructure of the economy – especially considerable investment in transportation. By the 1830s and 1840s, according to C. Feinstein (1978: VII, 40–1), investment in transportation came to rival (and even exceed) investment in industry and trade. A good deal of this went into the railroads, which for the purposes of this chapter may be treated as a special form of industrial enterprise deserving attention.

In Great Britain, as subsequently elsewhere, railroads were relatively large enterprises, organized from their inception as private corporations with limited liability. From the 1830s on, they raised large sums of capital through the sale of shares and (increasingly) bonds in what was rapidly becoming a national capital market. A striking feature of this development was the apparent ease with which such large sums – rising to over one quarter of total investment and nearly 5 per cent of estimated gross domestic product in the 1840s – were raised, with oversubscription of new issues characteristic, though there were moments when the bottom fell out of the market and neither shares nor bonds could be placed. The flow of funds to railroads was sensitive to general capital market conditions, it seems, with shifts in the rate of return on railroad securities relative to other financial investments (especially government bonds) playing an important role; but it does not seem to have been capital scarcity in any absolute sense so much as wavering expectations about returns – expectations shared by railroad companies and investors alike – which slowed down new issue activity.[7] Another striking feature was the fact that it was particularly from the rapidly growing centers of manufacturing and trade in the North of England, and within these centers from merchants and manufacturers, that the bulk of railroad capital flowed. S. Broadbridge (1970: 130) has stressed the role of Lancashire in this respect and remarked that 'Lancashire railways alone could not absorb the excess of [the region's] capital.' This can be taken as an argument for Marx's view, quoted above, which saw the accumulation of investment-seeking capital as an inevitable accompaniment and chronic problem of regions undergoing rapid industrial expansion. In Eric Hobsbawm's (1962: 45–7) formulation these huge investments in railways appeared irrational 'because in fact few railways were much more profitable to the investor than other forms of enterprise'. His answer to the question of why, then, so much railway money was forthcoming is simple: 'The fundamental fact about Britain in the first two generations of the Industrial Revolution was, that the comfortable and rich classes accumulated income so fast and in such vast quantities as to exceed all available possibilities of spending and investment.' The relevant indicator was, as Cottrell (1980: 46) notes, 'a declining rate of return on low-risk securities'. It is probably not too far-fetched to argue, as suggested earlier, that the public discussion of limited liability and the easing of incorporations embodying that legal privilege in the 1850s were also related more closely to the needs of capitalists for investment outlets than to industrial demands for finance. Even if a 'capitalist lobby' connected with the relevant legislation cannot be unambiguously identified, it seems clear that the institution of incorporation with limited liability was initially important mainly as a means for dividing family wealth accumulated in industry and trade and for providing a gateway through which increasingly lethargic capital might exit and entrepreneurial talent enter.[8] Nevertheless, taking British development of this mid-Victorian period as a whole, it is clear that the principal outlet found for domestic money capital was capital export, which by the 1860s already amounted to nearly a third of total domestic investment and which moved abroad to a large extent in the form of portfolio investment (Cottrell 1980: 46; Feinstein 1978: 91). This is a point to which we must return.

Turning to German development during the first part of the nineteenth century one is struck by important similarities with British experience despite some great structural differences. Similarities are to be seen in the probable predominance of self-financing and/or working capital needs among industrial firms, in indications of a relative surplus of money capital over investment opportunities, and in the substantial initial financing impact of railroad building in the 1840s.[9] The first similarity is based, to be sure, on no more than a thin sample of enterprise evidence of doubtful representativeness: the Krupps, the Haniels and the famous Gutehoffnungshütte, Harkort, Stinnes, Delius, and similarly subsequently prominent firms tend to dominate the record.[10] However, since the evidence is virtually unanimous and since documentation of the later experience of industrial corporations – which had, after all, greater opportunities and incentives for external finance – also reveals the predominance of self-financing, the probability is high that this was a real similarity (Feldenkirchen 1982a; Rettig 1978). Nevertheless, as in the British case, heavy reliance on self-financing by no means excluded the widespread use of short-term current-account credits extended by trading partners or private bankers, and there were times and instances in which the volume of such credits reached dangerous – indeed fatal – proportions.[11] A second resemblance between German and British financial conditions in this period lay in the apparent relative abundance of savings. As in Britain, fiscal policy led to debt retirement and pressure on long-term rates of interest, while large-scale wealth transfers from peasants to landed estate owners (as the result of the conversion of 'feudal' obligations) further swelled the liquid funds in search of outlets.[12] One important result or indicator of this accumulation of money capital was the export of capital through the purchase of foreign (mainly government) securities brought onto the Berlin capital market in the 1815–45 period (Brockhage 1910).

Railroad-building, finally, initiated the development of a national market for enterprise capital in Germany in the 1840s just as it had in Great Britain in the 1830s. German railroads were also corporate enterprises enjoying limited liability, and their demands upon savings came to exceed those of all other borrowers – including the government – in the 1840s. In spite of their relatively large size, German railroads may have represented smaller net demands on savings than appears at first glance, for they yielded considerable profits almost immediately after they began operation and their profits absorbed some – probably significant – share of additional capital issues (Fremdling 1975: especially pp. 123ff.; Eichholtz 1962; Beyer 1978). This suggests a parallel to the British experience.

However, German railroad-building and finance before the 1870s did differ from its British counterpart in two respects. First, railroads were relatively more important in the German economy. Table 1 sets out some crude estimates of annual average investment in Prussia by sector. Most of the expansion of the 1840s (around 43 of 53 million Marks in the 1840s as against 6 of 23 million Marks in the 1830s) reflected railroad investment and far overshadowed industrial and commercial investment – even if we allocate, say, 30 per cent of non-agricultural building to the latter, it is no more than half of transportation investment for the 1840s and this is far below the corresponding British figure.[13] That fact is perhaps not surprising but it is nevertheless worth mentioning, for it heightens the German financial achievement. Second, railroad financing in this period paved the way for the pattern which would subsequently become characteristic of German 'mixed' banking. As early as the 1830s, we find private bankers prominently represented in the initial railroad organizing committees; in the 1830s and subsequently we find those same bankers underwriting the capital issues of companies formed, marketing the securities with their customers and correspondent banking firms in commercial cities all over Germany, advancing subscribers the initial payments on their shares and also advancing funds to the railroad companies themselves in anticipation of the proceeds of the issues they were steering. It is perhaps not necessary to add that those proceeds generally were held in accounts maintained by the railroad companies with the very same bankers.

Table 1. *Annual net investment in Prussia by sectors, 1816–49 (in millions of Marks in 1913 prices)*

	Agriculture	Non agricultural buildings	Transport	Industry	Total
1816–22	85.5	28.7	7.0	2.8[a]	125.0
1822–31	70.4	18.7	8.8	5.1[a]	103.0
1830/1–40	109.6	52.0	22.5	5.6[a]	189.0
1840–9	59.9	69.2	73.7[b]	7.0	209.8

Notes:
[a]'Guesstimate' based on extrapolation of capital-product value trend 1830–4 to 1816 using value-of-product data.
[b]Railway investment in 1840 estimated at 15 million Marks.

As additional safeguards for their considerable organizational and financial contributions the bankers tended to occupy key positions on the boards of directors of the railroad companies. This eased the task of managing the railroad's finance (including the planning of further issues) and the continuity of this arrangement was insured by the bankers' ability to mobilize a majority of shareholders' votes at regular or extraordinary meetings through the machinery of proxies or powers of attorney. Railroad financing, however, tended to be too large a task for any single banking firm and was almost from the start a cooperative arrangement involving anywhere from several to dozens of bankers. It was this fact which limited the influence of individual bankers over the railroad companies, though cartel-like arrangements could offset such limits to some extent (Fremdling 1975; Eichholtz 1962; Tilly 1966: chapter 7; and Steitz 1974).

In short, we have here all the ingredients of German mixed banking to which Schumpeter attributed decisive positive achievements in a later phase of development. The banker truly appears here as the 'ephor' of development, and it is interesting to note that Schumpeter himself – apparently not aware of the role of private banker as predecessors of the corporate banks – was puzzled by the great advances of German railroading in the 1840s.[14] In any case the connection outlined makes the advent of massive railroad-building in the 1840s a very important event in European financial history.

III

The railroads, then, established the first major links between business enterprise and national capital market in both Great Britain and Germany. In the second half of the nineteenth century those connections were widened and intensified in both countries. By the beginning of the twentieth century, however, certain clear differences were emerging: the German industrial sector grew more rapidly than Britain's and its demands upon the capital market expanded relative to that of British domestic industry; and as a counterpart to this development the British market financed much more foreign investment. The task of this part of the paper is to discuss these and other differences and, if possible, to relate them to differences in enterprise development patterns.

Although the discussion which follows develops in terms of the contribution of the capital market to industrial growth in the two countries, in keeping with our general theme, the question of Marx's and Schumpeter's views on the subject also calls for attention. In this latter connection I should at once restate the obvious: namely, that Schumpeter's observations on the nexus between capital market and industrial finance have the advantage of hindsight not available to Marx (whose historical laboratory extended no further than Britain in the 1860s). Nevertheless, Marx's work shows considerable prescience concerning one of the most important issues: the possibility that corporate enterprise utilizing limited liability and raising share capital through the stock market could considerably widen the scope of capitalist development while at the same time altering the latter's character. Marx described this as 'the abolition of capital as private property within the limits of the capitalistic system itself' (Marx 1964: III, 452). By this he meant the separation of ownership and control and resultant conflicts between shareowner and management, between capitalist owners and production directors (which was not quite the same thing as a conflict between capitalist and entrepreneur in the Schumpeterian sense inasmuch as Marx did not distinguish between capitalist and entrepreneurial 'functions'). Marx believed that a concomitant of the growth of corporate enterprise would be the growth of a new kind of financial aristocracy – the proliferation of 'parasites' in the form of promoters, speculators, swindlers, straw men, etc. – who would be creating a system of private production without the control of private property (Marx 1964: III, 454).[15]

What was missing from Marx's analysis was a discussion of the potential links between capitalists and corporate business management, in particular a discussion of the capital market. It is interesting that this aspect of Marx's theorizing about capitalism was developed further in the Marxist tradition by Rudolf Hilferding (in his *Finanzkapital*). That is interesting because, as mentioned above, Hilferding and Schumpeter drew very much upon the same theoretical and historical sources, with Hilferding seeing in the 'Finance Capital' a new set of socio-economic institutions transcending industrial capitalism (and promising to stabilize it) while Schumpeter continued to see an important division between entrepreneurs and financial capital only temporarily obscured by the 'trust movements' and concentration in the financial sector from the late nineteenth century on. A good deal of the difference between the two appears to turn on their interpretations of interlocking directorates, with Hilferding seeing these as partial evidence of the control of 'finance' over production and Schumpeter rejecting such a notion.[16] In any case, if the Marxist–Hilferding theory were correct, one would expect to find industrial growth positively related to enterprise size and enterprise growth increasingly dominated by capital market conditons, whereas the Schumpeterian interpretation would seem to imply the continued importance of independence between finance and industry and the dependence of industrial growth upon innovation – involving new things and new entrepreneurs. In the context of an Anglo-German comparison of industrial finance this can be taken to mean that whereas the Marx–Hilferding view will interpret German–British differences in the light of differing degrees of financial influence Schumpeter's theory interprets such differences as a result of differences in innovation – including innovations in the financial field.

The financial systems of both countries developed powerfully between 1870 and 1914. According to R. Goldsmith (1969: 113–14), the value of assets of financial institutions issued in Britain and Germany between 1861 and 1913 grew about $11 billion and $20 billion respectively, while the value of all securities held by wealthholders in 1912 was $29 billion and $21 billion – about two to three times the size of estimated national incomes in the two countries. By the beginning of the twentieth century (1901–13), British wealthholders were acquiring publicly issued securities at a rate of about 6 or 7 per cent of national product per year, while German savers acquired at a rate of about 4 per cent. For assets of financial institutions the positions of the two countries were reversed, with Britain's accumulation in the 1901–13 period approximating 3 per cent of the national product and Germany's between 8 and 9 per cent (Goldsmith 1969: 118–119). This difference deserves attention later on; but for the moment the point to be stressed is the disproportionately great expansion of finance markets in both countries – a generally typical feature of growing economies in the nineteenth century.

One very important part of financial growth involved the market for corporate securities, particularly – but not exclusively – those operating in and out of the major monetary and banking centers of London and Berlin. Because of their great weight, these centers absorb the bulk of attention in the rest of this chapter. That imposes a restriction on the generality of conclusions which can be drawn, for in both countries industrial enterprises relied largely upon internal sources to finance expansion – even corporate enterprises did so, and they represented a minority of industrial enterprise – and when they did turn to external sources it was not typically the London or Berlin markets that they tapped, but financial institutions in their immediate geographic surroundings.[17] Nevertheless, the central markets of concern here *were* of more than negligible importance for the growth of industrial enterprise in the two countries, as we shall attempt to show. Moreover, they have frequently served as the basis for comparative assessments in the historical literature to which this chapter is thus also addressed.

Table 2. *New issues of securities in London and Berlin, 1882–1913 (in millions £ and Marks)*

	London			Berlin[a]		
Year	(1) Domestic industry	(2) Foreign	(3) Total	(4) Domestic industry	(5) Foreign	(6) Total
1882	23.6	49.8	145.6	—	—	—
1883	12.9	45.5	81.2	78	299	754
1884	20.0	57.0	109.0	79	530	905
1885	5.4	55.9	78.0	81	510	899
1886	14.7	56.2	101.9	66	485	1.015
1887	20.6	65.8	111.2	123	410	1.008
1888	22.0	101.2	160.3	223	667	1.985
1889	32.6	107.1	207.0	356	584	1.742
1890	24.3	101.3	142.6	255	386	1.521
1891	22.6	51.2	104.6	59	245	1.218
1892	14.2	32.3	81.1	28	172	949
1893	5.9	25.2	49.1	93	342	1.266
1894	18.0	48.9	91.8	129	338	1.420
1895	21.3	57.6	104.7	263	300	1.375
1896	54.9	37.3	152.7	376	489	1.896
1897	55.2	36.7	157.3	376	608	1.944
1898	51.5	51.0	150.2	664	891	2.407
1899	37.2	45.9	133.2	935	203	2.611
1900	60.7	26.1	165.5	640	271	1.777
1901	35.2	27.0	159.3	357	210	1.631
1902	35.4	62.2	153.8	342	454	2.111
1903	29.5	60.0	108.5	260	242	1.666
1904	26.1	64.6	123.0	470	232	1.995
1905	28.5	110.6	167.2	667	1.008	3.091
1906	27.5	73.0	120.2	837	221	2.741
1907	27.6	79.3	123.6	604	153	2.212
1908	45.5	117.9	192.2	915	228	3.416
1909	18.7	150.5	182.4	1.005	349	3.590
1910	42.8	179.8	267.4	640	545	3.022
1911	12.5	142.7	191.8	830	459	2.709
1912	29.4	144.6	210.9	1.293	270	2.934
1913	—	149.7	196.5	739	603	2.646

Note:
[a]Market prices.
Sources: London: Mitchell and Deane (1962: 462); Simon (1968: 38–9); own calculations from London *Economist* and *Investor's Monthly Manual*, 1882–1913. Berlin: Spiethoff (1955: table 3).

The point of departure is the new issues market. Table 2 offers some comparative estimates of total annual new issues in the London and Berlin markets, dividing them into foreign and domestic securities on the one hand, and 'industrial' and 'other' securities on the other. The most significant piece of information is that foreign issues dominated the British market absolutely and relatively: for the period as a whole and in 22 of 32 individual years observed. Foreign issues were much less important for the Berlin market, and exceeded domestic issues in only two years (1884 and 1885). The reverse is true of domestic industrial issues, where Berlin led London by a large margin, relatively speaking.

This chapter concentrates on domestic industrial issues and thus neglects possible indirect effects of foreign investment upon domestic industrial enterprise growth. It is worth remarking, however, that the fact of dominance of foreign issues alone has given rise to the judgement that the London capital market was biassed against domestic industrial enterprise in this period, with disastrous results for British industrial growth – a record which can be contrasted with the much more positive treatment of German domestic industrial needs in the Berlin market.[18] This must be borne in mind in the discussion which follows, though the interpretation itself may be wrong.

What about British industrial issues themselves? At then-existing exchange rates (about 20 Marks to a pound) London's domestic industrial issues exceeded Berlin's by a fair margin until around 1900; thereafter Berlin moved ahead. However, if one takes *ex post* domestic investment expenditures as an indicator of demand for finance and compares British with German data (as in Table 3) one comes to the rather surprising conclusion that the London capital market did more for British investors than Berlin was doing for German ones.

Of course, *ex post* investment data reflect not just the demand for finance but also its supply. British domestic investment was relatively low (as can be seen when one compares the British and German figures on a 20:1 basis) and one important reason for this could be that finance was in short supply.[19] There are, in fact, indications that in both countries domestic investment was sensitive to capital market conditions. B. Eichengreen's econometric results for Britain strongly suggest the importance of industrial share prices for domestic investment, 1870–1913, and roughly similar calculations for German industry over the same period point in the same direction (Eichengreen 1982: 87–95).[20] Thus the relatively more buoyant and stable German stock prices as a possible explanation for greater industrial issue activity – and greater domestic investment – ought not to be dismissed out of hand.[21] However, it should be pointed out that merger activity in both countries has also been shown to have been sensitive to movements of the industrial share prices in this period; but in this case the British response was by far the more vigorous one (Hannah 1974; Tilly 1982). The question is therefore one of explaining different

Table 3. *Net investment and new issues of industrial securities in London and Berlin, 1882–1913 (annual averages in millions of £ and Marks)*[a]

	United Kingdom (£)		Germany (M.)	
	Net investment	Industrial issues[b]	Net investment	Industrial issues[c]
1882–5	58.5	15.5	1565	100.3
1886–90	43.8	22.8	2288	212.2
1891–5	57.8	16.4	2406	122.6
1896–1900	108.0	51.9	3918	666.8
1901–5	137.2	27.2	4246	440.2
1906–10	89.2	32.4	5776	815.0
1911–13	89.0	28.3	6800	967.3

Notes:
[a]In current prices.
[b]Corresponds to category 'Capital created'.
[c]Market prices.
Sources: Net investment – United Kingdom: Feinstein (1961); Germany: Hoffmann c.s. (1965). New issues – London: own calculations from data in London *Economist and Investor's Monthly Manual*, 1882–1913. Berlin: Kleiner (1914).

kinds of response to a given financial stimulus – in addition to the needs for an explanation of the latter as well.

Before discussing one possible interpretation of the question just raised we turn to the somewhat easier, though by no means simple, task of describing the industrial issues themselves. Table 4[22] summarizes their distribution by sectors and permits a comparison with sectoral rate of growth, 1882–1913. The higher German growth rates in most sectors and in the aggregate – the weighted growth rate for Germany was 4.4 per cent per year as compared with Britain's 2.6 per cent, 1880–1913 – are no surprise (sectoral growth rates were weighted by sectoral shares in output in 1907). What is worth noting, however, is that in both countries the capital markets supported the more rapidly growing sectors. Weighting sectoral growth rates with output and new-issue shares yields higher rates of growth in both countries: 5.1 per cent for Germany and 2.9 for Britain. *Given* the rates of growth, Britain could not have improved her relative position by imitating the German new-issue structure, i.e. by allocating more funds to heavy industry and less to breweries and railroads. It is true, of course, that such a hypothetical reallocation might have shifted both sectoral growth rates and their output weights. Nevertheless, the calculation indicates that the market was not obviously locked into the stagnant sectors.

In order to discuss the sectoral distribution of new issues (and also any hypothetical alternative) it is necessary to examine a second characteristic of

Table 4. *Sectoral distributions of new issues and sectoral growth rates in United Kingdom and Germany, 1882–1913*

Sector	United Kingdom		Germany	
	Share in new issues %	Annual rate of growth %	Share in new issues %	Annual rate of growth %
Mining and metal production	5	2.2	30	4.88
Quarrying	2	1.92	1	3.97
Metalworking, engineering	13	3.36	12	5.96
Chemicals	5	4.86	7	6.39
Textiles	6	1.68	3	2.78
Leather, paper and woodworking	2	2.41	3	3.07
Construction	1	0.81	4	4.05
Food, drink, etc.	5	2.47	1	2.82
Breweries and distilleries	22	2.76	5	1.92
Gas and water	3	3.69⎱	20	9.75
Electricity	3	9.91⎰		
Transportation	33	2.98	14	5.55
Other[a]	20	—	4	—

Note:
[a] For the United Kingdom this corresponds to issues which could not be identified sectorally.

Sources: New issues – United Kingdom: as Table 3; Germany: as Tables 2 and 3 and own calculations from *Der Deutsche Ökonomist,* 1883–97, and *Vierteljahresheft der Statistik des Duetschen Reiches,* 1889–1913.
   Sectoral growth rates – United Kingdom: Feinstein (1972) and Lewis (1978); Germany: Hoffmann c.s. (1965: 333ff.).

the market – namely the expected rates of return they offered investors. This can be done on basis of M. Edelstein's estimates of 'realized rates of return' on securities traded in the London market, 1870–1913 (Edelstein 1976). They show that the market signalled a redistribution in the direction indicated above (toward heavy industry and away from railroads); no such redistribution was forthcoming, however, and large differentials persisted. Given the great weight in the British market of those financial dinosaurs – the railroads – and given their virtual absence in Germany due to nationalization, one is tempted to see in the latter a measure which had – or in Britain's case *might* have had – enormous consequences for the flow of funds to industry via the capital market. Unfortunately, however, a study of rates of return in the

Table 5. *Share of new enterprises in industrial new issues, London,* *1883–1905*

	1883	1889	1900	1905
1. Number of new issuers	77	120	152	36
2. Number of all issuers	97	146	174	101
3. Share of new issuers (%)	51	68	52	28

Source: Own calculation from sources as given for Tables 2 and 3.

Table 6. *Concentration of industrial new issues in London and Berlin,* *1883–1905 (share of top 10 per cent of issuers in total issues)*

	1883	1889	1900	1905
1. London				
(a) No. of enterprises	97	136	174	101
(b) Share of top ten (%)	41	39	46	38
2. Berlin				
(a) No. of enterprises	38	139	128	108
(b) Share of top ten (%)	68	28	45	45

Source: Own calculations.

German capital market comparable to Edelstein's study for London does not yet exist and the question can only be raised.

A third comparable feature of new industrial issues concerns the question of risk. The riskiness of industrial securities was presumably related to the age and size of the enterprises issuing them: for investors, small enterprises meant small issues and a 'thin' resale market. Such securities were relatively illiquid, and hence 'risky' investments. One way of comparing the performance of the London and Berlin markets is to simply identify the age and size of the issuers and their share in total issues. In fact, such identification is not an empirically simple matter, but Tables 5 and 6 nevertheless make an attempt for selected years. The results suggest that the German market was somewhat more likely to prefer the securities of larger, older enterprises. In 1900 and 1908, for example, we find 25 and 31 per cent of all issuing firms accounting for 57 and 62 per cent of the sum total registered in Berlin – much higher than the comparable British figures. However, the differences are not large enough to support an unambiguous judgement. Data on corporations are rather more definite in this respect. If one compares the founding of corporations with data on the admission of securities to trading on the stock exchange and new issues, one discovers that relatively few industrial enterprises ever reached the main

Table 7. *Joint-stock companies, founding and stock exchange listing,*
1887–1907 (capital in millions of Marks)

	Founded total[a]		Companies with listing			
			total		within 6 months	
Sector	No.	Capital	No.	Capital	No.	Capital
Mining and metal production	152	499.3	35	199.3	11	71.4
Quarrying	336	291.6	54	46.9	12	25.8
Metalworking	549	1.067.8	147	285.9	34	91.5
Chemicals	167	298.4	23	41.1	3	2.3
Water, gas and electricity	189	124.5	16	10.5	3	4.6
Textiles	192	289.9	43	64.9	9	14.9
Leather, paper and woodworking	180	160.7	32	28.6	9	8.3
Breweries	382	279.2	82	59.9	30	40.9
Food, drink, etc.	227	186.0	30	23.4	4	10.7
Other	215	62.5	26	21.7	7	9.9
Total	2.589	3.259.9	488	782.2	122	280.3

Note:
[a] Without Transport.
Sources: Unpublished tables of Jacques Beuchat, Münster 1982. *Deutsche Ökonomist*, Jgg. 1887–1908.

capital market in Germany. That, at least, is the lesson of Table 7: not quite one-quarter of the companies founded in the 1887–1907 period penetrated the central market. This statistic may be compared with British statistics for 1912–13 (Lavington 1921: 201). According to these data, only 477 of 3477, or 14 per cent, of newly founded companies were 'public', i.e. intended to issue securities to be placed in the London market. That would seem to indicate greater conservatism on the British side, but in fact one must recognize that in Germany far fewer corporations with limited liability and tradable shares were founded than in Great Britain in this period: between 1890 and 1913 around 200–300 per year as compared with 4000–5000 per year. To make the comparison meaningful, one has to throw in the German limited companies without tradable shares – the *Gesellschaften mit beschränkter Haftung* – which raises the number of newly founded companies in Germany by a couple of thousand per year, 1892–1913, and reduces the share of new companies having recourse to the formal capital market to about 3 per cent, for less than one-fourth of the British figure. The suggestion, then, is that the British capital market was not less, but *more* likely to serve the interests of newly founded, risky enterprises than its German counterpart. That is an interesting finding, I think, for if one were to interpret Schumpeter as seeing a close relationship between new firms and innovation – and there is some evidence to this effect – then the reported facts would seem to falsify his 'model', for by his own admission there was relatively little innovation in Britain during this period (certainly less than in Germany) (Schumpeter 1934: 66–7; and 1939: I, 400, 429–30).

Risk and innovation, however, are not necessarily closely and positively related to one another; nor is it always the case that they are inversely related to age or size of enterprises. Only case studies can give us appropriately differentiated answers. For the moment we can only note the ambiguity and cite a few examples. For instance, it is interesting to see that at the beginning of the twentieth century innovative enterprises in that innovative branch, the electro-technical industry, were among the largest issuers of securities on the Berlin market (in 1900 seven of the fourteen largest); only a few years later three of the seven firms had already disappeared.[23] In the British market at about this time new enterprises were also among the largest issuers, but here they tended to belong to traditional industries such as brewing, textiles or paper manufacturing and, moreover, some of the most important of the new firms created were in reality combinations of older firms merged to better achieve market control. But although they thus did not represent innovation of a Schumpeterian kind, they were nonetheless risky investments in the sense that they yielded shareowners either losses or unusually low dividends (see the data and interpretation in Hannah (1974) and also the rates of return in Edelstein (1976: especially pp. 318–19)).

A fourth – and perhaps the most important – characteristic of industrial new issues which can be compared across the two capital markets is the distribution of securities by type: common stock (or ordinary shares), preferred stock and fixed-interest bonds. Tables 8 and 9 provide an overview. The dominance of fixed-interest securities in the London market as a whole has frequently been noted: what seems especially remarkable is the extent to which that dominance came to characterize industrial issues as well. One reason for this lies in the development of British company law. After much debate the Companies Act of 1900 introduced restrictions on the promotion of limited companies which particularly affected the issue of shares (see the London *Economist*, 1902, pp. 474 and 074 for one assessment; for the general background and details, Cottrell 1980: especially pp. 68–75). In any case, the contrast between London and Berlin in this respect – visible in Tables 8 and 9 – is unmistakable. Moreover, these figures understate the difference since a larger percentage of the British common stock issued represented 'vendor' shares which did not move into the hands of 'outside' investors at all, while after 1900, well over half (Cottrell 1980: 163). Table 10 reveals an additional dimension of this contrast: by classifying new issues in both markets according

Table 8. *Structure of industrial new issues in the U.K., 1882–1913 (in £000)*

	Ordinary shares	Preferred shares	Debenture	Total
1882	15.476	4.063	4.059	23.598
1883	8.449	1.458	2.949	12.850
1884	11.066	4.187	4.795	20.048
1885	4.027	814	600	5.441
1886	8.910	2.682	3.080	14.672
1887	11.597	5.877	3.103	20.577
1888	13.024	1.682	7.261	21.967
1889	17.811	2.496	12.265	32.572
1890	20.725	719	8.281	29.725
1891	19.203	99	5.565	24.867
1892	10.622	717	2.830	14.169
1893	3.444	1.215	1.201	5.860
1894	9.123	2.540	6.369	18.032
1895	14.682	854	5.813	21.349
1896	29.308	7.115	18.424	54.847
1897	22.200	12.314	20.613	55.187
1898	29.534	6.903	15.105	51.542
1899	14.587	10.792	15.669	37.171
1900	22.270	17.665	20.743	60.578
1901				
1902				
1903				
1904	5.412	7.889	9.354	22.655
1905	2.787	2.400	8.697	13.884
1906				
1907				
1908				
1909				
1910				
1911				
1912	12.940[a]	16.485[a]	37.457[a]	66.882[a]

Note:
[a] Include some foreign issues, from London *Economist*, p. 157.
Source: As Table 3.

to percentage of ordinary shares and comparing them with rates of return and interest rates in subperiods (based on the German business cycle), the greater flexibility of the German market, its responsiveness to the stockprice dividend–interest rate differential, becomes clear. These are important differences which require some comment.

The significance of the differences lies in the fact that in Germany industrial enterprises in search of capital were able to transfer a larger share of their

Table 9. *New issues of domestic industry and foreign securities in Germany, 1883–1913 (in million of Marks)*

	Ordinary shares	Industrial preferred shares	Debentures	Foreign Shares	Foreign Debentures
1883	68.0	5.3	45.8	37.5	262.4
1884	34.5	3.6	53.8	38.4	481.4
1885	37.9	10.2	42.0	56.4	453.3
1886	48.9	9.0	17.8	18.0	467.2
1887	79.2	13.5	35.0	10.2	433.3
1888	185.8	8.8	31.0	77.4	590.0
1889	313.0	29.5	23.9	49.8	534.2
1890	183.7	18.5	63.2	22.9	362.8
1891	27.0	1.2	29.4	14.9	229.9
1892	18.8	0.3	17.0	4.0	167.7
1893	28.0	1.9	71.0	—	342.5
1894	69.7	11.1	58.2	46.0	338.0
1895	223.7	2.2	45.5	17.6	300.3
1896	343.3	27.4	91.5	76.9	488.7
1897	313.0	14.9	67.8	24.9	608.0
1898	528.6	9.9	160.8	18.8	690.9
1899	867.4	2.2	123.6	30.3	203.5
1900	505.8	10.9	263.8	89.6	185.7
1901	165.5	1.8	208.1	10.9	199.4
1902	186.9	45.6	166.8	14.6	438.9
1903	180.7	18.1	66.9	33.4	208.3
1904	348.7	14.9	118.7	45.7	186.4
1905	543.0	9.1	127.1	134.2	974.3
1906	654.4	10.6	192.1	106.7	114.1
1907	337.6	54.3	173.8	38.4	114.3
1908	606.5	12.3	317.9	22.8	205.2
1909	743.8	16.2	278.0	34.6	314.2
1910	499.0	10.1	137.0	78.4	467.2
1911	541.5		317.3	92.7	367.2
1912	904.8	1.0	396.6	53.2	217.1
1913	530.0		210.7	48.2	555.8

Source: *Deutsche Ökonomist*, Jg. 1883–97; *Vierteljahresheft der Statistik des Deutschen Reiches*, 1898–1913.

financial risks onto the investors than was possible in Britain. Industrial enterprises came through 'hard times' more easily if their liabilities were not dominated by fixed-interest claims. There are two ways of looking at this difference. One view stresses investor preferences. Faced with investor preferences favoring fixed-interest securities, as were characteristic in Britain, industrial enterprises were likely to respond by behaving cautiously, spending less, having less recourse to the capital market than was warranted in the

Table 10. *Rate of return on ordinary shares, bond rate and share of issues of ordinary shares in total industrial issues, London and Berlin (in %)*

| | | Berlin | | | London | |
	% Shares	Rate of return on shares	Bond rate	% Shares	Rate of return on shares	Bond rate
1883–86	50	12.74	3.82	61	7.16	2.99
1887–9	80	19.67	3.63	56	11.24	2.95
1890–3	38	− 5.50	3.70	72	2.47	2.84
1894–1900	76	11.66	3.48	47	7.32	2.58
1901–3	51	7.43	3.57			
1904–6	76	9.34	3.60	22[a]	6.73[a]	2.81[a]
1907–8	64	− 1.34	3.80			
1909–12	70	7.91	3.80			

Note:
[a] 1904–5.
Source: Own calculations as for Tables 2 and 3; Edelstein (1976); Tilly (1980a).

German case, where industrial shares dominated. This could explain why Berlin overtook London in the issue of industrial securities after 1900. There is another interpretation, however. It stresses the interest of industrial entrepreneurs in maintaining control over 'their' enterprises. Issuing mainly preference shares and debentures was a way of financing growth without facing a loss of control to 'outside' shareholders. This nexus is fairly well documented – for British as well as German enterprises (Cottrell 1980: 166–7; Feldenkirchen 1982b: 38–74, especially 44; Rettig 1978:243–6). For German enterprises as a whole the use of ordinary shares as a financial vehicle was, as already noted, much more prominent than in Britain, and German listed enterprises which grew very slowly tended to be relatively reluctant to issue shares.[24] But why the national differences? The answer, I suggest, lies in the relationship between banks and industrial enterprise, in a variant of Hilferding's 'Finance Capitalism': thanks to the development of company law in Germany since the 1880s and to stock exchange practice, banks and shareholders generally were well informed as to the financial status of most listed industrial companies; and banks were also, by virtue of their ability to dominate shareholder meetings and appoint directors, in a position to influence policy, to break down the resistance of enterprise management to issue new shares, not least of all because they were so frequently able to offer attractive issue terms (Tilly 1980b). In Britain, at least prior to 1900, insiders organizing new enterprises or enlarging existing ones had a distinct information advantage over the general investor, but, as Kennedy has recently argued, this could only be exploited for very limited times and at the long-run expense of not being able to fashion a permanent market for industrial securities calling for more than a minimum of risk-bearing (Kennedy 1982: 105–14). Thus the two interpretations merge into one: British investor preferences in favor of fixed-interest securities reflected the paucity of information and relatively weak financial controls on the operations of company founders and insiders. Cottrell (1980: 164) suggests, in addition, that in terms of yields 'outside' holders of ordinary shares did not do as well, on the average, as holders of preference shares and debentures, at least in the 1870 period.

We may sum up this part of the chapter with two seemingly somewhat conflicting claims: first, the British capital market appears to have been more open to new industrial firms, less concentrated on large, established firms and at least up to 1900 not clearly more risk-averse than its German counterpart; second, however, the British capital market provided domestic industrial enterprise with less equity financing and less flexibility, indeed from around 1900 onward with less finance in general, than the German market did. Since this provisional conclusion is rather a puzzle, it is necessary to pursue its implications further – the task of the following section.

IV

New issues of securities on the formal capital market were by no means the main source of industrial finance in Britain or Germany in the 1870–1913 period. The point may be obvious, but it deserves repeating. According to one source cited by Cottrell, public offers of securities financed no more than 10 per cent of 'domestic industrial development' in Britain in 1907; and Lavington, writing on the years 1911–13, estimated the share of domestic investment which was financed through the sale of new securities in the capital market at between 20 and 25 per cent.[25] In Germany at this time the same share was certainly not higher and probably a good deal lower, possibly lower than 10 per cent.[26] For Germany, this financial 'contribution' is dwarfed by that estimated for the banking system as a whole for the same period: with a share of more than 40 per cent its contribution was more than four times as large (Hoffmann c.s. 1965: 812–13). That is, the formal capital market was only part of a larger financial system. To say that is not to belittle that market's contribution to the financing of industry, but to stress that its functioning depended on its links to the rest of the system.

With this point in mind, let us return to the puzzle mentioned at the conclusion of the last section. Cottrell and Kennedy solve that 'puzzle' by seeing in the openness of the British capital market to new enterprises and their promoters evidence of the absence of institutions capable of taking a discriminating, long-run view of enterprise development potential; it was unable to filter out less promising projects. A major defect was that promoters rarely developed a routine client relationship with the enterprises they helped launch, and tended to see in promotions 'a major "killing" to be milked to the limit, for there was no certainty of what tomorrow had in store'. 'Promoters, the stock exchange, and investors were prepared to support "mania" waves of flotations' in good times, but when the booms were over the firms created, many of them weak ones, were on their own – as were the investors (Cottrell 1980: 187, 189; Kennedy 1976). It is clear, as suggested earlier, that the 'counter-model' is the system developed by the German 'mixed banks'. For these banks ran the promotion and issue business in a careful, routine way and in conjunction with the rest of their banking business. Above all, the current-account connection with many of the firms whose securities they marketed gave them additional information on those firms going beyond what the more stringent German company laws prescribed in any case. The banks had a direct interest in seeing that their clients would survive and thrive, not only because of the current business that would bring but also in order to satisfy the customers – mainly depositors – to whom such securities were marketed. Thus a good deal of continuous financial work went on outside the formal capital market in the 'German system' before, during and subsequent to actual stock exchange flotations.

The question then becomes a search for an explanation of why and how the German banks came to occupy the position of being able to work so effectively in both the formal capital market and the area of 'normal', current banking business. The rest of this section discusses two important factors: (1) the banks' own share capital; and (2) their links to the central bank, the Reichsbank.

One of the sources of the strength of the German banks was undoubtedly their willingness to mobilize equity capital on a large scale and their ability to do so on relatively attractive terms. Although German banks increasingly worked with funds mobilized in the form of deposits, the growth of their own share capital accounted for a much larger share of the growth of their business than it did in the British case. Table 11 arrays some of the relevant indicators. After all that has already been said, the different rates of growth to total assets will come as no surprise. If we then compare 'realized rates of return' on banking shares in both countries we also find confirmation of the frequently noted fact that the relatively large use of equity by the German banks helped produce relative rates of return for shareowners which compare unfavorably with those produced by the British banks:[27]

(a) Equity, British banks, 1870–1913 . . . . 5.18
Equity, British domestic shares, 1870–1913 . . . . 6.44
Bond rate, British Consols (3%), 1880–1912 . . . . 2.86

(b) Equity, German banks, 1871–1910 . . . . 6.53
Equity, German domestic non-bank equity 9.35
Bond rate, Reich and states 3.65

Moreover, the comparison favors the British banks since the German sample is much larger and contains many more slower growers than presumably the British one does.[28] In this connection, it is interesting to remark that the seven

Table 11 *Indicators of banking growth, United Kingdom and Germany, 1880–1910*

(a) United Kingdom[a]

Years	(Millions of £)				Annual Rates of Growth			
	Total assets	Paid-up capital	Cash and call money	Loans + advances	Total assets	Capital	Cash call	Loans + advances
1880/2	297	51	57	157				
1890/2	462	68	89	232	4.4	2.9	4.5	3.9
1900/2	681	80	154	337	3.9	1.6	5.5	3.7
1910/12	837	81	209	399	2.1	0.1	3.1	1.7

(b) Germany[b]

Years	(Millions of Marks)				Annual Rates of Growth			
	Total assets	Paid-up capital	Cash and call money	Loans + advances	Total assets	Capital	Cash call	Loans + advances
1883	2961	796	554	1109				
1890/2	3135	1248	938	1780	5.9	5.6	6.6	5.9
1900/2	6895	2354	1851	4131	7.9	6.3	6.8	8.4
1910/12	15505	3649	3792	9345	8.1	4.4	7.2	8.2

Notes:
[a]Joint-stock banks in England and Wales, from Table (a) 1.2 in Sheppard (1971: 118–19).
[b]German *Aktienkreditbanken* from Deutsche Bundesbank (1976: table 1.01, pp. 56–7).

largest Berlin banks generated a rate of return of 4.51 over the 1871–1910 period that was even absolutely lower than that of the British banks.

The point being made here is that relatively low rates of return for shareholders also represented relatively cheap capital for banks and that dividends can be seen as costs from the bank's point of view. By repeatedly going to the market for capital the banks braked increases in bank share prices, but due to this relatively greater growth of German bank capital, German bank yields stood much further below industrial share yields than British bank yields did. One way of looking at this difference is to see it as the expression of investor preferences: German capitalists held bank shares in such esteem that the offer of sub-normal returns by the banks sufficed to attract the necessary funds (Weber 1922:319). Bank shares were seen as a means of diversifying portfolios and size a positive factor. In this connection it is interesting to note, as hinted above, that the larger the bank, the lower the rate of return. The thesis, then, is that the interest of the banks – apparently unconstrained by fears of loss of managerial control – in exploiting this market position explains their relatively buoyant growth.

The offered explanation, however, may be incomplete: the liquidity preferences of the non-bank public may be relevant. It is well known that the 'banking habit' was much less developed in Germany than in Britain throughout the period in discussion. One accompaniment of this difference was the greater importance of the use of coin and central bank notes in Germany. The following estimates of the share of coin and currency in the total money supply of the two countries illustrate the difference (for the U.K.: Sheppard 1971; for Germany: Tilly 1973: H. 4).

	U.K.	Germany
1880	0.30	0.66
1890	0.20	0.54
1900	0.17	0.45
1910	0.14	0.33

It is plausible to argue that this differential could help explain why interest rates were higher in Germany and also why the costs of mobilizing deposits relative to the costs of raising share capital were higher.

In any case, their relatively large capitals allowed the German banks to engage in the promotion and issue business on a fairly large scale without unduly straining their credit positions (Hilferding 1910: 227). They did not generally hold large amounts of industrial shares in their portfolios for long stretches of time, but their capital resources did permit them to hold on and refrain from forced sales if that appeared desirable. This must have had positive consequences for the enterprises whose securities they issued and could be one of the reasons for the relatively strong and stable growth of German industrial share prices referred to earlier. Many observers have said it did, e.g. J. Riesser (1910: 279–88, 305–8), A. Weber (1922: 225–71, especially 233–4) or Lavington (1921: 109–10, 210–11).

It almost goes without saying that the large cushion of capital also lay behind the well-known readiness of the German banks to supply generous overdraft facilities within the current-account arrangement. They were less likely to worry about the relation between advances and deposits than the British banks; and the ratio (loans + advances/deposits) was in fact much higher for the former (for the U.K.: Sheppard 1971: 118–19; for Germany: Deutsche Bundesbank 1976: 56–7):

	1880–90	1900–13
Germany	1.42	1.12
U.K.	0.51	0.48

The importance of the current-account facilities for industrial enterprises as a flexible form of short-to-medium-term credit has been so often stressed that the point requires no further documentation here. What is worth noting in our connection is that such an arrangement eased decision-making about the mobilization of long-term capital and in particular about the timing of new issues. Within limits, one could wait for the proper moment to go into the market; that must have contributed to the buoyancy of the latter.

A second important source of strength in Germany's mixed banking sector was its virtually unlimited access to the central bank – the Reichsbank. Returning for a moment to Table 11, we note the relatively strong growth of loans and advances and relatively weak growth of cash and liquid assets held by the German credit banks; just the opposite characterized the development of the British banks. The German banks could get by with less liquidity and 'lend to the hilt' if demands warranted because the Reichsbank provided extremely liberal rediscounting facilities. In fact, they were so liberal – though not cheap – that bills of exchange held by the banks or their acceptances could be seen as substitutes for central bank notes (Borchardt 1976: especially p. 46; and McGoldrick s.a.). This was in contrast to the Bank of England, which frequently resorted to credit rationing.[29] This central bank behavior tended to stabilize the business cycle in Germany, for through its discount policy the Reichsbank tended to attract business in upswings and repel it in downswings, which meant a substitution of central bank money or gold coin for short bills, or what was, in effect, *potential* central bank money. (The reason for this was that the Reichsbank discount rate was generally higher than the market rate, but it rose and fell proportionately less than the latter.) With this stabilizing guarantee behind them, the German banks did not have to live with the fear of illiquidity which combining commercial and investment banking activity might otherwise – e.g. under the British set of arrangements – have dictated.[30]

V

To complete the chapter it is now necessary to summarize nineteenth-century Anglo-German differences with respect to the financing of industrial enterprise and, if possible, to relate those differences to Marxist and Schumpeterian theories. That is not too easy a task, even if one wishes to do no more than describe differences; and the present author is convinced that it is necessary to draw some analytical conclusions from the observed differences. But first to the differences themselves.

The descriptive findings can be reduced to three sentences. First, the basic difference between British and German industrial finance lay in the relation between investment and commerical banking, in the closeness of the links between formal capital market and current banking activities. Second, Marx assigned much less importance to financial intermediation than either Hilferding or Schumpeter. Third, Schumpeter saw the importance of finance as the prerequisite of innovation whereas Hilferding stressed the centralized control of industrial enterprise which finance and especially the development of a national capital market made possible.

The first finding has generated an analytical proposition: that the development of British industry before 1914 suffered from the lack of close links of the German kind between formal capital market and commercial banking activities.[31] The evaluation of this proposition requires not only a resummary of the historical facts of the case but also an explicit discussion of two methodological issues: the problems of temporal specification and of *ceteris paribus* conditions. The following makes an attempt to reweave the summarized facts into the discussion of these two issues.

Economic historians have a healthy tendency to see the economic development of a given period as deriving from economic changes of a previous one. Indeed, that is the hallmark of the historical school of economics from which economic history evolved. The merit of this way of looking at things lies in its restraining effect upon the economist's ahistorical tendency to interpret a given set of temporally simultaneous circumstances (e.g. those accompanying economic depression) as complete system. The danger of this habit, however, is that historical developments subsequent to a given period may be read back into it. What we have in the case before us is, at the worst, the backward projection of all of the twentieth-century problems of the British economy and the successes of the German economy into the late-Victorian period; at the least we have a rereading of the Victorian period in the light of the Edwardian era and the implicit extension of the 20 years preceding World War One to cover the entire Kaiserreich.

One method for reducing this danger is to attempt to specify the temporal pattern of differences more closely. Two points can be made, I think. First, with hindsight, it now seems clear that the differences between British and German banking go back to the railroad financing of the 1830s and 1840s. Virtually all of the subsequently important elements of 'mixed banking' emerged in Germany at this time – and not in Britain. However, the difference as yet effected only a miniscule share of German industry (outside of railroads) and contributes virtually nothing to an explanation of industrial growth differ-

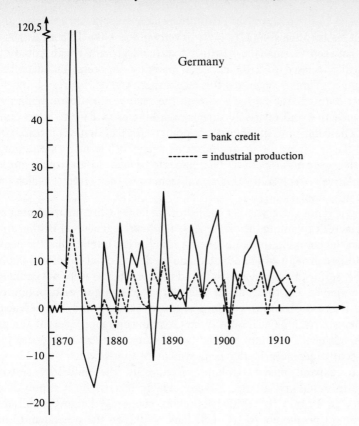

Figure 11

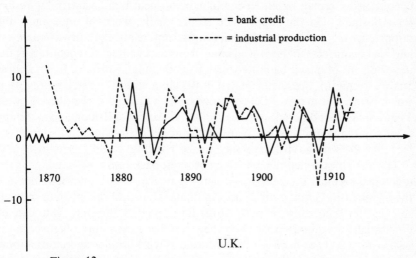

Figure 12

Sources: Germany: Hoffmann *et al.* (1965). U.K.: Industrial Production: Feinstein (1972), Bank Credit: Sheppard (1971).

ences between the two countries until much later – at the earliest, say, the 1890s. That leads to the second point: it is only in the 1900–13 period that a difference between German and British industrial growth which could be (hypothetically) related to a difference in banking structure and activities clearly emerged. Table 3 suggested this fact earlier. And as Figures 11 and 12 now illustrate, this is the period in which the relative slowdown in British industrial growth – and relatively sluggish banking growth – was most concentrated. These data and other evidence point to the fact that never before or since were the credit banks so significant as agents of Germany's economic growth as they were in this period.[32] If a case is to be made for the role of mixed banks as relative growth factor this would seem to be the period to which the argument must apply.

However, it is not clear whether the historical facts justify the treatment of banks as a factor explaining the differences in industrial growth in Britain and Germany in the period in question. Such a comparison implies that the bank 'contribution' to growth can be isolated and identified. That is unfortunately not yet the case, for things other than the commerical banks were not equal in the two economies. On the demand side, both the level and distribution of investment and industrial growth suggest (as in Tables 3 and 4) differences between the two. Nationalized railways in Germany and high levels of foreign portfolio investment in Britain may be two reasons for these differences, for they represent differences in the employment of funds which affected the incentive to expand mixed banking activities in the industrial sector. Differences in company law are a factor which affected both supply and demand, for in Britain its relative looseness encouraged many small entrepreneurs and promoters to try their luck, while, on the other hand, the relatively strong position of shareholders in Germany (from 1884 on) encouraged German banks to combine investment banking with the rest of their business. On the supply side alone, finally, we note once again the importance of relatively cheap equity capital and relatively expensive deposits and also easy access to the central bank in Germany as factors encouraging the development of mixed banking which were missing in Britain. In sum, these factors strengthen the suspicion that in Britain not only 'mixed banking' itself was missing, but many of the conditions which favored it elsewhere as well. That implies that differences in the industrial growth of Britain and Germany from, say, the 1880s to World War One are not likely to have resulted from the fact that Britain had not developed mixed banking as did Germany.

The last point which remains to be brought back into the discussion is the difference between the Marxist–Hilferding interpretation and Schumpeter's theory. British–German differences in financial institutions play an obvious role in the theorizing of both Hilferding and Schumpeter. This can be illustrated, for example, by the way they treat evidence of this difference in the business cycle. Thus both see Britain's role as world trader and international banker as the fundamental cause of Britain's distinct cyclical pattern.

Hilferding, however, suggests that the 'backwardness' of the British banking system is an important contributing factor, while Schumpeter feels that, because of Britain's role as international financial and trading headquarters, innovations – particularly the key innovations of the Third Kondratieff (1898–1913) such as electricity – are incapable of seizing hold of the British economy directly as they had in Germany, with the result being a business cycle shaped less by changes in industrial structure than by international trade and monetary changes (Schumpeter 1939: I, 403, 406, 429–30, 432, 435–40; Hilferding 1910: 383, 392–3). Schumpeter (1939: I, 435) himself summed up the matter as follows:

Our sketch suffices to show that England's economic history from 1897 to 1913 cannot, owing to the comparative weakness of the evolution (in our sense) of her domestic industries, be written in terms of our model .... Instead, we have a picture of induced developments and growth ... financed by the returns to accumulated wealth partly invested abroad and, because the feeders of the system were spread over the whole world, particularly sensitive to foreign booms and slumps, which, during those years tended to become the dominant factor in the English business situations.

This difference of opinion on the business cycle can be generalized, I think. Schumpeter's remarks on the business cycle as on innovation and on financing in the two countries imply a definite and negative answer to the question of whether differences in financial institutions explain differences in industrial development in Germany and Britain. They could not do so because, in the terminology of the previous discussion, differences in demand for finance were so great. As Schumpeter (1939: I, 430) said of the British capital market, 'the main reason why we find so little public financing of domestic innovation is that there was not much to finance.' Hilferding's *Finanzkapital* offers a contrast to Schumpeter, despite certain similarities. Hilferding's 'Finance Capital' is not a *deus ex machina*, to be sure, and he is at pains to show how its evolution and functioning depend upon the wider socio-economic environment (including appropriate government policies such as protective tariffs). For Hilferding, 'Finance Capital' is not simply a set of capital market techniques, easily learned, whose efficiency could be readily evaluated at chosen points in time, but a whole system of social and economic relationships. Nevertheless, the tenor of Hilferding's remarks strongly suggest that it is in the financial sphere – in the interlocking directorates, in devices such as proxy voting and non-voting preference shares, in the execution of mergers by means of stock substitution, etc. – that one must look to explain how the (then) modern economy functions. Financial institutions, that is, play a strategic role in the development of the economy, with Germany clearly the prototype of a well-functioning modern economy, one which profited from its vigorous financial institutions. Implicitly, he seems to be saying that Great Britain's well-explained inability to develop such institutions is a reason for her different economic state.

Before concluding the discussion it may be useful to point out that recent historical research into the role of the large mixed banks in financial industrial enterprise – centerpiece of *Finanzkapital* – suggests that Hilferding exaggerated the influence of 'Finance Capital' in Germany itself. Many important and successful industrial enterprises maintained their independence of financial institutions up to and beyond World War One. One reason why they could do so was the continued financial strength of individual entrepreneurs and business families; another was continued competition among financial institutions – including competition among the 'great banks' themselves.[33] Not even these large representatives of 'Finance Capital' were the monolithic structure he saw them to be.

It is in a certain sense ironic that the Marxist disciple, Hilferding, should develop the Master's thought to the point that he ends up saying that financial institutions were not only much more important for the development of capitalism than Marx himself had believed, but even the ultimate solvent of that system's contradictions, whereas Schumpeter, perhaps capitalism's most brilliant protagonist, should conclude that the system was doomed, in part because the concentration and centralization of enterprise control related to financial activities tended to destroy, not its economic efficiency, but its non-economic social and political, even its cultural, supports. But that is no doubt the type of irony that Schumpeter, in all his work, savored.

Notes

1 To state this is not to deny the importance of other differences between the two. For Marx, economic development was a crowning achievement of capitalism but it reflected and was transcended by the class struggle. For Schumpeter, in contrast, economic development was the very essence of capitalism, with class antagonisms an unfortunate and possibly unavoidable product of its development. And there are of course a number of significant points of agreement in their work, e.g. their emphases on the capitalist producer rather than consumer demands as key to understanding capitalist development.

2 Although critical of the Peel Banking Act, etc., Marx was not fully in the 'Banking School' camp. On this and other points of monetary doctrine, see Fritsch (1968).

3 Documentation of these points follows in the next section.

4 This book first appeared in German in 1911. See also p. 126, where Schumpeter insists on the importance of money in economic development as being much more than a 'veil' but the very instrument by which decentralized shifts in control over productive resources are effected. For this reason, the money market can be seen as the headquarters of the capitalist economy.

5 See in addition to Hilferding (1910), Sweezy (1971: 303ff.). I also obtained some valuable insights from an unpublished paper on Schumpeter by the late Herbert Kisch (1976). This paper points out that Böhm-Bawerk's seminar included (1905–6) not only Hilferding but also Emil Lederer and Otto Bauer – leading lights of Austro-Marxism. It is possible that the contemporary vogue of elite sociology absorbed by Schumpeter and worked into his concept the 'entrepreneur' (Mosca, Pareto, Michels, Le Bon) was a response to Marxist thought. See also, März (1976: chapter 3).

6 The standard works are: Cameron (ed.) (1967: chapters 2 and 3); Crouzet (ed.)

(1972); Chapman (1979: 50–69); Pollard (1964); Pressnell (1956); Mathias (1973); and the fine, recent summary of detailed research and of the summaries by P. Cottrell (1980: especially chapters 1–2 and 8).

7 For discussions of the early railroad capital market in Britain see Clapham (1926: chapter 9); Gayer, Rostow and Schwartz (1953: I); Broadbridge (1970). See also Hughes (1960: 198).

8 See Shannon (1954: 358–79 and especially 376–7); Cottrell (1980: chapter 3 and especially pp. 45–54); Jeffreys (1938). Of course, it was not to industry that capital mobilized by limited liability flowed, but toward insurance, utilities, finance, etc., but the point in the text stands.

9 The *locus classicus* would still seem to be Borchardt (1961, now reprinted with newly supplemented footnotes in Borchardt 1982). See also Tilly (1980a).

10 See Kocka (1978: 492–589 and especially 536–43); also a survey for the western provinces of Prussia, Rhineland and Westphalia in Coym (1971); Klein (1971); and Winkel (1970).

11 In 1848, for example, the largest private banking house, A. Schaeffhausen & Co. in Cologne, was forced to suspend payments, in part because of the illiquidity of its extensive advances to Rhenish–Westphalian industrial firms. This was an unusual situation, to be sure, but not with respect to the quantity of industrial credits. See Krüger (1925: especially pp. 55–6); for further examples Tilly (1966).

12 On this see Winkel (1970 and 1968); Moll (1972); and the older work by Brockhage (1910). Agricultural profits in 1820–50 may have also exceeded new investments in agriculture in Prussia. See Berthold, Harnisch and Müller (1970: IV, especially pp. 277–89).

13 The 30 per cent adjustment corresponds to the relationship between non-agriculture residential housing and industrial + commercial building investment in Britain for the 1840s as estimated by Feinstein (1978: 40–1). The Prussian data are from Tilly (1978a: VII, 427).

14 Schumpeter (1939: I, 350), commenting on the 'great' corporate banks of the later period after having discussed German railroad expansion, adds: 'This financial apparatus was a powerful help to railroad development from the beginning of the second Juglar onward, but during the forties it had not yet come into existence. Nor, as far as the writer knows, was capital import from England of much importance then. Hence, financing from genuine savings must have played a much greater role than it did later.'

15 In a larger sense, Marx saw such institutions as serving the centralization of capital and hastening capitalism's end. See Marx (1906: I, 686–9).

16 Hilferding's position is most clearly stated in Hilferding (1910: chapter 8, pp. 130–44, and chapter 14, especially pp. 298–303). Schumpeter's views can be found stated in Schumpeter (1939: I, 405), where he describes the notion of the financial rule over industry as 'a newspaper fairy tale, almost ludicrously at variance with facts'. A page or so later he argues for the persistence of the entrepreneurial function and its ability to assume new guises even where 'finance capital' seems to dominate things: 'innovation in the formative stages of trustified capitalism will regularly produce ... events [such as takeovers] ... owing to the fact that large-scale financial operations of a type entirely lacking in the mechanism of innovation in competitive capitalism are in this case necessary for the entrepreneur to set his hand on the wheel.'

17 On self-financing of German corporations see Feldenkirchen (1982a) and Rettig (1978); for Britain, see Cottrell (1980: chapters 7 and 8).

18 See Kennedy (1976) for one statement of the argument with most of the relevant literature. See also Kindleberger (1964: 61–8) for a still useful discussion of the issues.

19 In the early twentieth century Germany's estimated rate of investment was close to 20 per cent of social product – nearly four times the estimated British rate (excluding foreign investment) (Hoffmann c.s., 1965). The German figures contain inventories as well but exclude agriculture. Correcting for this would not alter the relative orders of magnitude.

20 Strictly speaking, Eichengreen is arguing that domestic investment was a response to industrial share price movements, a relationship which is consistent with a model in which those prices reflecting money and capital market conditions indicate expected net returns to investment. The German calculations are less sophisticated. On the one hand, there is a close relationship between non-agricultural investment and both new issues of industrial securities and industrial share prices, 1886–1913. On the other hand, for a sample of 48–50 listed companies, 1880–1911, real changes in share prices were among the most significant determinants of annual fixed investment. See Rettig (1978: chapter 9); also Tilly (1978a; and 1982: 629–58).

21 Between 1880 and 1913 the real rate of growth of industrial share prices was roughly 75 per cent in Germany and about 35 per cent in Britain. Data for Germany from Tilly (1982) and Hoffmann c.s. (1965); for Britain from Hannah (1974) and Feinstein (1972). In both cases the price deflator used was an index of capital goods prices.

22 It should be noted here that one reason for the inclusion of Table 4 in the present discussion is its usefulness as a crude indicator of the sectoral distribution of bank credit in Germany during the 1880–1913 period. Despite reams of paper on the 'great banks', virtually no data on that distribution have ever appeared. Since the banks were understandably more willing to extend credit to companies whose shares could be marketed on the stock exchanges than to others, this distribution should approximate the sectoral distribution of credit. Solid evidence to the contrary is at present lacking – but welcome.

23 The largest 14 issuers in 1900 were the following (at market prices in 1000 Marks):

Gelsenkirchener Bergwerksverein	19.200
Helios Elektrizitäts-AG	19.465
Siemens u. Halske	25.259
Gesellschaft f. elektr. Untern.	15.150
Deutsche Gesellschaft f. elektr. Untern.	10.050
Hapag	19.290
Elektriz.-AG Schuckert	29.505
Union, Elektriz. Ges.	18.705
Grosse Berliner Strass.-Ges.	54.780
AG Schalker Gruben-u. Bergbau-Ges.	17.340
Rheinische Stahlwerke	30.518
Zellstoffabrik Waldhof	14.393
A.E.G.	14.963
Farbwerke L. Brüning, Hoechst	18.056

24 There are some important exceptions to this rule, e.g. A. Thyssen's enterprises. See Jeidels (1905: 18ff.).

25 Cottrell (1980: 189) cites Ayres' London Thesis. Lavington's estimate is based on a much higher level of domestic investment (ca. £200 million) than Feinstein's figures, cited in Table 3, allow (Lavington 1921: 201–5).

26 The figures in Table 3 contain bond issues which replaced older securities. If one accepts the estimate of Table 7, roughly one-quarter of Germany's joint-stock companies appealed to the stock exchange for funds, but listed companies were about three times the size of the average company. If we therefore multiply the estimate made by Hoffmann c.s. (1965: 812–13) of total funds raised annually by

joint-stock companies by 0.75 we get a figure of around 450 million Marks per year for 1900–13, or somewhat less than 10 per cent of annual net investment (and also rather lower than the estimates of Table 3).

27 Cottrell (1980: 244); Weber (1922: 307–21). The realized rates of return for example of British banks and for British equities are from Edelstein (1976). The rates of return for German banks are from a sample of 62 banks analyzed in an unpublished paper by the author, those for German domestic non-financial equities from Rettig (1978). The bond rates are from Sheppard (1971) for the U.K., and for Germany from Deutsche Bundesbank (1976).

28 The sample in Edelstein (1976) contains 19 banks.

29 And not in an easily predictable way, as e.g., the *Investor's Monthly Manual* (*I.M.M.*) complained in 1899. See *I.M.M.*, Nov. 30, 1899; for the Bank of England's policy in respect to the British joint-stock banks see Goodhart (1972: especially pp. 100ff.).

30 McGoldrick's unpublished paper makes the point that the Reichsbank was, in effect, stabilizing gold flows and, by so violating the 'rules of the game', contributing to Germany's strikingly stable monetary growth over the period.

31 Kennedy (1976) brings the argument and some of the supporting literature in a relatively explicit form.

32 It was above all in the 1895–1913 period that the mixed banks clearly emerged as Germany's most important intermediaries. See Goldsmith (1969). In the 1920s the 'great' Berlin banks had become relatively more important as intermediaries, but German industrial growth could not be sustained; and in the post-1945 period the large banks played a relatively modest role.

33 The recent work in the vein cited includes Kocka (1978: especially pp. 565-70); Feldenkirchen (1982a: e.g. pp. 124–7) and Pohl (1982: especially pp. 258–72).

10 Imperialism and Social Class (Apologies to Marx and Schumpeter): Imperial Investors in the Age of High Imperialism

LANCE E. DAVIS AND ROBERT A. HUTTENBACK

Despite the fact that a British Prime Minister – and a Liberal at that – equated imperialism with patriotism, imperialism remains a nasty word, and British imperialism appears to carry a particularly unpleasant connotation.[1] Nor is that view limited to distraught Argentinian generals railing against imperial ventures in the South Atlantic; George Bernard Shaw, for example, wrote in his *Man of Destiny*:

There is nothing so bad or good that you will not find an Englishman doing it; but you will never find an Englishman in the wrong. He does everything on principle. He fights you on patriotic principles, he robs you on business principles, he enslaves you on imperial principles.

While a consensus appears to support Shaw's interpretation of the British imperial experience, and while any set of political maps indicates or student of high-school geography knows that the empire expanded by more than a third (36 per cent) between 1860 and 1910, the important question still remains: what caused Crown and Parliament to add such slightly tarnished jewels as Cairo, Khartoum, Johannesburg, and Kuala Lumpur to the imperial diadem? Was it merely the random outcome of a series of mindless acts, as some have charged, or was it the foreordained result of some cunning master plan? If in fact it was a plan, who were the planners and what motivated their actions?

On those questions debate has never ceased, and even the fact that today the Falkland Islands represent almost two-thirds of the overseas empire has caused the intensity of the argument to diminish only a little. While participation in the debate was not limited to them, a list of actors would have to include Joseph Schumpeter on the one side and the Marxian economists, if not Marx himself, on the other. This chapter attempts to bring some new empirical evidence to bear on one aspect of that debate between Schumpeter and the new Marxists.

I

Since most of Marx's work was written before the era of 'high imperialism', it is not surprising that Marx himself was relatively, but not entirely, silent on the subject. All neo-Marxist interpretations begin with his observations that the tendency for profits to decline can for a time at least be ameliorated by the opportunities for trade:

If capital is sent to foreign countries, it is not done because there is absolutely no employment at home. It is done because it can be employed at a higher rate in the foreign country .... Capitals invested in foreign trade are in a position to yield a higher rate of profits because, in the first place, they come in competition with commodities produced in other countries with lesser facilities of production.... In the same way a manufacturer, who exploits a new invention before it becomes general undersells his competitors and yet sells his commodities above their individual value.... On the other hand, capitals invested in colonies etc., may yield a higher rate of profit for the simple reason, that slaves, coolies, etc., permit a better exploitation of labor.... These higher rates of profits...sent home...enter into the equilization of the general rate of profit and keep it up to that extent. (Marx 1909: III, 278–9, 300)

Thus the law of falling profits is weakened but not suspended.

But Marx, while recognizing the possible benefits to capitalists from overseas trade in general and such trade with colonies in particular, never made imperial expansion an enunciated political component of his economic theory. Schumpeter (1950b: 52), for example, concludes his comments on Marxian theories of imperialism with the caveat 'Marx himself does not put too much stress on the resulting tendency toward monopolistic restriction of output and the consequent tendency toward protecting the domestic game preserve against the intrusion of poachers from other capitalist countries. Perhaps he was too competent an economist'. In fact, Marx did not conclude that imperial expansion was necessarily in the best interest of the British capitalist. On the impact of a large Indian loan he wrote:

It is true that successive loans by the Indian Company in the London Market would ... prevent ... the further fall in the rate of interest; but such a fall is exactly required for the revival of British industry and commerce. Any artificial check put upon the downward movement of the rate of discount is equivalent to an enhancement in the cost of production and the terms of credit, which in the present weak state, English trade feels itself unable to bear. Hence the general distress of the announcement of the British loan. (Marx and Engels 1960: 124–8)

Similarly, in his general assessment of the benefits derived by Britain from its occupation of India he argues (ibid.: 86–90) that while:

It is evident that individuals [and here he enumerates 3,000 stockholders in the East India Company, 10,000 military officers and civilian bureaucrats, and 6,000 private speculators and traders out of an upper- and middle-class population of about 6,000,000] gain largely by the English connection with India, and of course their gain does increase the sum of national wealth. But against this a very large offset is to be made. The military and naval expenses are paid out of the pocket of the people of England on Indian account ... and it may well be doubted whether, on the whole, this dominion does not threaten to cost quite as much as it can ever be expected to come to.[2]

While Marx's attitudes towards colonies and imperial expansion and their relation to capitalist development may be somewhat in doubt, the same is not true for those of his followers. Whether the world had changed, or the latter-day Marxists saw something that Marx himself did not recognize, it is certainly true that for the half century after 1885 socialist thought was dominated by the discussion of the relationship between capitalism and imperialism. In the intellectual history of economics' Karl Rodbertus is usually given credit for first enunciating the new paradigm, although Marx might complain about calling Rodbertus a 'Marxist' (Heimann 1945: 138–9).[3] To Rodbertus the underlying force was underconsumption, but his theory is equally applicable to any crisis that produced a surplus of goods that an already glutted home market could not absorb. The capitalists' desire to secure sales outside that market leads to economic imperialism. Writing some thirty years later in 1910 Rudolph Hilferding (1910: 412) made much the same point, but perhaps in more familiar terms:

The policy of finance capital pursues a threefold aim: First, the creation of the largest possible economic territory, which, secondly, must be protected against competition by tariffs, and thus, thirdly, must become an area of exploitation for the national monopoly companies.

The elements – finance, monopolies, tariffs, and political action – were welded into a single scenario of capitalist development. In Engels' (1937: 117) words 'Colonization today ... is purely a subsidiary of the stock exchange.' And in those of Bukharin (1966: 107), 'this policy of finance capital is imperialism.' The intellectual circle was completed by Rosa Luxemburg, who concluded that imperial expansion was a necessary part of the historical process. Capitalism, she felt, could only survive as long as there were buyers for the goods unsaleable within the capitalist economy; therefore, the system must expand or die, 'yet in expanding it destroys itself because the precapitalist markets are now absorbed in the orbit of capitalism. When this happens the whole system will come to an end' (Heimann 1945: 165–7).[4] 'Imperialism is the political expression of the accumulation of capital in its competitive struggle for what remains open of the noncapitalist environment' (Luxemburg 1951).

The foundation of the neo-Marxist argument was laid, and nowhere was that argument more cogently synthesized than in the work of Lenin (1939: 89):

If it were necessary to give the briefest possible definition of imperialism we should have to say that imperialism is the monopoly stage of capitalism. Such a definition will embrace the following five essential features: (1) The concentration of production and capital developed to such a high state that it created monopolies which play a decisive role in economic life; (2) The merging of bank capital with industrial capital, and the creation, on the basis of this 'finance capital' of a 'financial oligarchy'; (3) The export of capital, which has been extremely important as distinguished from the exports of commodities; (4) The formation of international capitalist monopolies which share the world among themselves; (5) The territorial division of the world among the great powers is completed.

Thus by 1920 the intellectual reaction of the scramble for colonies and the cotemporal surge of symbolic capital out of the United Kingdom produced a well-articulated theory that concluded that it was the capitalist's search for markets and raw materials that had led to the political penetration and subsequent colonization of most of the world's underdeveloped regions.

In no science, and least of all in economics, does a set of facts admit to only a single interpretation. It is not, therefore, surprising that others found alternative explanations of colonialism. Among those with a very different but no less well-articulated position was Joseph Schumpeter. It was not that Schumpeter denied either the geographic expansion of the British empire or the magnitude of the outflow of financial capital from the island nation. In his discussion of the 'third Kondratieff' – a cycle caused in most of the world by innovation of electricity and electrical equipment – 'the English case presents a striking contrast.' So striking that he terms the period the 'neo-mercantilist' Kondratieff:

The strong increase in capital exports ... complements this. Foreign, and particularly colonial enterprise and lending was the dominant feature of the period. Rubber, oil, South African gold and diamonds, Egyptian cotton, sugar, irrigation, South American (Argentinian) land developments, the financing of Japan and colonial communities (municipalities, particularly Canadian) afford examples of the way in which England, more than through domestic development, took part in the industrial process which carried the Kondratieff prosperity. The London Money market concerned itself mainly with foreign and colonial issues to an extent never equaled in England or in any other country. The great issuing houses in particular, almost exclusively cultivated this business managing, sometimes rigging, the market for it. (Schumpeter 1939: I, 430–1)

These words could have been written, but perhaps not so well, by either Hilferding or Lenin.

Similarly, Schumpeter recognized that Britain had become a very expansionist imperial power in the last years of Victoria's reign, and again there is little to choose between his and Lenin's summary of events. Both, for example, point to Chamberlain as the living incarnation of the 'political imperialist' (Lenin 1939: 78–9; Schumpeter 1955: 14). The difference in their conclusions rests in part on their interpretations of events after 1900 and even more on their analysis of the forces that motivated those political imperialists. As for the former, Lenin mentions no change in the British political policy but Schumpeter (1955: 14) finds a complete rejection of imperial expansion by the British electorate after the Boer War:

So complete was the defeat of imperialism that the Conservatives under Bonar Law in order to achieve some degree of political rehabilitation, had to strike from their program the tariff on food imports, necessarily the basis for any policy of colonial preference.

But the alternative readings of history are not the main sources of difference between the Austrian Finance Minister and the Russian First Secretary. Of more importance are their explanations of the change in the political posture of the western nations. To Lenin (1939: 78–9) the motivation was economic:

It is not without interest to observe that even at that time these leading British bourgeoisie politicians fully appreciated the connection between what might be called purely economic and the political–social roots of imperialism. Chamberlain advocated imperialism by calling it a 'true, wise, and economical policy', and he pointed particularly to the German, American, and Belgian competition which Great Britain was encountering in the world markets. Salvation lies in monopolies, said the capitalists as they formed cartels, syndicates, and trusts. Salvation lies in monopolies, echoed the political leaders of the bourgeoisie, hastening to appropriate the parts of the world not yet shared out.

To Schumpeter, on the other hand, motives and causes were different. He observes (Schumpeter 1955: 74–7):

where free trade prevails *no* class has an interest in forceable expansion .... Where the cultural backwardness of a region makes normal intercourse dependent on colonization, it does not matter, assuming free trade, which of the civilized nations undertakes the task of colonization. Dominion of the seas, in such a case, means little more than a maritime traffic police. Similarly, it is a matter of indifference to a nation whether a railway concession in a foreign country is acquired by one of its own citizens or not – just as long as the railway is built.

Instead:

in a purely capitalist world, what was once the energy for war becomes simply energy for labor of any kind. Wars of conquest and adventurism in foreign policy in general are bound to be regarded as troublesome distractions, destructive to life's meaning.... A purely capitalist world, therefore, can offer no fertile soil to imperialist impulses. (ibid.: 69)

Imperialism is rooted in the:

inherited dispositions of the ruling class ... in the vital needs of situations that molded peoples and classes into warriors if they wanted to avoid extinction – and in fact the psychological dispositions and social structures acquired in the dim past in such situations, once firmly established, tend to maintain themselves and continue in effect long after they have lost their meaning and their life preserving functions. (ibid.: 59, 64–5)

But, of course, there are some capitalists who will support these bellicose activities:

the entrepreneurs in the war industries, in the broader sense, possibly also the large land owners – a small but powerful minority,

and monopoly capitalists:

a social group that carries great political weight, undeniable economic interest in such things as ..., an aggressive economic policy, an aggressive foreign policy, and war, including wars of expansion with typical imperialist character. (ibid.: 74–5, 83–4)

Thus:

the orientation towards war is mainly fostered by the domestic interests of the ruling classes, but also by the influence of those who stand to gain ... whether economically or socially .... Imperialism thus is atavistic in character. (ibid.: 65)

The lesson history seems to teach is that imperialism stemmed mainly from warriors and aristocrats, while only a fraction of the pressure for imperial expansion was engendered by the capitalist class.

Thus it appears that there are three distinct views of the imperial process (the Marxist, the neo-Marxist, and the Schumpeterian); who was correct? This paper attempts to shed some light on one aspect of that question by identifying the groups who invested in imperial enterprises and who, therefore, stood to gain from any political control that Britain may have exercised over her colonies and dominions.

To Marx (1909: III, 384–93), foreign investment was dominated by merchant capital, and is, therefore, a part of an earlier mode of production. To Marx, therefore, to the extent there was an economic foundation to imperial adventure it was the 'private speculators and traders' who were the imperialists. To the neo-Marxists, imperialism is an integral part of finance capitalism and imperial investment is 'simultaneously banking and industrial capitals' (Bukharin 1966: 116). To these groups some would add the 'so-called middle class whose livelihood depends directly or indirectly on the imperial connection, ranging from clerks in city offices to colonial administrators, and an inflated *rentier* element which thrived on the yield on foreign investment' (Dobb 1940: 248).

Finally to Schumpeter it was the ruling classes, the military, and the landed aristocracy together with some 'promilitary interests among the bourgeoisie' (Schumpeter 1955: 97). So was foreign investment in the hands of the merchants, financiers and industrialists (and perhaps the middle class) or the aristocrats and warriors?

II

Before beginning an examination of the structure of ownership it seems useful to pause and consider some economic data that place the Marx–Lenin–Schumpeter controversy in historical perspective. The neo-Marxist scenario suggests that empire profits were far above those at home and that capitalists in Britain responded to that incentive and invested in the paper securities of enterprises located in those protected markets.

First as to the profitability of empire, Table 12 provides a measure of the profits earned by a sample of 476 British firms that operated at home, in the empire, and 'abroad' during the period 1860 to 1912.[5] The evidence indicates that while there were substantial profits to be earned from empire investments in the early years, that differential was reversed after 1880. In the later years empire investments yielded substantially less than alternatives at home and in the foreign sector. While returning 2.1 times as much as home investment and 1.8 times as much as foreign in the years between 1860 and 1884 over the next thirty years empire returns were only about three-fifths of those available at home and three-quarters of those available in parts of the world not painted

Table 12. *Rates of return* – All firms (standardized assets)

	United Kingdom	Foreign	Empire	Empire, United Kingdom	Empire, Foreign	Foreign, United Kingdom
1860–4	4.6	8.7	12.7	276	146	189
1865–9	3.8	4.6	8.6	226	187	121
1870–4	5.9	6.8	8.1	137	119	115
1875–9	3.2	3.3	11.1	347	336	103
1880–4	3.8	1.5	3.6	95	240	39
1885–9	3.6	4.2	2.0	56	48	117
1890–4	3.2	1.4	1.0	31	71	44
1895–9	3.9	1.9	1.9	49	100	49
1900–4	3.3	1.8	1.2	36	67	55
1905–9	2.0	1.9	2.1	105	111	95
1910–12	2.4	3.4	3.1	129	91	142
All years	3.7	3.6	5.1	138	142	97
1860–84	4.3	5.0	8.8	205	176	116
1885–1912	3.1	2.4	1.8	58	75	77

red. As to foreign investment, it too was more profitable than domestic until the early 1880s, but not again until the end of the period.

As to the export of capital, the story told by both Lenin and Schumpeter appears to be somewhat at variance with the facts. Table 13 displays estimates of the composition of the new finance that passed through the London market between 1865 and 1914. Over that period a total of almost £6.0 billion in stocks and bonds (or in the British vernacular: stocks and shares) were issued.[6] The annual volume was subject to substantial cyclic variation, but the trend was upward. In the early years the annual total was only about £50 million, but by the outbreak of the First World War it had risen to almost £225 million. The actual composition, however, does differ somewhat from what Schumpeter and the neo-Marxists believed. Overseas investment was very important, however, over the entire period domestic activity attracted about one-third of the total – nor was the figure far different for the period of the 'third Kondratieff'. Of greater importance for the present argument, however, is the level of financial exports to the empire. Overall the Dominions, colonies and India received about 35 per cent of all overseas finance and something less than a quarter of the total flow. The largest recipient was not the dependent empire, it was instead the colonies with responsible government (Canada, New Zealand, Australia, and South Africa) that took the lion's share. The dependent empire (India and the dependent colonies) received about one pound in eight of overseas finance but less than one in twelve of the total. (Even that figure, however, is biased upward by the relegation of the Transvaal and the Orange Free State to dependent status for a few years after the Peace of

Table 13. *Capital called London market (intermediate estimate) £000s*

	Responsible government Total	Avg/yr	Dependent empire Total	Avg/yr	All empire Total	Avg/yr	All identified overseas Total	Avg/yr	Total identified Total	Avg/yr
1865–69	17239	3448	32510	6502	49749	9950	134981	26996	268101	53620
1870–74	31011	6202	12660	2532	43670	8734	187470	37494	305718	61144
1875–79	61404	12281	25894	5179	87296	17459	357189	71438	463434	92687
1880–84	87504	17501	35149	7030	122652	24530	346108	69222	484230	96846
1885–89	105280	21056	36649	7330	141928	28386	434923	86985	602510	120502
1890–94	72944	14589	32908	6582	105831	21166	329885	65977	471676	94335
1895–99	61896	12379	48163	9633	110558	22112	318310	63662	546091	109218
1900–04	68739	13748	97593	19519	166331	33266	377681	75536	790486	158097
1905–09	175305	35061	98860	19772	274164	54833	765303	153061	951228	190246
1910–14	270574	54115	95257	19051	365831	73166	884287	176857	1126408	225282
All years	951896	19038	515643	10313	1468010	29360	4136137	82723	6009882	120198

Percentage shares

	Responsible gov't of Overseas	Total	Dependent empire of Overseas	Total	All empire of Overseas	Total	Overseas of Total
1865–69	12.8	6.4	24.1	12.1	36.9	18.6	50.3
1870–74	16.5	10.1	6.8	4.1	23.3	14.3	61.3
1875–79	17.2	13.2	7.2	5.6	24.4	18.8	77.1
1880–84	25.3	18.1	10.2	7.3	35.4	25.3	71.5
1885–89	24.2	17.5	8.4	6.1	32.6	23.6	72.2
1890–94	22.1	15.5	10.0	7.0	32.1	22.4	69.9
1895–99	19.4	11.3	15.1	8.8	34.7	20.2	58.3
1900–04	18.2	8.7	25.8	12.3	44.0	21.0	47.8
1905–09	22.9	18.4	12.9	10.4	35.8	28.8	80.5
1910–14	30.6	24.0	10.8	8.5	41.4	32.5	78.5
All years	23.0	15.8	12.5	8.6	35.5	24.4	68.8

Table 14. *Geographic distribution overseas capital (minimum estimates)* (%)

	Lenin[a]	Total overseas		All empire of total		Dependent empire of total	
		1865–1914	1900–14	1865–1914	1900–14	1865–1914	1900–14
Europe	5.7	10.8	9.1	0.0	0.0	0.0	0.0
North and South America	52.9	54.1	56.3	11.3	16.8	0.3	0.2
Asia, Africa, Australia	41.4	35.1	34.6	26.6	25.2	11.6	14.4
Total	100.0	100.0	100.0	37.9	42.0	11.9	14.6

	All empire of continent total		Dependent empire of continent total	
	1865–1914	1900–14	1865–1914	1900–14
Europe	0.0	0.0	0.0	0.0
North and South America	20.5	28.3	0.4	0.2
Asia, Africa, Australia	74.0	70.5	30.9	31.0

Note:
[a] Lenin (1939: 64).

Vereeniging.) Given the independent economic policies – policies that included some of the world's highest protective tariffs, and tariffs aimed largely at British business, pursued by the self-governing dominions – it is difficult to justify any argument that would include them in the class of 'exploited colonies'. In fact few Marxist economists do (Lenin is an exception). The data themselves are clear. For example, Lenin (1939: 64) alludes to a geographic distribution of British overseas finance: Europe 6, America 53, and Asia, Africa and Australia 41 per cent. He then continues: 'The principal spheres of investment of British capital are the British colonies.' He dates his figures from 'about 1910' so comparison is not simple, but the figures from the London capital market tell a somewhat different story (see Table 14). Overall Lenin's figures for Europe are a little below the 'London' estimates and those for Asia, Africa, and Australia somewhat above, but the differences are not substantial. It appears that around the turn of the century the empire constituted about 40 per cent of all overseas finance but the dependent empire only about a third of that. While the dependent empire did represent slightly more than 30 per cent of the total flowing to Asia, Africa, and Australia, it constituted less than one-tenth of one per cent of the European and less than one-half of one per cent of the American transfers. The 'exploited' colonies, while certainly absorbing some of Britain's savings, do not appear to have been the tail that wagged the dog, let alone the dog itself. Still, profits were earned on empire investment, and the question remains – who earned those profits?

III

The Company Acts of 1856 and 1862 required the corporations to file annually a statement of their equity structure and a list of their stockholders. The latter included not only names, but most often addresses and occupations as well. It is these annual reports to the Board of Trade that provide the basis for the study. The three samples (domestic, foreign, and empire firms) were drawn from the corporations listed in the *Stock Exchange Annual Yearbook* (*SEAYB*) at some time between 1883 and 1907. Companies were placed in one of the three sectors on the basis of information in that chronicle, or, when that information was inadequate, the original prospectuses and the financial press provided the basis for the assignment. Firms were classified by industry on the basis of the classifications made by the editors of the *SEAYB*.[7]

The industries were the same as those used by the editors in the year 1903 except that no insurance firms were included. The industries are (1) commercial banks, (2) breweries and distilleries, (3) canals and docks, (4) commercial and industrial, (5) financial, land, and development, (6) financial trusts, (7) gas and light, (8) iron, coal, and steel, (9) mines, (10) railroads, (11) shipping, (12) tea and coffee, (13) telephone and telegraph, (14) tramways and omnibusses, and (15) waterworks. The Stock Exchange lists, however, include only empire 'tea and coffee' companies and only foreign and empire 'telephone

Table 15. *Firms in sample by location and industry*

	Home	Foreign	Empire	Total
Commercial banks	4	5	6	15
Breweries and distilleries	6	6	6	18
Canals and docks	5	2	1	8
Commercial and industrial	14	9	22	45
Financial, land, and development	7	10	21	38
Financial trusts	2	5	5	12
Gas and light	4	3	8	15
Iron, coal, and steel	7	6	11	24
Mining	5	4	15	24
Railroads	0	6	11	17
Shipping	1	4	1	6
Tea and coffee	0	0	10	10
Telephone and telegraph	0	4	2	6
Trams and omnibusses	5	5	5	15
Waterworks	0	5	3	8
Total	60	74	127	261

and telegraph' companies and 'waterworks'. Moreover, for technical reasons no British railroads were included in the sample. Table 15 displays the number of firms in each location and industry. There was a total of 261 firms with 80,235 stockholders in the sample. Of that total 15,218 invested in British, 20,972 in foreign and 44,045 in empire enterprises.

The occupational categories are largely self-explanatory. Initially all stockholders were classified into thirty-three occupational categories. The thirty-three were divided into twelve 'super occupations', and the twelve were again subdivided into the general categories business, elites, and others.[8] There were some (less than 2 per cent) multiple occupations. In those cases, any occupation took precedence over deceased or retired, all but deceased and retired precedence over 'women', all but those three took precedence over 'peers and gents', and all but those four took precedence over MPs. Thus a baronet who was also retired and a shipbuilder was included as a shipbuilder (manufacturer). Anyone who was listed as an MP had no other occupation except, perhaps, deceased, retired, or peers and gents. For other joint occupations, the first listed was given precedence, but dividing the shares between occupations does not affect the result. Shares held jointly by several persons were divided equally between the occupations of the joint holders.

One additional caveat. There are some problems with nominee holders. They did exist, and they are difficult to identify. The phrase 'and another' is easy, but that classification is significant only in the case of railroads. In addition it is clear that stocks were often held in the name of a banker, a stockbroker, solicitor, an employee, a wife, or a relative; and these present a more difficult problem. Subsidiary studies do, however, indicate that the problem may not be too serious. Nominee holders were less common than on the continent, and when they did exist they tended to be most often used by peers and gents and shareholders in empire and foreign firms. For those firms there may be some overstatement of the proportion held by brokers, women, clerks, and bankers and an underenumeration of the holdings of peers and gents. It has probably become evident by now that throughout the taxonomy was designed to minimize the holdings of the elites and to maximize those of the business community. Thus any conclusions about elite participation can be viewed as reflecting the 'worst case' (i.e. it is a minimum estimate of their investment). On the other hand, statements concerning business participations may overstate the contributions of that group.

For the analysis of the geographic distribution of stockholders, Great Britain has been divided into nine regions (the North, Yorkshire, Lancashire, Midlands Industrial, West, East, South and Southwest, Home Counties, and London). Within London, addresses in 'EC' appear to present a problem. Not only was it the most common location of nominee holders, but more importantly, shareholders often used their banks and brokers as convenience addresses. Therefore, London averages have been calculated both with and without that district. The former probably overstates the importance of the metropolis, but since there were many shareholders who lived or worked in the city, the latter certainly understates its importance. If the record listed only a city or town and no county, and if there were more than one place with that name, the address was, in the absence of other information, assigned to the town with the largest population.[9]

The measure discussed in this paper is the percentage of the value of shares in domestic, foreign, and empire firms owned by certain occupational groups and by persons living in certain locations.[10] Since the Marx–Lenin–Schumpeter debate focuses on the effects of stock ownership on economic and political behaviour, ideally one would want a measure of the importance of each class of securities to each group of holders (e.g. the ratio of the return (dividends + capital gains), on empire investments to the total income of the person in the group in question). Unfortunately, those data are not available; and the measure employed herein is at best a proxy. As such, however, the measure chosen has at least one desirable characteristic. It is generally recognized that the middle class were far more numerous than the upper class. Dudley Baxter (1869), for example, estimated that only three out of a hundred Britons not in the labouring element were actually in the upper class, but no one is likely to believe that it was any lower than five or ten to one. Thus, if the upper class held a larger fraction of the equities of empire business, it is almost certain that the empire income for each member of the class was greater than it was for a typical butcher, baker, or candlestick-maker.

Table 16. *Distribution of stockholders by class, status and industry (%)*

	All firms				Fin. trusts				Shipping				Canals & docks			
	UK	For.	Emp.	All	UK	For.	Emp.	All	UK	For.	Emp.	All	UK	For.	Emp.	All
Business	48.3	28.9	26.8	32.4	40.6	23.5	23.0	26.4	46.5	53.5	44.9	50.1	52.2	28.3	20.8	42.3
Elites	28.2	38.7	36.5	35.2	36.2	30.6	37.3	34.1	33.2	17.6	21.0	21.4	18.5	43.3	14.9	24.3
Other	22.0	31.3	36.6	31.7	23.2	45.9	39.6	39.5	20.3	21.4	34.0	24.2	29.2	28.5	64.3	33.4

	Commercial banks				Gas & light				Tea & coffee			
	UK	For.	Emp.	All	UK	For.	Emp.	All	UK	For.	Emp.	All
Business	53.9	37.0	21.9	35.5	49.6	28.6	26.0	32.8			34.7	
Elites	41.1	41.7	56.5	47.5	22.0	17.6	45.2	33.5			27.9	
Other	5.0	21.2	21.6	17.0	28.4	53.8	28.7	33.7			37.4	

	Brew. & dist.				Iron, coal & steel				Tel. & tel.			
	UK	For.	Emp.	All	UK	For.	Emp.	All	UK	For.	Emp.	All
Business	67.9	19.8	30.3	39.3	48.7	31.4	25.1	33.5		6.6	18.8	
Elites	20.2	36.5	42.2	33.0	33.8	43.8	44.2	41.1		76.9	13.5	
Other	12.0	43.7	27.5	27.7	17.5	24.8	30.8	25.4		16.5	67.3	

	Com. & ind.				Mines				Trams & Omnis			
	UK	For.	Emp.	All	UK	For.	Emp.	All	UK	For.	Emp.	All
Business	59.2	42.3	44.5	39.3	27.9	32.1	30.4	30.2	34.6	17.7	16.9	23.1
Elites	13.9	35.9	24.4	23.4	45.2	40.0	23.9	31.0	41.7	43.1	38.7	41.2
Other	20.5	21.7	31.1	26.0	26.9	28.3	45.7	38.9	23.7	39.3	44.4	35.8

	Fin., land & dev.				Railroads				Waterworks			
	UK	For.	Emp.	All	UK	For.	Emp.	All	UK	For.	Emp.	All
Business	29.3	17.3	13.9	17.7	32.4	36.4	13.7	21.7	37.5	37.5	26.3	
Elites	36.3	36.5	45.1	41.4	35.7	35.7	45.8	42.2	41.1	41.1	44.5	
Other	34.8	39.7	41.0	39.5	27.9	27.9	40.6	36.1	21.4	21.4	29.2	

Table 17. Stockholders average investment by class, status and industry (£)

	All firms				Commercial Banks				Brew. & dist.				Com. & ind.				Fin land & dev			
	UK	For.	Emp.	All	UK	For.	Emp.	All	UK	For.	Emp.	All	UK	For.	Emp.	All	UK	For.	Emp.	All
Business	624	2534	1606	1489	1203	1407	874	1091	824	404	947	714	416	1471	2019	1170	1377	1938	508	1045
Elites	912	2109	2804	2370	1672	1560	1008	1143	449	471	685	551	801	1804	1550	1395	6159	1666	1312	1772
Other	361	1134	3221	2081	416	2337	585	743	239	522	3210	1110	277	335	918	600	414	1928	670	759
All	639	1783	2671	2045	1258	1610	856	1028	607	475	1440	725	435	978	1529	1043	1761	1208	836	1060

	Fin. trusts				Gas & light				Iron, coal & steel				Mines				Railroads			
	UK	For.	Emp.	All	UK	For.	Emp.	All	UK	For.	Emp.	All	UK	For.	Emp.	All	UK	For.	Emp.	All
Business	720	6846	465	2645	217	2064	1195	1101	702	1078	518	720	754	3826	1068	1444	10161	10161	5987	6483
Elites	1108	5127	645	1899	266	865	1332	1178	530	928	584	677	695	507	522	540		3007	10641	10000
Other	1175	961	343	766	192	911	2480	1606	343	654	742	619	1135	2636	1008	1381		9479	12445	12217
All	1069	2619	503	1486	219	979	1740	1371	557	874	609	674	824	1279	887	1023		6056	10467	10082

	Shipping				Tea & coffee				Tel. & tel.				Trams & Omnis				Waterworks			
	UK	For.	Emp.	All	UK	For.	Emp.	All	UK	For.	Emp.	All	UK	For.	Emp.	All	UK	For.	Emp.	All
Business	122	3219	1887	1706				1580		1375	692	1121	101	1565	513	437		1323	1330	1326
Elites	247	842	1586	810				571		4859	759	1431	105	3437	859	804		2264	1661	1861
Other	58	829	4991	580				858		3949	23391	18114	97	730	812	518		1256	7667	4003
All	117	1907	2019	1172				930		3984	5082	4846	102	1879	761	629		1620	2582	2141

	Canals & docks			
	UK	For.	Emp.	All
Business	916	5254	2866	1546
Elites	1941	3538	527	2384
Other	410	1748	917	656
All	921	3519	1528	1490

IV

Table 16 reports the occupational composition of the stockholders in the 261 firms classified by location (domestic, foreign, and empire) and industry. The figures refer to percentages of the *value* of shares held. Table 17 provides information on the average size of holding classified in the same way. The 'all firms' category provides some general insight into the types of persons who held shares and provides a standard against which to compare the distributions of particular industries. While the average investment was £2045, domestic investments were smaller than foreign and foreign smaller than empire. Moreover, while there was some difference in level, that ordering holds for both 'elites' and 'others', but in the case of businessmen average foreign investments were higher than empire. In the case of domestic and foreign holders, the differences do not appear to reflect the presence of a few large holders, but for the empire it appears that, in part at least, the higher average is associated with a few very large holdings.

Within the business community, all groups except merchants had a much greater affinity for domestic than foreign or empire shares. On average they held about 50 per cent of domestic, but only three-fifths that fraction of overseas shares. Among businessmen, only merchants held as high a proportion of overseas as domestic shares; for other businessmen the ratio was about one to two and for manufacturers one to three. Given the importance of overseas commerce in the British economic matrix and the proclivity of businessmen to invest in 'what they know', it is hardly surprising that the merchants appear to have behaved somewhat differently from their peers. In fact, it may appear strange that their behaviour was not more deviant.

The second group, the elites, appear to have pursued a markedly different investment strategy. They held less than 30 per cent of domestic, but just less than 40 per cent of foreign and empire shares. The largest group in that category, the peers and gents, held about a fifth of the value of domestic, but a quarter of foreign and empire securities. Smaller but still substantial proportions were held by the financial community – 4 per cent domestic, 8 per cent foreign and empire. The other subgroups were much less important, but it is interesting to note that the military displayed a slightly greater preference for foreign than for empire investment. So much for Schumpeter's warriors.

The third general group, 'Others', is very diverse and generalizations have little meaning. However, the pattern displayed by some of its constituent groups appears worthy of note. The tiny holdings of 'labourers' indicate that 'people's capitalism' had made very little headway in the late nineteenth century, but it is interesting that workers held any shares at all. 'Other firms' held 4 per cent domestic, 8 per cent foreign and 14 per cent of empire holdings. While at times these presented interfirm holdings of nascent multi-nationals, such was not usually the case. Instead, they were most often blocks of shares

Table 18. *Industry relatives (% industry in location/% all firms in location)*

	Commercial Banks				Brew. & dist.				Com. & ind.				Fin. land & dev.				Fin. trusts			
	UK	For.	Emp.	All	UK	For.	Emp.	All	UK	For.	Emp.	All	UK	For.	Emp.	All	UK	For.	Emp.	All
Business	112	128	82	110	141	69	113	121	123	146	166	151	61	60	52	54	84	81	86	81
Elites	146	108	155	135	72	94	116	94	49	93	67	66	129	94	124	118	128	79	102	97
Other	23	68	59	54	55	138	75	87	93	69	85	82	158	127	112	125	105	147	108	125

	Gas & light				Iron, coal & steel				Mines				Railroads				Shipping			
	UK	For.	Emp.	All	UK	For.	Emp.	All	UK	For.	Emp.	All	UK	For.	Emp.	All	UK	For.	Emp.	All
Business	103	99	97	101	101	109	94	103	58	111	113	93	96	126	51	67	96	185	168	155
Elites	78	45	124	95	120	113	126	117	160	103	65	88	118	92	125	120	118	45	58	61
Other	129	172	78	106	80	79	84	80	122	90	125	123	92	89	111	114	92	68	93	76

	Tea & coffee				Tel. & tel.				Trams & Omnis				Waterworks				Canals & docks			
	UK	For.	Emp.	All	UK	For.	Emp.	All	UK	For.	Emp.	All	UK	For.	Emp.	All	UK	For.	Emp.	All
Business			129			23	70		72	61	63	71		130	98		108	98	78	130
Elites			76			199	37		148	111	106	117		106	122		66	112	41	69
Other			120			53	184		108	126	121	113		68	80		133	91	176	105

Table 19. *Industry relatives (% industry in location/% industry in UK)*

	All		Commercial Banks		Brew. & dist.		Com. & ind.		Fin. land & dev.		Fin. trusts		Gas & light		Iron, coal & steel		Mines	
	For.	Emp.	For.	Emp.	For.	Emp.	For.	Emp.	For.	Emp.	For.	Emp.	For.	Emp.	For.	Emp.	For.	Emp.
Business	60	55	69	41	29	45	71	75	59	47	58	57	58	52	64	52	115	109
Elites	137	129	101	137	181	209	258	176	101	124	85	103	80	205	130	131	88	53
Other	143	166	424	432	364	229	106	152	114	118	198	171	189	101	142	176	105	170

	Shipping		Trams & Omnis		Canals & docks	
	For.	Emp.	For.	Emp.	For.	Emp.
Business	115	97	51	49	54	40
Elites	53	62	103	93	234	81
Other	105	167	166	187	98	220

held by commercial and private banks, financial, land and development companies, and financial trusts. Together these groups accounted for over one-half of interfirm holdings. Lastly, women held almost 8 per cent of domestic, 5 per cent of foreign, and 6 per cent of empire shares.

What can be inferred about the proclivity of business and elites to invest in the empire? There are at least two possible measures of the demonstrated industrial 'taste' of the two groups. On the one hand it is possible to compare holdings in single industry with average holdings across all industries (see Table 18). On the other, it is possible to contrast empire with domestic investments (Table 19). To the extent that both measures lead to similar results it should be possible to suggest something about investment choice, and therefore, perhaps, interest in the empire.

In the case of businessmen, it is quite clear that, to the extent that they invested in the empire at all, their tastes ran strongly to commercial and industrial and shipping firms and probably to mines and tea and coffee plantations as well. Mines aside, it appears that when the business community turned its attention to the empire, it tended to place its resources in activities related to business at home. Concomitantly, it appears that the group showed a disinclination to invest in commercial banks, canals and docks, financial, land and development companies (and probably financial trusts as well), railroads, telephone and telegraph companies, and trams and omnibusses. Here the unifying principle is less clear, but there seems to have been a hesitancy to invest in financial enterprises and in transportation.

It is possible to extend the argument by examining the relationship between investment in these 'outlying' industries in the empire and investments by the same groups in the foreign sector. Given the demonstrated proclivity to invest in some and not in other activities, were these tendencies a reflection of empire-related factors or just of overseas investment in general? In general it appears that businessmen tended to invest abroad in activities that were somewhat related to their commercial activities, but they display no particular affinity for empire as opposed to overseas investment. On the other hand, while they tended to stay away from financial and local transport investments in the empire, they were more willing to invest in those activities in the foreign sector.

The elites show a preference for empire investment in commercial banks, breweries, gas and light companies, railroads, and waterworks. At the same time they appear to have been less willing to invest in mines, shipping lines, and tea and coffee plantations. In the case of the commercial and industrial sector, their behaviour is mixed. If the measure is domestic habits, then empire investments were high; but in terms of 'normal' elite investment behaviour in the empire, their commitments to trade and commerce were very low.

A comparison of elite overseas investment patterns indicates that of the five 'favoured' activities, the empire appeared particularly attractive for investments in commercial banks, gas and light companies, and waterworks and fairly attractive for railroad investment. In the case of breweries it appears that overseas investment was appealing but that the empire was not particularly so. When it came to the commercial and industrial sector, the empire was apparently far less attractive than the foreign sector. It appears then that the empire attracted the investments of the elites in railroads, public utilities, and banking, but, if they were interested in directly supporting the production and distribution of commodities, they looked elsewhere.

A word might now seem in order about the stockholders in our sample whose shareholdings were of considerable value and about whom we have biographical information. Nineteen of these held shares in a single sample company worth between £25,000 and £50,000; twenty-two had holdings whose value lay between £50,000 and £100,000 and thirty-five securities valued at more than £100,000. Of this last group, twenty-two were peers and gents; ten, merchants; and three, bankers. The single greatest investment came to £804,000. It was in Dalgety and Company and not surprisingly was held by Frederick G. Dalgety.

The most popular security for the large investors was, however, the Bengal Nagpur Railroad. No less than eighteen (sixteen peers and gents) purchased shares in that Indian enterprise. Joseph Christy and James Alexander were the two largest holders of Bengal Nagpur stock with shares valued at £600,000 each. Thomas Sutherland, chairman of the board of P. & O., held shares to the value of £400,000. Two prominent British Jews also had large holdings in the railroad. Nathan de Rothschild (created the first Jewish peer, the son of Lionel de Rothschild – the first Jew to take a seat in the House of Commons and the man responsible for generating the short-term funds necessary for the British purchase of the controlling interest in the Suez Canal) owned shares worth £200,000. Leonard Lionel Cohen, the son of another early Jewish member of Parliament, owned shares valued at £300,000.

Next to Bengal Nagpur Railroad, the most popular investment for the over £100,000 cohort was the Merchant's Trust. Included on its shareholders list were seven men – four merchants, two bankers, and a 'gentleman' – each of whom controlled between £100,000 and £150,000. Included among the shareholders in the greater than £100,000 class were also two members of the Gibb family, both partners in Antony Gibb and Sons–Alban and Vicary; and Sir John Willoughby, fifth baronet, a soldier who served in Egypt and Matabeleland and who accompanied Dr Jameson on his famous and ill-fated raid into the Transvaal.

Of the twenty-two investors in the £50,000 to £100,000 range, fifteen were peers and gents; four, bankers; four, businessmen or manufacturers; and one a soldier – Major-General John Clark, who had served primarily in India and owned £94,800 worth of shares in the Bengal Nagpur Railroad. The favourite investment of the £50,000 to £100,000 group was the Merchant's Trust – seven held those shares. Sir Everard Hambro, one of the directors of the Bank of England and the son of the noted banker, Baron Hambro, owned shares to the value of £94,500. John Hays Hammond, the famous mining engineer who had been the special expert for the US geological survey team that had surveyed the California gold fields in 1880 and a consultant to Cecil Rhodes, invested £90,000 in the Bulawayo Waterworks. Of the nineteen shareholders in the £25,000 to £50,000 range on whom we have biographical information, nine were peers and gents. Among that group railroads were a favourite choice.

It is evident that experience in the empire helped motivate investment in the colonies, usually in an area where the investor had served. Thus General Clark, who had been stationed in India, held shares in the Bengal Nagpur Railroad. Sir John Willoughby, long involved in Rhodesia, invested in the Bulawayo Waterworks as did Rhodes' advisor, John Hammond. James Alexander, who, it was noted, held the largest block of Bengal Nagpur stock, had been the last agent for India in London. Thomas Russell, who lived in Eaton Square in London but had been defense minister for New Zealand, held £82,258 worth of shares in the New Zealand Mines Trust. However, Lieutenant-General George Jackson, who had served in the Punjab, preferred to place his trust in London's Maypole Dairy!

Of the total of 80,000 odd shareholders, 323 were MPs who sat sometime between 1860 and 1912. Together they held 1.5 per cent of the value of all stock in the sample. Since the total number of sitting MPs in those years was less than 4,000, these stockholders represent about 8 per cent of the total membership. It is difficult to judge exactly the degree that MP participation compares with that of others of similar circumstance, but it appears to have been substantially higher. There were, after all, only *126,000* corporate charters granted in the UK between 1856 and 1912. Moreover, of the 104 firms in which MPs held shares, only about a dozen were domestic. Foreign and empire securities were apparently more attractive.

V

Table 20 displays the geographic distribution of shareholders. No matter whether 'east Londoners' are included or not, the most important conclusions are placed into immediate and very sharp focus. Any thought that British domestic firms depended to any extent on overseas investors is immediately dispelled; and the contribution of those investors to British enterprise in the foreign and empire sectors, while larger, was far from a dominant one. Under the most generous assumption (removal of all 'EC' residents), overseas shareholders accounted for no more than 0.5 per cent of domestic, 25 per cent of foreign, and 18 per cent of empire issues. If 'EC' owners are included, the overseas proportion declines to one-sixth of foreign, and one-tenth empire.

In the Celtic fringe, Irish investment in no sector exceeded 1.5 per cent. The Welsh and the Scots, however, made a substantial contribution to domestic industry, and the latter owned almost 4 per cent of foreign and more than 7 per cent of empire securities. The pattern suggested by the Scots and Welsh

Table 20. *Geographic location of stockholders (all firms) (%)*

	UK	Foreign	Empire	All
Asia	0	1.1	0	.3
Europe	.4	8.3	2.3	3.6
N. Africa & Middle East	0		0	
N. America	0	4.8	0	1.3
S. & Central America	0	1.5	.1	.5
Other empires	0	0	0	
Total	.4	15.7	2.4	5.7
Empire				
D. Gov.	0	.1	1.7	.8
R. Gov.	0	0	4.6	2.3
India	0	.2	1.8	.9
Total	0	.3	8.1	4.0
London				
EC	9.7	33.0	38.2	30.4
Other	10.6	16.8	20.1	17.2
Total	20.3	50.7	58.3	47.6
Regions				
Home	4.1	4.2	6.1	5.5
Lancashire	9.4	8.0	2.1	5.5
Midlands	7.9	2.3	2.5	3.7
Rural east	2.3	.7	1.1	1.3
Rural west	6.2	2.3	3.1	3.5
South & southwest	8.5	2.3	3.8	4.4
North	5.0	1.3	.5	1.8
Yorkshire	13.8	3.0	1.6	4.8
Total	57.2	24.1	20.8	30.5
Total England	77.5	74.8	79.1	78.1
Celtic				
Scotland	8.1	4.2	7.1	6.2
Ireland	1.3	1.0	.8	1.0
Wales	9.7	.6	.6	2.7
Total	19.1	5.8	8.5	9.9
Total UK	96.6	80.6	87.6	88.0
Unidentified	3.0	3.4	1.9	2.3

experience is underscored when attention is focused on England. Depending on the measure chosen, as much as one-fifth or as little as one-eighth of domestic shares were held in London and the rest were owned by stockholders living outside the metropolis. Domestic shares were very broadly held with stockholders spread fairly evenly from Land's End to John o' Groats. There was greater than average concentration in the south and south-west, in Yorkshire, and in the north and less than average ones in the Home counties and the east, but British industry was truly domestic industry.

In the case of the foreign sector, only Lancashire, of the non-metropolitan regions, stands out. Residents of the capital, however, held one-quarter of the foreign shares if EC is excluded and one-half if it is not. In the case of the empire, there was no secondary concentration in Lancashire, and, depending on the measure, the London proportion ranges from one-third to three-fifths of the total.

If holdings are adjusted for population differences, it appears that a Londoner was more likely to invest in equities than his 'country' cousin, but there was also a sharp contrast between London and the rest of the country when it came to selecting where to invest.[11] A Londoner was about twice as likely as a non-metropolitan resident to make an investment in domestic equities; but the population-adjusted index for London was only slightly higher than the Yorkshire (the next highest) figure. Those same Londoners, however, were twelve times as likely to buy foreign securities as their non-metropolitan countrymen and eighteen times as likely to buy empire securities. Nor were there other regions with indices close to London's. In the foreign sector, Lancashire residents displayed the second highest investment propensity (thanks to the citizens of Manchester and Liverpool), but that figure was only one-sixth the London number. In the case of the empire, the scenario is repeated. Residents of the Home counties bought empire shares more frequently than any other non-metropolitan group (and one can wonder whether many were not actually Londoners), but their average was only one-seventh that of London.

One conclusion is obvious. While Britain was a very important market for equities, sociologically it was not one capital market but two. Domestic firms enjoyed the savings of London residents, but they could not have survived without the accumulations of investors in Cornwall, Birmingham, and rural Rutland. In 1901, 26 of England's 31 million people lived outside the capital, but, in terms of foreign equities, the 26 million's contribution was only one and one-half times as large as that of the capital's residents, even if the entire holdings of EC residents are removed from the sample. Moreover, in the case of the empire sector the contributions of the two groups (one five-and-a-half times as large as the other) were almost equal. If the EC residents are counted, then the 4.6 million London residents contributed twice as much to foreign and two and one-half times as much to empire finance as all the rest of England.

Overall, foreign investors aside, it is apparent that London residents had a tendency to invest in foreign and empire firms, but residents of the United Kingdom outside that city were inclined to put their accumulations to work in domestic enterprises.

Table 21. *Index of relative holdings by occupations (UK = 100)*

	UK	Foreign	Empire
Business			
Merchants	100	182	75
Manufacturers	100	25	15
Professional and management	100	61	66
Miscellaneous	100	78	30
All Business	100	86	47
Elites			
Financiers	100	245	104
Military	100	56	77
Miscellaneous	100	163	258
Peers and gents	100	96	161
All elites	100	110	146

VI

It appears that there were substantial differences between the domestic 'public imperialists' and those who bought shares in overseas companies, and even substantial differences between investors who chose the empire and ones who preferred investments in lands not owing allegiance to the British Crown. Given the data it is difficult to investigate the composition of the 'investment portfolios' of the occupational groups; however, Table 21 provides an index of relative holdings for the elite and business classes.[12]

While there were some important inter-occupational differences, businessmen as a whole were twice as likely to invest in domestic as foreign securities. Of that group, merchants held the highest proportion of their 'portfolios' in overseas investments, but as far as the empire was concerned their proportions were still below those held by any 'elite' subgroup. That was, however, not true for foreign investments; the merchants displayed a very strong affinity for those securities. Financiers aside, they were more likely to invest abroad than any other group. (Dropping merchants from the calculations reduces that foreign index for the business group from 86 to 50.) Manufacturers, on the other hand, displayed the least interest in overseas and particularly empire investment. Members of that group were seven times as likely to invest in domestic as empire securities.

The elites, on the other hand, appear to have been somewhat more likely to invest in foreign (the index is about 10 per cent higher) but very much more likely to invest in empire than in domestic issues. In the latter case the index was almost 50 per cent above the domestic level. Oddly enough, the military

Table 22. *Relative attractiveness, elites/business by industry*

	UK	Foreign	Empire
Commercial banks	131	84	189
Breweries and distilleries	51	138	102
Commercial and industrial	40	63	40
Financial, land, and development	212	158	238
Financial trusts	152	97	119
Gas and light	76	46	128
Iron, coal, and steel	119	130	129
Mines	277	93	58
Railroads	—	73	245
Shipping	122	25	34
Tea and coffee	—	—	59
Telephone and telegraph	—	870	52
Trams and omnibusses	206	181	168
Waterworks	—	82	124
Canals and docks	61	114	53

appear to resemble the business group far more than the other elites. The generals and admirals displayed a fairly strong preference for domestic as opposed to any overseas investments. The financiers seem to have much preferred foreign investment, but their index for empire commitments was only slightly above the domestic level. Miscellaneous elites showed the strongest preference for overseas investment, they acquired foreign securities at rates more than half as high again as domestic and empire shares at rates two and a half times as great. Finally, the largest group, the peers and gents, display no particular affinity for foreign shares (their index was slightly less than 100) but a strong (more than 60 per cent above domestic) preference for empire investments.

The conclusions are quite clear. Businessmen did invest abroad, but their major interest was the domestic economy. While the merchants should have been concerned with foreign political developments, all groups were likely more concerned with domestic than empire problems. For the 'elites' as a whole the opposite was true, although the military officers were an exception. If, however, the success of empire ventures was linked to policies at home, the elites (and particularly the miscellaneous and peers and gents) must have been more concerned with those policies than their counterparts in the business sector.

There were, of course, some substantial inter-industry deviations from the 'all firms' average. Businessmen were more heavily involved in some industries and the elites in others. A measure of relative affinity is presented in Table 22.[13] A number larger than a hundred suggests that the industry was relatively

Table 23. *Index of relative holdings by location*

	UK	Foreign	Empire
Non-UK	100	1058	416
London			
EC	100	208	148
Other	100	102	198
Total	100	159	171
Regions			
Home	100	83	61
Lancashire	100	115	43
Midlands	100	21	27
Rural east	100	224	186
Rural west	100	50	72
South & southwest	100	37	62
North	100	18	11
Yorkshire	100	11	9
Total	100	54	46
Total England	100	93	99
Celtic			
Scotland	100	85	145
Ireland	100	195	116
Wales	100	10	12
Total	100	52	69

attractive to the elites and relatively unattractive to the business community. For numbers less than a hundred, the opposite holds.

The elites' interest in empire was strongest in commercial banks, financial, land, and development companies, and iron, coal, and steel firms plus the 'public utilities' – gas and light, railways, tramways and omnibusses, and waterworks. Businessmen, however, tended to focus their empire investments in the 'private' sector: in canals and docks, commercial and industrial, mining, shipping, and tea and coffee plantations. While the empire connection was important, these were competitive industries and profits must have depended far less directly on the particular form of the political structure.

It has also been possible to examine the geographic distribution of stockholders and those distributions are summarized in Table 23.[14] Overseas residents showed no inclination to invest in domestic securities; those in foreign countries placed most of their accumulations in foreign firms, and colonial residents turned almost entirely to empire firms. The average figure for the Celtic fringe would suggest that those investors looked much like the typical non-metropolitan Briton, but that average masks very different behaviour by the citizens of the three 'nations'. The Welsh were more English than the English and seldom invested in any non-domestic securities. The Irish were, as might be expected, far more catholic in their tastes; on the average, however, they preferred empire to domestic and foreign to empire shares. The Scots displayed a little more interest in foreign equities than the typical non-metropolitan Englishman, but they still preferred domestic investment. On the other hand their preference for empire shares was as strong as an EC resident, and that was quite strong indeed.

Interest, however, must center on the English investors (they accounted for more than 90 per cent of the total); and there were clearly two Englands: London and the provinces. To the extent that equity holdings provide an adequate measure of total investments, a Londoner's portfolio held less than one-quarter domestic, more than one-third foreign and two-fifths empire securities. Within Greater London the EC residents were strongly attracted to foreign investments and relatively strongly attracted to the empire (the portfolio ratios were 22, 45 and 32). Outside the city, the empire was very popular but those investors appear to have been largely indifferent when it came to choosing between home and foreign investment.

In the provinces, the domestic index is more than twice that for foreign and empire holdings. The foreign sector figure was much inflated by the residents of Lancashire and the rural east while that latter area and the Home counties keep the empire index as high as it was. The provinces were not, however, all identical. In the north, in Yorkshire, and in the Midlands the domestic proportions ranged from more than two-thirds to 90 per cent and averaged almost 80 per cent. Elsewhere the domestic figure was much less, although, with the exceptions noted, still far above the ratios recorded in London. Empire proportions average 13 per cent in the four northern regions (the North, Lancashire, Yorkshire, and the Midlands), but were almost three times that level in the three southern (east, west, and south and south-west). Even in the country the 'London Disease' appears to have infected the contiguous regions.

Table 24 provides an indication of the relative attractiveness of particular industries to London and provincial investors (figures greater than 100 indicate a metropolitan and less than 100 a provincial bias).[15] The results are less sharp than for the occupational distributions, but in the empire, Londoners had a propensity to invest in financial, land, and development companies, in the unregulated sector, and railroads and waterworks among the public utilities. The non-London communities, while gazing abroad far less frequently than their London peers, looked in different directions when their eyes did turn outward. In the empire their investments clustered about the non-regulated part of the economy. They displayed above-average indices for four of the five goods-producing sectors (brewing, mines, iron, coal, and steel, and tea and coffee) and in addition they invested above typical amounts in commercial banks and shipping. In the 'public' sector they showed greater than 'average' interest in gas and light and telephone and telegraph companies.

Finally, given the 'two nation' character of imperial investment, it appears

Table 24. *Relative attractiveness of industries*

	UK	Foreign	Empire
Commercial banks	55	86	55
Breweries and distilleries	34	105	60
Canals and docks	51	436	3387
Commercial and industrial	67	80	97
Financial, land, and development	329	106	158
Financial trusts	139	35	93
Gas and light	82	241	61
Iron, coal, and steel	59	99	81
Mines	163	63	88
Tea and coffee	—	—	60
Railroads	—	120	192
Shipping	103	12	84
Telephone and telegraph	—	22	40
Trams and omnibusses	141	349	99
Waterworks	—	382	177

useful to examine the composition of the occupational 'portfolios' in the two regions. In that way it may be possible to determine if empire investors in London came from an occupational distribution similar to country investors or if members of the same occupational group behaved differently. Table 25 provides some insight into that question. In that table an entry greater than 100 indicates that the securities in question were preferred more by Londoners than by their cousins and a number less than 100 indicates a country preference.[16] If the behavior of the investors was similar to both regions, the ratios should be close to 100.

For one group (businessmen) at least, it is apparent that Londoners behaved very differently. In every subcategory, London businessmen invested far less often in domestic industry and far more frequently in the empire. The 'miscellaneous business' category aside, the same preference appears to hold for foreign investments as well. In the business sector as a whole, the ratio of London to non-London indices stood at less than one-fifth for domestic and more than one and one-half for empire investment.

For the elite group, the 'urban–rural' differences are much less clearly marked. Every subgroup appears somewhat more willing to invest in the foreign sector than were their counterparts outside London, but there is no such uniformity of feelings in the domestic and empire sectors. In the former, although the overall elite ratio for London is well below that for the provinces, both the military and miscellaneous groups tended to invest in domestic activities relatively more often than their country counterparts. In the case of empire investment the rates were identical for Londoner and non-Londoner alike. In London, financiers and peers and gents appear to have viewed

Table 25. *Relative attractiveness home, foreign and empire by occupation and location (ratio is London to non-London)*

	UK	Foreign	Empire
Business			
Merchants	16	126	130
Manufacturers	39	134	193
Professional	20	114	130
Miscellaneous	2	38	653
Total	19	118	158
Elites			
Financiers	57	101	108
Military	135	111	93
Miscellaneous	128	156	88
Peers and gents	48	111	104
Total	66	114	100

domestic investment as slightly more attractive than did their rural confrères, but the opposite was true for the other two groups.

Altogether it appears that the London bias towards overseas investment while in part accounted for by the somewhat greater concentration of elite investment in the metropolis (peers and gents accounted for about 5 per cent more of London than of 'rural' investment) can in large measure be traced to the lure that overseas investment had for London businessmen, particularly the merchant community (London manufacturers were twice as willing to invest in the empire than were their country cousins; however, neither group invested much). That lure was clearly much weaker outside the capital, and the farther one travelled north from London the weaker it became.

Who then was correct? To a certain extent both Marx and Schumpeter. The empire capital was partly mercantile, but it was largely London mercantile. Similarly a large part of the finance was supplied by the elites and here it appears Schumpeter was correct. However, the warriors do not appear to have shared those same proclivities. Finally, there is little evidence to support Lenin and the other neo-Marxists. Neither the business community as a whole, manufacturers in particular, nor even the financiers were heavily into imperial investment. They were far more involved in domestic enterprise.

Notes

1 'Imperialism, sane imperialism, as distinguished from what I may call wild-cat imperialism, is nothing but this – a larger patriotism': Lord Rosebery to the City Liberal Club, May 5, 1899 (he was, of course, no longer Prime Minister).

2 The figures for the middle- and upper-class populations are from Baxter (1869: 119). Dudley Baxter puts the population of the United Kingdom in 1867 at 30 million of which he argues 23 million are the working class and 6.7 million in the middle and upper classes.

3 Rodbertus' arguments can be found in 'Handelskrisen und Hypothekennot', in Rodbertus (1899: IV). Robert Brenner has suggested that Hegel be given credit for the restructured argument (Hegel 1967: 149–50).

4 Luxemburg's conclusions differ little from those reached a few years earlier by an economist of a very different persuasion, John A. Hobson.

5 Of the 476 concerns, 241 are from a random sample of corporations whose shares traded on the London Stock Exchange sometime between 1883 and 1912. The second group (235 firms) includes partnerships and sole proprietorships as well as corporations, and also includes records for the years 1860 to 1882 as well as 1883 to 1912. Inclusion, however, is based on no systematic sampling unless one believes that the existing and available records provide a random sample of the firms that existed in the past.

6 Of that total, 98 per cent has been identified by region and indirect evidence suggests that the bulk of the remainder should be classified with the domestic issues.

7 All firms listed in the index in any year ending in three or seven were brought together and duplicates eliminated. This purged master list became the universe from which the three samples were drawn. For firms still in existence in 1973 the records remain in the Companies Record Office in London and Edinburgh. For them, although some files had been misplaced, no serious problems were encountered in finding the records of the firms selected. The same was true for a small number of now defunct firms whose records still remain in the possession of the CRO. The records of most defunct firms, however, had been turned over to the Public Record Office. For firms registered in Britain and Wales, records are held in London and constitute the basis for PRO series BT-31. Records of Scottish firms are held in Edinburgh as PRO series BT-2. For these latter (Scottish) firms, all records had been preserved, and there was no problem in finding the desired stockholder lists. In the case of defunct English and Welsh companies, however, there were serious problems. In the first place, records had been saved for only every fifth year. In the second place, for 'small' firms the PRO had retained only a 5 per cent sample of firms registered. For concerns whose records had been destroyed replacement was made by choosing the firm of similar location and industry nearest to the originally selected firm in the *Yearbook* that first listed the selected firm. Moreover, since our interest was in 'public imperialists' (as opposed to persons who organized imperial enterprises), the focus was on the lists three or four years after the date of information. In the case of the defunct, English and Welsh companies, however, the PRO's selection procedure limited the choice. As a result, some lists are from firms only two years old and some from firms as much as six.

8 Business included (1) trade and commerce (merchants, sales and agents, and retail trade and business services), (2) manufacturing (manufacturers, engineers, brewers), (3) professions and managements (management, education, creative arts, legal, medicine, entrepreneurs, publishing), and (4) miscellaneous (agriculture, marine, transport and communication, and mining). The elites subsumed (1) finance, (2) military, (3) miscellaneous elites (government employees, religion, Members of Parliament (not otherwise identified), and land and property owners), and (4) peers and gents. Finally the classification 'Others' encompassed (1) labor (craftsmen, labor, personal service, and skilled labor), (2) miscellaneous (retired, deceased, and unknown), (3) other firms, and (4) women. The category 'peers and gents' includes anyone who had a title, an honorary title (e.g. JP or DL) or who classified himself as a 'gent'.

9 If, for example, the company was the Aberdeen Land and Cattle Company, and, if one of the towns in question was in Aberdeen, that county was chosen. Similarly, if the stockholder in question was next on the list after an entry with the same town name, but with county included, that county was chosen. The sources for county classifications were Bartholomew (1932) and Cassell (1899).

10 For each firm the percentage is calculated and then those percentages are averaged across all firms in an industry-location. Thus each firm, no matter what its size, carried equal weight.

11 For these calculations the percentage holdings have been divided by population to produce an index of acquisitions.

12 The data are constructed by first calculating the home, foreign, and empire distribution of the 'average stockholder'. Second, the holdings of each occupational group were expressed as a fraction of that 'typical' percentage; and finally, the foreign and empire figures were compared with domestic.

13 $$\frac{\%\ \text{industry-elite}}{\%\ \text{in 'all' industry-elite}} \Bigg/ \frac{\%\ \text{in industry-business}}{\%\ \text{in 'all' industry-business}}$$

14 $$\frac{\%\ \text{of the value of shares sectors foreign or empire held in location X}}{\%\ \text{of the value of shares of all UK securities held in location X}}$$

15 $$\frac{\dfrac{\%\ \text{of UK foreign or empire in industry X held in London}}{\%\ \text{of UK foreign or empire in 'all' industries held in London}}}{\dfrac{\%\ \text{of UK foreign or empire in industry X held in non-London}}{\%\ \text{of UK foreign or empire in 'all' industries held in non-London}}}$$

16 $$\frac{\dfrac{\text{value held by London merchants in UK}}{\text{total value held by all London merchants in UK, foreign and empire}}}{\dfrac{\text{value held by non-London merchants in UK}}{\text{total value held by non-London merchants in UK, foreign and empire}}}$$

11 Capitalists and Entrepreneurs: Prototypes and Roles

KURT W. ROTHSCHILD

I

If one sets out to discuss the differences between certain objects, these objects must have something – indeed, quite a lot – in common. There is little point in comparing a daffodil and a human being; but it makes sense to look at the differences between ape and man.

What, then, is it that Marx, Schumpeter and Keynes have in common that makes comparisons between them relevant and fruitful? I believe that the most important *specific* characteristic which sets them off against a great number of other important economists is – apart from their far-above-average erudition and intelligence – their endeavour to see in economics not a narrowly defined special subject but an aspect of human activities to be studied in the context of general historical and social development. Their major contributions are guided by what Schumpeter has so aptly called 'vision'. While – as Schumpeter stresses in his *History of Economic Analysis* (Schumpeter 1954) – *some* vision is unavoidable as a starting-point for all theoretical (innovatory) work, its importance is greatly enhanced when the aim is to cover the 'grand dynamics' of economic events. 'When we are concerned with nothing more ambitious', he writes (ibid.: 570),

than to formulate the way in which – on the plane of pure logic – economic quantities 'hang together,' that is, when we are concerned with the logic of static equilibrium or even with the essential features of a stationary process, the role of Vision is but a modest one – for we are really working up a few pretty obvious facts, perception of which comes easily to us. Things are very different when we turn to the task of analyzing economic life in its secular process of change. It is then much more difficult to visualize the really important factors and features of this process than it is to formulate their modi operandi once we have (or think we have) got hold of them. Vision (and all the errors that go with it) therefore plays a greater role in this type of venture than it does in the other.

Vision in a wider sense is in the view of Schumpeter, to which one can easily subscribe, *one* of the hallmarks of a great economist. And he had no doubt that it was a clearly recognisable characteristic of both Marx and Keynes. 'Marx saw [the] process of industrial change more clearly and he realized its pivotal importance more fully than any other economist of his time. This does not mean that he correctly understood its nature or correctly analysed its mechanism .... But the mere vision of the process was in itself sufficient for many of the purposes that Marx had in mind' (ibid.: 39). And as regards Keynes he finds a vision of stagnation tendencies in modern capitalist society pervading his entire work. 'In [the] pages of the *Economic Consequences of the Peace* we find nothing of the theoretical apparatus of the *General Theory*. But we find the whole of the vision of things social and economic of which that apparatus is the technical complement. The *General Theory* is the final result of a long struggle *to make that vision of our age analytically operative*' (ibid.: 268; italics in the original). And, finally, there is no difficulty in detecting a special Schumpeterian vision of the capitalist process which made a very early and compact appearance in his *Theory of Economic Development* and reappeared again and again in his later writings, notably in his *Business Cycles* and in *Capitalism, Socialism and Democracy*.

A wide and historical vision of the capitalist process necessarily implies a dynamic viewpoint, even when static and stationary models are fused for the analysis of particular problems. It is this combination of historic and dynamic elements in their scientific endeavours which provides a common platform for Marx, Schumpeter and Keynes. This attitude prevented them from looking at economic processes in a purely formal, static and mechanistic way, and forced them to pay attention to the 'motive power' of the economic process. That means – in capitalist society – to have a look at the 'undertaker', the capitalist–entrepreneur–manager. In this respect they (and, of course, some others) differ quite clearly from the general run of 'classical' and 'neo-classical' equilibrium economists in whose mechanistic, self-regulating systems capitalists, workers and the like more or less disappear as social, historic and individual entities. They all can be replaced by simple utility-maximising calculating machines.

Thus Messner speaks of the '*Fehlstart*' (wrong start) of classical economics in its neglect of the importance of the entrepreneur and his role in modern economic life, and continues: 'The economic theory of Manchester liberalism lost sight not only of the entrepreneur, but of the individuals in general. One studied exclusively the relationships between prices, wages, rents and profits' (Messner 1968: 9; quoted in Weber 1973: 25). Or, as Macdonald (1960: 31) puts it: 'The entrepreneur appears in the classical literature in a relatively emasculated form. In the writings of the strict classicists, such as Ricardo and McCulloch, he almost disappears. Although Mill, following Say, admits "the wages of superintendence" as distributive claim, he otherwise leaves the entrepreneurs as a type of automaton.'

The 'capitalist' (in the widest sense) is certainly not absent in the writings of Marx, Schumpeter and Keynes. He takes on a distinctive role: this – as has been said – the three authors have in common. But the ways they look at this role – their 'vision' – are certainly not the same and reveal important differences between them stemming from their environment, the period in which they lived, and, of course, from their different personal viewpoints. The rest of this short essay will try to indicate these differences in the hope that this may be a small contribution towards understanding the differences between the three Great Men.

II

Before starting with a comparison of 'the capitalist' under Marxian, Schumpeterian and Keynesian perspectives, a short terminological departure is necessary in order to avoid misunderstandings. Following Redlich (1949) I shall distinguish three types of entrepreneurial functions, which are here personified, but may be found in various combinations in single individuals, in groups, and in larger organisations. These three types are:

capitalist: supplier of funds
entrepreneur: innovator, ultimate decision-maker
manager: supervisor and coordinator.

Other terms can be and are used (e.g. Keynes' rentiers for pure 'capitalists'), but the division itself should be clear enough and does not need any elaboration as far as our investigation is concerned. To simplify matters I shall speak of the 'capitalist' without any further addition when I want to deal with the 'undertaker' in general, combining all three functions. If I want to distinguish the capitalist function in its narrower sense from the other functions I shall either speak of the 'rentier' or the differentiation will be clear from the context.

III

Let us start off, then, with Marx. In his case, certainly, the functional differentiation of entrepreneurial activities mentioned in the previous section is, in strong contrast to Schumpeter and Keynes, of little importance.[1] Marx's preoccupation with a compact capitalist has several roots. There is, firstly, his dichotomic, dialectical style of thinking which tends to attack problems through concentrating on two essential, focal and opposite phenomena. *The* worker is confronted by *the* capitalist. Secondly, there is the obvious historical factor. In Marx's times the owner–capitalist, the person or family who combined all three functions in one individual or in one small non-specialised group, was a representative phenomenon. And, thirdly, there were Marx's special research interests.

He was drawn into economic analysis by his urge to study the social problem of badly paid and exploited workers. Once he had spotted the lack of productive property as a decisive characteristic in this distributional problem it was natural that his main interest turned to the relationship between property-owning capitalists and propertyless workers. Distributional problems *within* the property-owning class (and indeed *within* the working class) were of little consequence in this framework. This explains the neglect of income divisions between rent, interest and profit, but also between capitalist profits and capitalist 'wages' obtained for managerial activities. Marx was certainly aware of these managerial activities comprising organisation and book-keeping. In fact, these would be – in his opinion – the principal activities of the worker – owner in future socialist society. But the manager as a *separate* person in capitalist society did not seem worth noticing. Even if the funds-owning capitalist turns rentier and transfers the management function to a specialist, the latter is seen as a sociological annex of the capitalist class, closely connected with it by common interests so that his income becomes – as far as the research programme is concerned – part of the unimportant intra-class income distribution.

When we turn to this 'generalised' Marxian capitalist there is no doubt that Marx recognised his importance and central place in the dynamics of capitalist development. His eulogies (in the *Communist Manifesto* and elsewhere) regarding the rapid economic progress after capitalists had taken over from feudalism and the guild system can stand comparison with Schumpeter's epical pictures of the pioneer–entrepreneur.[2]

But *the way* he looks at this capitalist is fundamentally different from Schumpeter and Keynes. To understand this fully we must keep in mind Marx's era and *Weltanschauung* in which Darwinism, enlightened optimism and Historical Materialism take a central place. History unfolds itself in a secular process where in response to a changing milieu outmoded forms of human interrelationships are replaced by more viable forms. This process, which may be slow at times but given to sudden revolutionary changes, is seen as having a 'positive' direction from 'lower' to 'higher' forms of human existence. The deep and fundamental forces of environmental change lead to a constant and autonomous development of productive forces and technological capabilities ('economic interpretation of history') which ultimately demands and creates new forms of production relations, altered political and social frameworks with new ideologies and cultural outlooks.

The Marxian capitalist must be seen and understood against this background. The principal part in the great drama of historical and economic development is played by impersonal basic forces. Human beings are not so important as individual persons but as carriers of roles in the ongoing historical process. Marx is not interested in psychological niceties or differences which distinguish capitalists from non-capitalists or which might permit differentiation between different types of capitalists.[3] He is interested in the *prototype* of the capitalist, the 'representative' capitalist in the Marshallian sense. But in contrast to Marshall the capitalist is not seen first and foremost as the ruler of the enterprise acting on the micro-level, but as the person who fills the role allotted to him in the capitalist period. 'To be a capitalist is to have not only a purely personal, but a social status in production', it is said in the

Communist Manifesto (Marx 1973: 81), and in *Capital* we read: 'Except as capital personified, the capitalist has no historical value, and no right to that historical existence which, to use Lichnowsky's amusing expression, "ain't got no date". It is only to this extent that the necessity of the capitalist's own transitory existence is implied in the transitory necessity of the capitalist mode of production'. (Marx 1967: 739)

To some extent we can view the individuals in the Marxian setting – both capitalists and workers – as being *all* equipped with the same average human capacities. These capacities may be normally distributed around the mean (again among both capitalists and workers). The analysis is then centred on the average person (the 'mean'). Whether this person can fill the role of a capitalist or a worker is predominantly a question of historical precedent (feudal wealth, primitive accumulation plus inherited wealth, propertyless persons, evicted peasants, etc.) and perhaps also of 'a little bit of luck'.

Once thrown into the role of capitalist the individual's main task is to accumulate, to accumulate, to accumulate, if he wants to survive. He is forced to do so by the competitive rules inherent in the historically determined mode of production which drives him into action; this in turn provides the dynamics of the system. The activities of the capitalist, accumulation, investment, innovation, organisation (including the 'exploitation' of labour), are thus not due to any special entrepreneurial qualities, be they lust for adventure or social responsibility, greed or a high propensity to save, aggressiveness or superior capabilities; they reflect the way in which the 'normal' person reacts when he is 'thrown' into a special environment in a certain way and wants to survive. The same person, when given the role of the worker, would have to lead the more passive existence appropriate to this role.

It is self-evident that the worker is nothing other than labour-power for the duration of his whole life, and that therefore all his disposable time is by nature and by right labour-time .... Time for education, for intellectual development, for the fulfilment of social functions, for social intercourse, for the free play of the vital forces of his body and his mind, even the rest time of Sunday – what foolishness! (Marx 1976: 375)

IV

The capitalist as the driving force behind the dynamics of a technologically advancing historical system called 'capitalism': this is a common aspect in Marx and Schumpeter. But here the common ground ends; the rest is difference.

In contrast to Marx's 'normal' or 'typical' capitalist who combines property and entrepreneurial functions, Schumpeter has presented economic theory with his highly idiosyncratic picture of a sharply differentiated capitalist class. A dividing line is drawn between wealth-owning and property-managing capitalists on the one hand and innovating entrepreneurs on the other. There are some interdependencies: financial means ease the way into 'true' entrepreneurship, and entrepreneurial success leads to the accumulation of wealth. But these interdependencies are regarded as loose; in particular, the daring entrepreneur is typically seen as the New Man, who enters the scene with new ideas and borrowed money to carry out innovative changes: the creation of new products or qualities, the introduction of new technologies or marketing methods, the opening up of new markets or of new raw material sources, the reorganisation of market environments and market forms.

It is this 'entrepreneur', the pioneer, the business leader, who is the hero in Schumpeter's drama. The differences to Marx are obvious. With Marx the moving force is technological advance provided by the whole human race; the average capitalist, driven towards accumulation, is the tool of the autonomous developmental forces. In Schumpeter's world the average person – be he propertyless worker or property-owning capitalist – can be a conscientious manager of routine activities. The stationary economy of classical (and neo-classical) theory is well served by this type of person. But when it comes to an explanation of capitalist dynamics, the emergence of new combinations and the destruction of old ones, a special type of person is needed, the daring leader, the innovative entrepreneur.

While Marx looks at the 'representative', the average capitalist, Schumpeter is more concerned with the upper tail of the distribution of the capitalist class (in the wider sense).[4] It is this *relatively* small pioneer group of entrepreneurs who are the really dynamic force in capitalism because – in Schumpeter's words – it is 'a historical fact and a theoretical proposition ... that carrying out innovations is the only [!] function which is fundamental in history' (Schumpeter 1939: 102).[5] The rest of the industrialists, the 'ordinary' capitalists, are mere followers who – like Marx's capitalists – 'are driven to copying [the innovations] if they can, and some people will do so forth-with' (ibid.: 100). In a simplified way one could say that in the case of Marx it is capitalist development which creates the capitalist, while in the case of Schumpeter it is the entrepreneur who creates capitalist development.

As in the case of Marx, we can find a better access to Schumpeter's approach if we indicate the background and personal 'philosophy' of the author. Schumpeter was born and spent his formative years in a country which – in contrast to Marx's England – had seen neither a complete bourgeois nor a thoroughgoing industrial revolution. Feudal splendour and economic backwardness were prominent elements in Schumpeter's Austria. They both had a deep influence on his outlook. In Vienna, where he spent his youth, he was strongly influenced by a titled stepfather, educated at the exclusive Theresianum, and exposed to the splendour of the monarchy. In Czernowitz, where he got his first professorship, he was confronted with a backward region in an industrialising empire.

This background formed and sharpened Schumpeter's 'vision'. The established aristocracy with its traditional values appealed to Schumpeter's basically romantic and conservative temperament, while his economic insight told him that there was a scarcity of daring 'new' leaders, of enterprising persons who would provide the necessary push to a sluggish industrial development.[6] The consequence was that Schumpeter tended to expand an important distinction – that between the more enterprising type of capitalist and that of more routine-management-oriented type – into a deep and fundamental division. The pioneer–entrepreneur becomes the hero of the capitalist age, the creative driving force of development, the source of profit and all other property incomes (like interest) which would stagnate in a stationary society.[7] Like the aristocrat this hero is not just motivated by a desire for profit, but also or even foremost by a 'will to conquer', by a desire 'to found a dynasty', i.e by typical military and feudal elitist values.

The adventurous entrepreneur as opposed to the 'normal' capitalist[8] presents without doubt the main difference between the Schumpeterian and the Marxian view of the business leader. This is stressed by Schumpeter himself when he writes of Marx that 'he had no adequate theory of enterprise and his failure to distinguish the entrepreneur from the capitalist, together with a faulty theoretical technique, accounts for many cases of non sequitur and for many mistakes' (Schumpeter 1952b: 39).

This difference is also decisive for their views regarding the future of a capitalist society based on private property and free markets. *Formally* they have a common vision of a replacement of capitalism by some sort of socialism or semi-socialist order. But the *reasons* behind this view are quite different.

With Marx we have the continuous development of society's productive powers which creates a new environment 'demanding' new social relations. The private capitalist is no longer needed and becomes a brake on progress. His role in history has come to an end; management can be taken over by the workers. In Schumpeter's view a successful period of expansive private, unfettered capitalism will come to an end because – among other things – ideological and cultural developments will cause the exit of the 'daring entrepreneur'.[9] Capitalism in the Schumpeterian sense would then be replaced by a more regulated society, be it managerial capitalism, a 'labourist' or corporate economy, or – ultimately – a fully grown socialist society. They all would still need managers; but the age of the true entrepreneur would have gone.

V

If we can characterise – 'in desperate brevity' (to use a Schumpeterian phrase) – the Marxian capitalist as a historical and Darwinist phenomenon, and the Schumpeterian entrepreneur as a romantic hero, then we can summarise the Keynesian view as predominantly psychological: he sees the capitalist–investor's fate as an example of the *condition humaine* in a dangerous and uncertain world.

The concept and definition of the 'capitalist' in Keynesian theory overlaps the Marxian and Schumpeterian types. In the case of Marx the sharp dividing line lies between property-owning capitalists and propertyless workers. Keynes is here nearer to Marx than Schumpeter. The latter looks at the entrepreneur who is able to launch forward without means of his own, combining his creative talents with credited finance. Keynes is on the whole aware that *normally* it is only the well-to-do who have a realistic chance to take on the role of capitalist. For both, Marx and Keynes, the institution of inheritance is of some importance, and a short digression on this question might be in place.

In Marxian economics the legal right of inheritance secures the accumulation of wealth in private hands. It reserves the access to capitalist functions and privileges to the members of the capitalist class and is a tool for the preservation of a superior class position. But inheritance is of no consequence as far as the qualities or shortcomings of the individual capitalist are concerned. For Keynes the inheritance of wealth is not abhorrent in itself; but being more concerned with individual differences he sees – following an idea of Marshall – a danger in the selection principle involved in the institution of heredity. 'The hereditary principle in the transmission of wealth and the control of business is the reason why the leadership of the capitalist cause is weak and stupid. It is too much dominated by third-generation men' (Keynes 1971–83: IX, 299). In Schumpeter's case inheritance can play an important role as a motive force stimulating entrepreneurship in order to acquire wealth for 'forming a dynasty'. It also helps to explain the continued supply of 'average' capitalists who can play their imitative part on the basis of inherited wealth (which was created by past entrepreneurs).

Let us return to the Keynesian capitalist, and let us now compare his concept with that of Schumpeter. For Schumpeter – as we saw – the dividing line is drawn between the pioneer–entrepreneur and the imitative capitalist who will normally fulfil financial and managerial functions. Keynes also distinguishes sharply between two functions, but his line is drawn in a different place: between investing entrepreneurs and interest-drawing rentiers.[10] The first – whether he is innovating or imitating – is the person on whom the dynamics, both short-term and long-term, of the capitalist system depend. The rentier is 'functionless'. For the (very) long run Keynes advocates 'the disappearance of its [i.e. capitalism's] rentier aspect ... the euthansia of the rentier, of the functionless investor' (Keynes 1936: 376), not in order to destroy private capitalism, but to save it.

The Keynesian capitalist is thus typically a person in possession of some means who has the choice of turning entrepreneur or rentier (or a bit of each of them). The latter option has been greatly facilitated through the growth and increasing reliability of financial markets. With the availability of fairly safe and non-negligible interest-payments, real investment – the source of employment and economic growth – is no longer an obvious choice. The Keynesian capitalist is neither driven towards continuous accumulation by the force of relentless competition (like his Marxian cousin); nor is he normally the type of conquering hero with a will to power whom Schumpeter envisages. In fact, he is on the whole an individual who is always tempted to enjoy life and to be afraid of the uncertainties of the future. To 'go rentier' must, therefore, always be a rather attractive choice for many capitalists unless either (1) the gap between (safe) interest and (risky) investment returns is big enough to lure them towards entrepreneurial activities or (2) the outcome of investment activities is made more certain. The main Keynesian message was, of course, that 'free markets' do not necessarily create such conditions so that we cannot rely on capitalists and capitalism functioning in a smooth way.

As in the case of Marx and Schumpeter we can 'derive' Keynes' view of the capitalist and his problematique both from the *Zeitgeist* and from Keynes' personal background. Taking the latter first: it is probably safe to assume that Keynes' involvement in the Bloomsbury group and its philosophy sharpened his senses for individual emotions – love, fear, enjoyment, artistic creation, etc. – and prevented him from looking at the capitalist as a mere calculating machine. As far as the general environment was concerned he was faced by rather different conditions from those of Marx's early capitalism or of Schumpeter's semifeudal Austria. After the first world war the British economy was constantly plagued by special stagnation problems, and was burdened with an overdeveloped financial system and a long-accumulated debt problem. When the big depression set in with the bank crashes of 1931 the deep structural and protectionist changes in international trade affected Britain more than other countries and made uncertainty about the future a predominant problem.[11]

It is against this background that Keynes' sceptical views about the possibilities of a smooth capitalist process must be seen.[12] Marx's crises stem from a badly functioning system that prevents accumulation-hungry capitalists from following their urge. In Schumpeter's case stationary capitalism can function according to classical rules, but it needs the intervention of the innovative entrepreneur to upset the stationary equilibrium in order to initiate dynamic growth. In the Keynesian world the free, unregulated market cannot function smoothly because the future-oriented investment process is so loaded with uncertainty that human nature cannot easily cope with it. Investment, albeit irregularly, continues because it can offer high rewards but also (and mainly) because in addition to fear of risk and uncertainty there are also 'animal spirits'. 'Most, probably, of our decisions to do something positive, the full consequences of which will be drawn out over many days to come, can only be taken as a result of animal spirits – of a spontaneous urge to action rather than inaction, and not as the outcome of a weighted average of quantitative benefits multiplied by quantitative probabilities' (Keynes 1936: 161).

Uncertainty and expectations thus become central phenomena for the problem of entrepreneurship in the Keynesian paradigm. The stress on uncertainty is, of course, a decisive point in differentiating 'true' Keynesianism from classical theory and 'vulgar' Keynesianism.[13] But Schumpeter, with his interest in economic dynamics, had always been aware of the existence and importance of uncertainty. Thus, in conclusion, it may be in place to indicate the difference between Keynes and Schumpeter with regard to this point: capitalist and uncertainty.

There *is* a very decisive difference. Schumpeter accepts in principle the Walrasian–Marshallian equilibrium picture for a stationary or slowly changing economy. There may be exogenous frictions; but they are usually of a minor nature, and can be digested by the market mechanism and the manager–capitalists acting in these markets. This transparent world breaks down, however, 'as soon as we leave those precincts and allow the business community under study to be faced in – not simply new situations, which also occur as soon as external factors intrude but by – new possibilities of business action which are as yet untried and about which the most complete command of routine teaches nothing' (Schumpeter 1939: 98). It is the Schumpeterian entrepreneur who treads this dangerous ground where new structures and developments are born. 'If a new frame is to be constructed, the task changes its character .... The major elements in such an undertaking *simply cannot be known*' (ibid.: 100; italics mine).

Compare this with Keynes' view of uncertainty. Having lived through a time of vanishing investment opportunities, widespread bankruptcies, fickle demand developments, etc., he ceases to believe in the equilibrating forces of 'normal' markets. The problems of uncertainty is inherent in *all* future-oriented activities, and thus affects *all* investor–capitalists.

By 'uncertain' knowledge, let me explain, I do not mean merely to distinguish what is known for certain from what is only probable. The game of roulette is not subject, in this sense, to uncertainty; nor is the prospect of a Victory bond being drawn. Or again, the expectation of life is only slightly uncertain .... The sense in which I am using the term is that in which the prospect of a European war is uncertain, or the price of copper or the rate of interest twenty years hence, or the obsolescence of a new invention, or the position of private wealth owners in the social system in 1970. About these matters there is no scientific basis on which to form any calculate probability whatever. *We simply do not know* (Keynes 1937: p. 213–4; italics mine)

We can compare the two positions very succinctly. In Schumpeter's case uncertainty is looked for and *created* by the Schumpeterian pioneer–entrepreneur; it leads to creative destruction, new sources of profits and economic growth. In Keynes' case uncertainty is an all-pervasive and increasingly important phenomenon affecting the will to investment of all capitalist entrepreneurs; it hampers and endangers full employment and economic growth.

VI

Let me conclude: the figure of the capitalist, his role and his functions, are seen differently by Marx, Schumpeter and Keynes. Each of them stresses different *aspects* of capitalist activity as the central element in a dynamic capitalist society. The different approaches reflect differences in period and place, and, of course, varying viewpoints and *Weltanschauungen*. All three are aware of the possibly transient nature of 'mature capitalism' and realise that the respective prototype of the capitalist must (Marx), will (Schumpeter) or may (Keynes) change in the course of time. As to the way he will or can be changed they have, of course, different views. But this is another story.

Notes

1 'For Marx the capitalist was at the same time producer, merchant and banker' (Feig 1922: 42).
2 '[The capitalist] is fanatically intent on the valorization of value; consequently he ruthlessly forces the human race to produce for production's sake. In this way he spurs on the development of society's productive forces' (Marx 1976: 738).
3 Thus McClelland probably misunderstands Marx's approach when he writes: 'Marx seems to have been a bit premature in dismissing psychology as a major determinant in history' (McClelland 1961: 93).
4 Schumpeter's entrepreneur–hero is certainly an elitist type. But Schumpeter did not think in terms of genius. He thought that entrepreneurs are statistically less frequent, but not exceptional events. See Schumpeter 1939: 99.
5 Since the problem of rentiers vs. entrepreneurs remained foremost in Schumpeter's mind from his earliest to his latest works, appropriate quotations can be found in several writings. The choice of *Business Cycles* in this case has no special reason.
6 Most readers will be acquainted with the famous anecdote about Schumpeter who – so goes the tale – used to talk about his three big ambitions in life: to become the greatest horseman, the greatest lover and the greatest economist. Only two of these ambitions – so he used to say – had been fulfilled; but he never betrayed which of the three. While I am not able to provide the answer to this 'riddle' I should like to point out the mixture of aristocratic romanticism and economic–theoretical urge which lies behind those targets.
7 See Endress 1971: 43.
8 The difference between the two types can be very vividly described by a quotation from a novel by Mnacko (1970) where the general manager of a big chemical combine recalls the image of the 'Boss', the founder and former director of the firm: 'Occasionally it is not without envy that I think of the Boss. He had conquered, we enjoy. He had ideas, we administrate. He took on risks, we are worried. I react nervously to any small variation in production, markets, or research. He liked such unavoidable events, in fact, they were a big joke for him. What I regard as tasks and duties was for him an exciting game' (Mnacko 1970: 39; my translation).
9 'Capitalism ... means a scheme of values, an attitude towards life, a civilization – the civilization of inequality and of the family fortune. This civilization is rapidly passing away' (Schumpeter 1950a: 450).
10 Entrepreneur and rentier are the concepts used in the *General Theory*. In a draft for this work written in 1933 Keynes used the terms 'entrepreneur function' (centred in firms) and 'capitalists' from whom the firms rent their fixed capital equipment in return for an annual rent. See Keynes 1971–83: XXIX, 87.
11 See McDonald 1960: 139ff.
12 'The General Theory is the final result of a long struggle to make the vision of our age analytically operative' (Schumpeter 1952b: 268).
13 As early as 1926 Keynes wrote: 'Many of the greatest evils of our time are the fruits of risk, uncertainty, and ignorance' (Keynes 1971–83: IX, 291).

12 Marx and Bismarck: Capitalism and Government 1883–1983[1]

ANGUS MADDISON

I

The capitalist epoch began around the time of Marx's birth, and until the 1880s, when he died, the state's role was permissive not propulsive. The technical progress and increased rates of investment which produced accelerated and generalised economic growth in Western Europe from 1820 onwards were not primarily due to government encouragement. And governments did little else to promote supply-side potential, e.g. in the way of education or human resource development.[2]

Classical political economy advocated policies of *laisser-faire*, and these were generally pursued in both the social and the economic fields. It was therefore an era when technology offered large prospects for profit, when international markets were much more open to competition than in the preceding merchant capitalist epoch, when profits were untaxed, and there was an unlimited supply of cheap labour at more or less subsistence wages.

The distribution of the gains from capitalist development was unequal. The bourgeoisie grew in size. They and older landowning and professional elites were enriched. In the working class, average subsistence levels increased as the urban–rural ratio rose, but illiteracy, population pressure, a repressive poor law, legal constraints on union activity and political disfranchisement kept them hungry, insanitary, ragged and exploited.[3]

This was the socioeconomic system whose dynamics and tensions were so brilliantly described by Marx. The state was a nightwatchman whose expenditure was concentrated on a soldiery and police protecting property and the national frontiers. It seemed inevitable that such a system should someday crack, as its ultimate legitimacy was so threadbare.

Marx himself never conceived of the capitalist state as significantly promoting growth or alleviating social tension. When he did back political action within a capitalist framework it was not to urge the potential for welfare expenditure, but for regulatory intervention to shorten working hours to ten per day.

In 1883 Adolph Wagner enunciated his 'law' of a steadily rising proportion of public expenditure. Wagner was a *Kathedersozialist* who, like many

Table 26. *Total government expenditure as a percent of G.D.P. at current prices*

	1880	1913	1929	1938	1950	1960	1973	1981
France	11.2	9.9[a]	12.0	21.8	27.6	33.9	38.8	48.7
Germany	10.0[b]	17.7	30.6	42.4	30.4	33.4	41.2	47.7
Japan	9.0[c]	14.2	18.8	30.3	19.8	20.9	22.9	34.1
Netherlands	n.a.	8.2[d]	11.2	21.7	26.8	36.1	49.1	59.0
U.K.	9.9	13.3	23.8	28.8	34.2	32.9	41.5	46.4
U.S.A.	n.a.	8.0	10.1	18.5[e]	22.5	27.9	32.0	34.4
Average		11.9	17.8	27.3	26.9	30.9	37.6	45.1

Notes:
[a]1910–13. [b]1881. [c]1885. [d]1910. [e]1939.
Sources: 1950 onwards generally from *National Accounts of O.E.C.D. Countries,* various issues.
Otherwise as follows:
France: 1880–1938 numerator from L. Fontvieille, *Evolution et Croissance de l'Etat Française 1815–1969,* ISMEA, Paris, 1976, pp. 2118 and 2124–9. The current price physical product denominator (p. 1743 for 1880–1929) was increased by a coefficient of 1.43 to convert it to a G.D.P. basis, and five-year averages were unscrambled by interpolation. 1938 G.D.P. from *Statistics of National Product and Expenditure No. 2,* O.E.E.C., Paris, 1957.
Germany: 1881 and 1913 from S. Andic and J. Veverka, 'The Growth of Government Expenditure in Germany since Reunification', *Finanzarchiv,* January 1964, pp. 241–3.
Japan: 1885–1960 from K. Ohkawa and M. Shinohara, *Patterns of Japanese Development,* Yale, 1979, pp. 251–4 and 370–2.
Netherlands:1910–38 very rough estimate derived from *Tachtig Jaren Statistiek in Tijdreeksen,* CBS, The Hague, 1979, pp. 144 and 150. Trend movement derived from *rijksuitgaven* divided by net national product at market prices, adjusted by the 1950 coefficient of this ratio to government expenditure/G.D.P. ratio derived from O.E.C.D. *National Accounts* for 1950.
U.K.: 1880 government expenditure from J. Veverka, 'The Growth of Government Expenditure in the United Kingdom since 1870', *Scottish Journal of Political Economy,* 1963; 1913 from A.T. Peacock and J. Wiseman, *The Growth of Public Expenditure in the United Kingdom,* NBER, Princeton, 1961, p. 164. G.D.P. at market prices from C.H. Feinstein, *National Income, Expenditure and Output of the United Kingdom 1855–1965,* Cambridge, 1972, pp. T14–18.
U.S.A.: 1913–39 government expenditure from S. Fabricant, *The Trend in Government Activity in the United States since 1900,* NBER, New York, 1952, p. 27. G.N.P. from J.W. Kendrick, *Productivity Trends in the United States,* NBER, Princeton, 1961, p. 297; 1929 and 1939 G.D.P. from 'The National Income and Product Accounts of the United States: An Introduction to the Revised Estimates for 1929–80', *Survey of Current Business,* December 1980.

professors before and since, was distilling a tendency which he wanted to see rather than describing a phenomenon based on empirical observation (cf. Wagner 1967). But Wagner in fact adumbrated the characteristics of a welfare state. He favoured progressive taxation, public education, state control of railways, etc. Between 1820 and 1880 there was no observable tendency for increased public expenditure in capitalist countries as is clear from Table 26, but Wagner's prediction was better than his history.

II

In 1883, one could therefore discern three theories of the state's role in socioeconomic life. The dominant official view was the *laisser-faire* 'liberalism' of classical political economy (Smith, Malthus and Ricardo). Marx viewed the state as an apparatus to reinforce the exploitation of the masses by the ruling class. Wagner predicted that the state would legitimate capitalism by promoting social welfare, and intervention to sustain economic performance.

At that time it was not clear which interpretation would prove to be correct. Until recently, it appeared that Wagner's perception of capitalist performance was the right one. Governmental 'welfare state' expenditures grew from a typical 2 per cent of G.D.P. in 1883 to a typical 30 per cent in 1983. In the golden age of postwar growth to 1973, welfare capitalism was further augmented by a general commitment of Western governments to Keynesian type macroeconomic guidance to promote high levels of employment and resource use.

Since 1973, the Keynesian-type commitments in macropolicy have steadily wilted. Monetarist-type diagnosis and policies now dominate; they are in the pre-Keynesian *laisser-faire* tradition. Since 1973, 'liberal' critics of the welfare state have also gained tremendously in political power and in the U.K. and U.S.A. there has been a radical shift in governmental attitudes. Official action to dismantle the welfare state has as yet been very limited and does not parallel the revolution in macropolicy, but the change in emphasis is clear.

This paper is intended as a diagnosis of the growth of the welfare state since 1883. It examines the causal forces behind its expansion, and its impact in mitigating the social conflicts which Marx detected in the first decades of modern capitalist development. It also considers whether the welfare state has reached dysfunctional limits which impede economic performance and which might provide a rationale for its dismantlement.

On such broad issues, it is difficult to assemble convincing evidence. I have therefore augmented the historical record with cross-country analysis of developments in the five big capitalist economies plus the Netherlands.

III

Bismarck was the politician who pushed capitalism in a new direction. Given the Prussian tradition of paternalism and *Staatsräson* he had no *laisser-faire* inhibitions limiting state action in social and economic affairs. As the architect of German unification he had a clearer view of the need to legitimate his new creation than politicians in older countries who took this for granted. Germany also had the best-organised socialist movement and many academics, like Wagner, who felt that the state needed to play a more active role in mitigating the social tensions of capitalism.

Since Bismarck's day, the welfare state has expanded enormously under a variety of political pressures. It has grown incrementally, and not as a grand design or a neatly structured edifice which serves clearly defined goals. It has received major impetus from utopian socialists or social engineers with egalitarian goals. However, the present interpretation treats its growth as the outcome of a succession of *ad hoc* attempts to mitigate social tension and to satisfy claims of conflicting groups. It implies a different theory of the state from that of Marx, the liberals or the utopian socialists. It is not unlike Galbraith's view of countervailing power as expressed in his *American Capitalism*, or the view of Dahrendorf (1959) and Strachey (1956). This is the reason I call it Bismarck's era, because the motivation of politicians implementing the successive increments to the welfare state did not differ significantly from his.

Germany pioneered state insurance with three pieces of legislation. Sickness insurance was legislated in 1883 (extended in 1888) and provided income maintenance payments for workers during sickness absence who earned below a certain income threshold. In 1884 there was legislation providing compensation for industrial injury in occupations where there were substantial risks of this nature, and in 1889 a system of old age and sickness pensions was introduced. The first two schemes involved compulsory contributions by employers and workers and covered 12 million workers in 1890. The pension scheme was the only one which involved a government subsidy.

In the period from these reforms until the first world war, Western European countries generally moved in the German direction. The U.K. held on to the Malthus–Ricardo tradition until 1909 when the Welsh populist Lloyd George introduced state coverage for similar risks and also introduced unemployment insurance (which Germany did not have until 1927).

The pressure for such reforms in the U.K. came from the labour movement which grew strongly after the easing of restrictions on trade union activity and the gradual extension of the franchise. The evidence of poverty collected in the first social surveys (Mayhew, Booth and Rowntree) also helped, as did the activism of Fabian reformers like the Webbs who conducted inquiries into the Poor Laws. Beveridge's 1909 enquiry into unemployment had a significant impact and he was later a very influential advocate for a comprehensive welfare state and Keynesian policies to promote full employment (Beveridge 1909, 1942 and 1944).

The last quarter of the nineteenth century saw increased public provision of compulsory primary education, and in the beginning of the twentieth century some secondary education. There was limited state action to improve sanitation and promote public health, but generally no public provision of health services. The motivation for state action in these fields was similar to that in social insurance. There was also some awareness of education's role in improving human capital which in Europe probably went furthest in Germany, which promoted higher education and R. and D. earlier than other European countries.

State education was resisted in ecclesiastical circles and helped to provoke the *Kulturkampf* in Germany and the controversy surrounding the Jules Ferry laïcisation reforms in France. In all Western European countries there was some degree of compromise, by which the state left some role for church education and usually contributed substantially to finance it.

In the U.S.A., the tradition of rugged individualism held strong until 1935 when the social security system was introduced as part of Roosevelt's New Deal. Although American provision of social insurance still lags well behind that of the European countries, the U.S.A. went much further than Europe as an early provider of public education. This was in part because as an immigrant country, education was viewed as a powerful vehicle for national integration. U.S. tradition since Jefferson has always given strong emphasis to social mobility rather than social equality, and there was also a greater awareness than in Europe of the role of education in contributing to the supply potential of the economy.

In Japan, which in spite of location can appropriately be treated as a major bastion of Western capitalism, the role of the state in social insurance has been a good deal smaller than in Europe, partly because other social arrangements covered some of the risks. But the state has always played a major role in bolstering the supply potential. Ever since the Meiji restoration in 1867, Japanese government has promoted technical progress and industrial investment and spent heavily on a public education system which provides an ample supply of skills and social discipline. Since 1960, Japanese welfare state expenditures have risen very rapidly.

During the first world war, the role of the state increased enormously in absorbing resources directly for military purposes, in raising taxes, and in resource allocation. The degree of mobilisation was probably higher than in the Napoleonic wars, and the potential regulatory scope for state action within a capitalist framework was amply demonstrated. The outcome of the war was a shakeup in the social hierarchy, particularly in defeated countries such as Germany and Austria, the emergence of a communist state on the doorstep of Western capitalism, and a strong feeling after such large-scale and in retrospect such pointless sacrifices that the political legitimacy of all Western countries needed to be strengthened by universal suffrage in countries which had been subjected to general mobilisation.

Thus the forces that had fostered social insurance in prewar years were strengthened. The coverage of social insurance and public education grew. Most countries developed some kind of unemployment insurance and widened the coverage of 'public assistance', i.e. noninsured social risks began to be covered with less of the stigma of older attitudes towards the 'undeserving poor'. In some countries government involvement in enterprise activity increased, and in every country included in Table 26, government expenditure increased as a share of G.D.P. The war also brought a substantial regulatory role for government in housing markets and in some countries important public housing construction and rental programmes. In almost all countries, the tax structure had been extended in wartime to include income tax, and this feature persisted. In this sense, the expansion of war finance had perhaps had a certain ratchet effect as suggested by Peacock and Wiseman (1961).

However, this ratchet was only a very partial reason for government expansion as experience subsequent to the 1929 recession demonstrated that government's role could make a major leap forward in peacetime. Between 1929 and 1938 there was a massive increase in the relative importance of public expenditure in all the countries covered in Table 26. Germany and Japan both tilted sharply towards totalitarianism with much increased military spending and widespread control of industry. But in France, the Netherlands, U.K. and U.S.A., massive unemployment led to increased social spending, to 'structural' support programmes for industry, farm relief programmes, etc.

The second world war involved many Western governments in even bigger resource mobilisation efforts than the first, leading to higher levels of taxation, and to patterns of taxation which would produce a strong 'fiscal dividend' in the subsequent conditions of rapid economic growth and inflation. This was one factor facilitating finance of public spending in the postwar era. Nevertheless, the average proportion of G.D.P. spent by Western governments was lower in 1950 than in 1938. This was due in substantial measure to the dismantlement of the totalitarian state in Japan and Germany and to their demilitarisation. In other countries the government role had grown. In the U.K. there was a substantial growth in public spending due to the implementation of Beveridge's comprehensive social insurance proposals by the postwar Labour government, to the introduction of a national health service and education expansion. In France too there was a broadening of social insurance and health coverage, as well as a very generous pro-natal system of family allowances.

Progress in these directions also occurred in the Netherlands, but it was only later that the Netherlands together with Sweden became the top government spender. In the U.S.A., the increased role of government by 1950 was due to high military spending and the cold war. Social expenditure had not increased.

In the golden years of fast economic growth to 1973, the growth of government expenditure was concentrated in health, education, housing, the new area of the 'environment', and on social transfers. Expenditure on traditional public goods such as defence actually declined as international tensions eased.

In providing merit goods and social transfers, there was a certain 'bandwaggon effect'. Once these programmes grew beyond a certain size and involved large tax levies, there was a tendency for their coverage to become universal rather than to remain restricted to beneficiaries who would otherwise be in hardship. Middle-class voters could see that there were substantial benefits from participation in schemes which they had in any case to help finance, and any possible stigma of indigence which may have formerly been involved in participation in such schemes disappeared when their coverage was enlarged and benefits came as cheques in the mail rather than cash in the post office.

The persistent incidence of inflation and general practice of rent control made it difficult to make private provision for retirement or risk contingencies via insurance or small investments. This produced a greater reliance on indexed inflation-proof public schemes, at a time when changes in demographic structure were producing substantial increases in the proportion of retired voters.

Similar pressures brought about the growth in publicly financed health services. In this field there was a much bigger displacement effect than had ever been the case with education, with the state financing expenditures which had hitherto been private, though in most countries medical services are still *produced* in the private sector.

Another significant influence in raising the public share of G.D.P. was the fact that measured productivity in the service sector grows a good deal more slowly than in commodity production. This underlying tendency was reinforced by pressure from professional bodies to increase manning levels, e.g. the teachers' unions pressed for smaller classes, medical personnel in hospitals rose in numbers relative to the patients. In an era of general expansion, public servants were also able to preserve rather favourable salary scales.

In the Netherlands, a contributory factor in the exceptionally rapid rise in government spending was undoubtedly the natural gas bonanza which put large extra tax sources (about 6 per cent of G.D.P.) into the hands of government.

Finally, an important reason for expansion in transfer payments in the 1960s was the widened concern with poverty, whose nature was redefined. In the 1950s, the British tended to think that the postwar expansion of their welfare state had virtually abolished poverty and that progressive taxation had produced much greater equality. In 1951, Rowntree and Lavers found only 2 per cent of the population of York in poverty compared with nearly 18 per cent in 1936.[4] But in the 1960s British poverty was rediscovered and redefined. Titmuss (1962) was the leader of the movement in the academic world but it had wide support amongst the growing number of sociologists and social workers who formed the major lobby for the expansion of social coverage on a non-insurance basis, e.g. supplementary benefits. In 1970 Atkinson (1970), after a careful survey of the evidence, concluded that 9 per cent of the British population were living in poverty.[5]

The rediscovery and redefinition of poverty also occurred in the U.S.A. Galbraith (1952: 116) wrote: 'in recent times, for most people the biological minimums of food, clothing and even shelter have been covered as a matter of course. By comparison the further wants are comparatively unimportant.' But Harrington (1962) claimed that a majority of Americans was poor and later Jencks (1972) defined poverty as a relative not an absolute level of living. The academic lobby played a smaller role in influencing the Lyndon Johnson welfare expansion (Food Stamps, Medicaid, Medicare and A.F.D.C.) than academics did in influencing U.K. policy. The main reason was the widespread rioting by the black population in U.S. cities, who wanted something more material than civil rights legislation.

In the 1960s and 1970s there was a general move to universalise social benefits, so that the distinction between social insurance and social transfers had become rather blurred in Europe, and in the Netherlands virtually disappeared. In the U.S.A., where social insurance programmes are run on a trust fund basis, there is still a sharp distinction between insurance and 'welfare' payments, and the latter have less political legitimacy than in most of continental Europe. The U.K. is in a somewhat intermediate position with supplementary income payments and various *ad hoc* benefits playing a major role.

Some analysts view the social transfer system of Western capitalism as an anti-poverty programme, poverty being defined in terms of a minimum income geared to average earnings rather than subsistence needs. On these criteria it is not difficult to develop a 'churning' critique, showing that the massive transfer systems which do occur have not eliminated poverty (cf. Beckerman et al. 1979). However, the major purpose is not primarily to eliminate poverty, but to reduce social risk, provide guaranteed savings for old age and induce social solidarity. Bismarck still looms larger than Titmuss.

Since 1973, there has been another substantial leap forward in government expenditure. This has generally been smaller than in the 1930s, and has occurred to some extent because of the built-in stabiliser characteristics of advanced welfare states, for the government macropolicy stance has generally been restrictive. Unemployment compensation has obviously risen, though by less than would seem warranted by the extent of the problem. Other social transfers have risen, to some extent to disguise unemployment. Hence Dutch payments for 'handicapped' workers removed from the labour force rose from 2 to 4.3 per cent of G.D.P. from 1973 to 1980. In other countries there have been substantial extra payments for 'pensions' to workers persuaded to retire prematurely, and many supplementary (non-insurance) programmes have grown to augment the income of the unemployed.

IV

Table 27 classifies the present structure of government expenditure. The traditional domain of 'public' wants is not much larger now than it was in the 1880s. The big difference is in 'merit' wants[6] and income maintenance areas

Table 27(a). *Structure of government expenditure as percent of G.D.P. around 1980*

	France 1980	Germany 1980	Japan 1981	Netherlands 1978	U.K. 1979	U.S.A. 1978	Average
Total	46.9	48.5	34.1	57.8	43.4	33.8	44.1
Traditional commitments Debt interest	1.7	1.9	3.6	4.0	4.6	2.7	3.1
'Public wants' (defence and general government)	7.4	8.5	4.2	10.3	8.7	8.5	7.9
Modern commitments Economic services	3.4	5.3	6.0	3.8	3.9	3.4	4.3
'Welfare state' (merit wants and income maintenance)	34.4	32.8	20.3	39.7	26.2	19.2	28.8

Table 27(b). *Detail of welfare state expenditures as percent of G.D.P. around 1980*

	France 1980	Germany 1980	Japan 1981	Netherlands 1981	U.K. 1979	U.S.A. 1978	Average
'Merit wants'	15.9	13.8	12.6	(18.7)	13.9	9.0	13.8
(a) Education	5.7	5.1	5.0	7.1	5.4	5.7	5.7
(b) Health	6.2	6.5	4.7	6.6	4.7	2.5	5.2
(c) Housing	3.2	1.4	2.4⎱	(5.0)	3.3	0.4⎱	2.9
(d) Other	0.8	0.8	0.5⎰		0.5	0.4⎰	

	France 1981	Germany 1981	Japan 1981	Netherlands 1981	U.K. 1981	U.S.A. 1981	Average
Income maintenance	18.4	16.8	7.7	19.3	10.5	9.0	13.6
(a) Pensions	11.9	12.5	4.8	13.0	7.4	7.4	9.5
(b) Sickness cash benefits	1.2	0.7	0.1	1.9	0.3	0.1	0.7
(c) Family allocations	2.2	1.2	1.6	2.0	1.4	0.5	1.5
(d) Unemployment compensation	1.9	1.4	0.4	1.0	1.4	0.5	1.1
(e) Other	1.2	1.0	0.7	1.4	0.0	0.5	0.7

Source: O.E.C.D. Statistics Division, O.E.C.D. *National Accounts*, and Dutch national sources.

which together absorb amounts varying from under 20 per cent of G.D.P. in Japan and the U.S.A. where the government commitment is weakest to nearly 40 per cent in the Netherlands where (together with Sweden) it is highest.

In pre-Bismarck days these expenditures were almost universally less than 2 per cent of G.D.P.[7] They represent the major new role of government in capitalist society which Marx did not foresee and which have greatly softened the social impact of capitalism. In spite of very high levels of unemployment since 1973, capitalism has not been threatened by massive social discontent, or by development of antidemocratic political extremism. In fact, Western capitalism has become more democratic with the disappearance of the Greek colonels and the Iberian dictators.

Table 27 defines government in a national accounting sense, and therefore excludes public enterprise activity. The importance of this varies between countries a good deal, being now biggest in France amongst the countries listed and smallest in the U.S.A. Public enterprise usually operates on similar lines to private enterprise, except in the U.K. where it is not particularly efficient and has not helped capitalist growth.

Another problem of inter-country comparability arises from 'tax expenditures', i.e. derogations deliberately built into the normal system of tax liability as a form of subsidy for certain types of spending. Thus the U.S.A. gives tax derogations to people with children or for private pensions, health insurance and education spending. These are a substitute for government expenditure on these items which occurs in other countries. Table 27 may therefore somewhat understate the U.S. governmental role compared with that of Europe. In Germany tax expenditures amounted to 1.9 per cent of G.D.P. in 1980 and in the U.S.A. federal 'tax expenditures' alone were bigger at 5.7 per cent of G.D.P. in 1979.[8] However, it is very difficult to compare 'tax expenditures' because (1) they are a tax forgone rather than a tax collected; (2) they require definition of the 'normal' tax structure from which a derogation is granted, and (3) they require a definition of 'normal' income as distinct from expenses incurred in producing it.

Other problems in defining the scope of government expenditure arise from government loan guarantees or other devices to disguise off-budget loan activity.[9] However, Table 27 is based on national accounting conventions which are more comparable between countries than 'budgets', and less likely to conceal government off-budget loan activity.

It should be noted that the state is not nearly so important proportionately as an employer or producer as it is in terms of expenditure. Public employment averages about a sixth of total employment in our six countries, and carries out a somewhat bigger proportion of production.[10]

V

It is not easy to give an authoritative assessment of the role of government in social progress over the past century, because it is not possible to reconstruct a counterfactual framework, without this very pervasive influence.[11] However, there can be little doubt that government has improved and equalised social welfare by mitigating the hardships associated with unemployment, sickness and old age, and by improving health and education.

Kuznets has suggested that capitalist development at first involved increased inequality[12] and then took a U-turn towards increased equality. This conclusion is certainly correct for disposable income after taxes and transfers though it is less true for primary income.

Governments have helped equalise primary income over the past century by provision of more equal educational opportunity and permitting greater freedom for trade union bargaining. The bargaining power of workers has also strengthened since Marx's day by the termination of what Arthur Lewis (1954) called the phase of unlimited supply of labour (i.e. the wilting supply of labour from agriculture and, in the U.K. case, from Ireland).[13] This was not due to government action but is probably one of the main reasons why the bargaining power of workers is stronger in advanced capitalist countries than in the third world.

However, in the past two or three decades, the availability of social transfers has tended to increase inequality in primary income because it induces people to stop working, or to reduce their savings, and to set up separate household units which are only sustainable because of the existence of social transfers.

When post-tax, post-transfer incomes are considered, the most powerful equalising instrument seems to be the cash transfers provided by social security and welfare schemes. The tax systems of Western countries do much less to promote equality than their apparently progressive structures would suggest, and the big expansion of social transfers since 1950 has been financed mainly by rather regressive social security levies.

Around 1960, there was a spate of literature claiming that the welfare state had created social harmony within Western capitalism,[14] and that class conflict had disappeared because levelling processes had produced a middle-class social continuum in which the ruling class had been dismantled and the working class had acquired bourgeois status and aspirations. There was a widespread tendency in such circles to reject the word 'capitalist' as an appropriate epithet to describe Western society, and to come up with labels like 'post-industrial', 'post-capitalist', etc. In retrospect these views of social harmony seem naive, although Marx's prediction of continuous sharpening of class antagonism and material welfare between rich and poor has not proved correct.

In the 1960s and 1970s, conflicts within Western society became more obvious, though they were not of the type which Marx predicted. Major race riots in the United States were a reminder that the melting-pot theory was a myth and that major U.S. cities were not harmonious communities but ethnic ghettoes, with enough muggers and dope peddlers to make life unsafe for pedestrians.[15] There was a rediscovery of poverty in the early 1960s as already discussed. Student disturbances almost toppled the Gaullist regime in France in 1968, and New Left student radicalism shook universities to their foundations in many countries. Urban terrorism became an important menace in Germany and Italy. The women's liberation movement gained momentum. Union militancy became greater in many countries (see Crouch and Pizzorno 1978). In the 1970s, there was a sharp acceleration in the rate of inflation and a general failure of attempts to deal with this problem by techniques of social accommodation such as incomes policies and social contracts.

Although the growth of the welfare state has clearly improved and equalised welfare, there is now more doubt amongst latter-day Bismarckians than there was in the early 1960s about the degree of its success in mitigating social tension. There is also a substantial degree of disillusion amongst the utopian social engineers about the possibilities of 'rationalising' the welfare state to achieve egalitarian goals more efficiently. There is more awareness of and resistance to the tax burden of the welfare state. The tax backlash varies in intensity from country to country without any close association with the size of the burden, and resistance takes different forms – constitutional ceilings on tax revenue proportions in some U.S. states, and the underground economy in Italy.

These reactions against the welfare state are now powerfully reinforced by arguments that it, and big government generally, have had adverse effects on economic growth.

VI

In the 1960s when growth was fast there was big pressure to expand government. Now that growth is much slower and government expenditure grows more or less autonomously because of the structure of income maintenance systems, there is in many quarters a feeling that government spending has gone too far and should be turned back. This has been reinforced by the substantial budget deficits since 1973 and increasing public debts compared with 1960–73 when, on average, budgets were balanced and debt/G.D.P. ratios declined. This view has been most vocally expressed in the U.S.A. and U.K. which now have radical conservative administrations. This reflects both backlash hostility towards programmes for the 'undeserving' poor and old-fashioned fiscal worries about budget deficits and increased government debt.[16] The later arguments seem to predominate in the Netherlands, where the government is making cuts but where there has been no backlash against social security.

The other strand in recent discussion which is used as a rationale in favour of cuts is that government spending has reached dysfunctional levels, though this view is not correlated with the importance of government, and it is certainly not easy to substantiate. There is no clear relationship between the size of government and economic performance. Government spending absorbs a similar proportion of resources in Japan and the United States which have had very different growth records. Government size is a good deal higher in the West European countries than in the U.S.A. and again there is no apparent relationship between this phenomenon and comparative growth rates. Nevertheless worries about the role of government are widespread and not confined to conservatives.[17]

Warnings about the potential dangers of big government are not new. Schumpeter (1943) put forward a sociopolitical theory concerning the probable stifling of capitalist development which includes the disincentive effect of progressive taxation, a tendency to socialist controls, harassment of big business, as well as other features such as the bureaucratisation of entrepreneurship, the power of trade unions, and disillusion of intellectuals. Around the same time Hayek (1944) predicted that big government would lead to totalitarianism, and Colin Clark (1945) predicted disastrous results if taxation grew beyond 25 per cent of national income.

But in the postwar golden age, government grew well beyond Clark's 25 per cent threshold without any evidence of weakening economic performance or the breakdown predicted by Hayek or Schumpeter. And it is not at all clear that the slowdown in economic growth since 1973 has had much to do with the size of government. The proposition of Laffer, who supposes a sizeable acceleration in growth would occur if the government share were diminished, is pure speculation.

VII

It is difficult to reach strong conclusions on the influence of the welfare state on capitalist development because the evidence does not warrant them. Strong judgements on the question are influenced mainly by ideological positions, or predictions about what might happen in the future. The ideological positions vary in detail across countries, and the degree of concern about the welfare state is not always closely related to its relative size. Nevertheless five different ideological positions concerning the welfare state are distinguishable in most Western countries, and the following paragraphs attempt to characterise the current view of these groups – the liberals, the Bismarckians, the egalitarians, the neo-Marxists and the New Left.

(a) The Liberals   There is no evidence that high welfare state expenditure has been disastrous for economic incentives and economic growth as early-nineteenth-century *laissez-faire* liberals (relying heavily on Malthusian population assumptions) would have predicted. It is also striking that the degree of welfare commitment has been virtually ignored as a causal influence in the growth-accounting literature (Kuznets, Denison, Chenery, etc.). In most of the growth debates, the distribution of expenditure between private and public consumption, or the redistributive impact of government, has seemed to have been given as little consequence for growth as private

decisions to buy motor cars of different colours. Occasionally people of liberal persuasion such as Rueff have pointed to moral hazards in social security benefits such as unemployment insurance, but until recently the main liberal critique of the welfare state was that biases in voting procedure did not give the electorate what it really wanted (Buchanan and Tullock 1962), or that heavy reliance on the state gave bureaucrats too much power (Niskanen 1971). The recent emphasis of the liberal school on the dysfunctionality of the welfare state from the point of view of work incentives, savings and economic growth is a reassertion of the more fundamental type of critique which the *laissez-faire* school originally advanced. However, they have not produced acceptable evidence of very significant adverse impact on growth.[18] Their persuasive power derives perhaps more from current disillusion amongst former welfare state supporters of other political persuasions than the power of their own argument. And the new governments in the U.K. and the U.S.A. are as much concerned to increase rewards to property and work for their own anti-egalitarian sake as for their presumptive impact on economic performance.

(b) The Populist Middle Ground   In the postwar period until the 1970s, support for the welfare state was general over a fairly wide spectrum of politicians and bureaucrats in Western countries for pragmatic reasons. Such measures added to the legitimacy of the state by providing programmes broadly in the public interest. Economic growth provided the finance for such schemes without much political effort. It was acknowledged that public transfers involved a fair degree of 'churning', but bureaucratic dangers or incentive costs were not thought to be great. Within the group of political managers and administrators, attitudes have now swung closer to the liberal school, because tax revenues are less buoyant now that stagnation has replaced growth, welfare state commitments are very large and have a momentum of their own which is difficult to control.

Members of this group are now apt to give more emphasis to the wastes involved in 'churning',[19] and are more conscious of the practical difficulties of rationalising transfers through negative income tax or social security reform and the problems of checking manpower growth in public services.

(c) The Egalitarians   Amongst egalitarians, there has also been disillusionment with the welfare state, though there can be little doubt that transfers have been highly equalising. As far as transfers are concerned, egalitarians also complain that there is too much 'churning', that the net distributive impact is small relative to the amount of gross tax and transfer activity (Beckerman et al. 1979). Some of them would be content with smaller, more redistributive programmes.

In the merit goods field, there has also been a realisation that there are inherent limitations on the degree to which delivery of education and health services can be manipulated to serve egalitarian goals (Jencks 1979; Le Grand 1982).

(*d*) *The Neo-Marxists*   The neo-Marxists who have written about the welfare state have generally treated it as more than Bismarckian. They suggest that is has been necessary not only to make a capitalist economy legitimate or acceptable, but also that it was functionally necessary, e.g. education and health services are required to provide the skills and strength needed in productive workers. But they hold that the welfare state now has strong elements of dysfunctionality because its growth has strengthened workers' bargaining power, and higher taxes have squeezed profits. Attempts to remedy these problems by cutting back on welfare will reduce capitalist legitimacy and ultimately lower the quality of the labour force. The argument seems to be that the welfare state has prolonged the duration of the capitalist epoch but that now is a time of crisis and that its heyday is over (Gough 1979; O'Connor 1973).

(*e*) *The New Left*   The various New Left views are to large degree a revival of the viewpoint of the utopian socialists with an equally diverse range of interests. They have in common a heavy stress on self-starting schemes involving local initiative, and an attack on government provision as bureaucratic in form and psychologically repressive. Their discontent is concentrated more on public services than on transfers. Ivan Illich (1971 and 1975) is perhaps the most vociferous of this group and has attacked public education because it produces alienation, and public health services because they have created a significant degree of iatrogenic (doctor-made) illness. It is difficult to characterise the policy implications of the New Left. Those derivable from Illich do not differ much from liberal programmes for privatisation and vouchers such as Milton Friedman has advocated. In several countries, elements of the New Left have been incorporated into welfare state programmes in various ways. These range from leafraking measures to mitigate unemployment in the U.K. or U.S.A. to much wider participation to the Netherlands.

In spite of the growing disenchantment, with the welfare state over the past decade, it has continued to grow in all Western countries for four general reasons: (1) health and education services are provided by highly organised professional groups whose measured productivity (pupil/teacher, patient/doctor ratios) is in continuous decline, but whose relative wages have been well sustained; (2) demand for health and education is not seriously checked by user costs; (3) eligibility for pensions is growing for demographic reasons; (4) the proportion of pensioners with full entitlements is rising steadily in consequence of earlier social insurance decisions.

The odds are that Bismarck's creation will continue to grow for the same mixed reasons as in the past.

Notes

1 A lengthier and more quantitative statement of the present argument can be found in Maddison 1984.
2 Alexander Gerschenkron had a different viewpoint with regard to countries he regarded as latecomers to accelerated growth. See Gerschenkron (1965: 12–16). I think Gerschenkron exaggerated the difference in growth experience in Western countries and erred in describing France as 'relatively backward', Germany as a 'relatively late arrival' and Denmark 'very backward' in the middle of the nineteenth century. I also think he exaggerated the governmental role in propelling economic growth in the alleged latecomers. The only strong case is Japan.
3 I am here simply making the point, which seems incontestable, that inequality increased. I am not suggesting that working-class standards did not increase in absolute terms from 1820 to the 1880s.
4 See Rowntree and Lavers (1951) on poverty levels. Dudley Seers (1955) has also argued that there had been a major shift in income distribution because of tax changes. This induced Crosland (1956: 42–53) to downplay the importance of distributional issues. At the same time and using the same evidence Strachey (1956) produced a Marxist revisionist analysis of the historical development of welfare states and progressive taxation as social progress obtained by pressure of the labour movement in parliamentary democracies.
5 This new awareness of poverty was also present in other European countries, as reflected e.g. by the creation of the Swedish Low Income Commission; the book by Giscard's minister, Lionel Stoleru (1977).
6 The terms 'public' wants and 'merit' wants are taken from Musgrave (1959).
7 It is interesting to note Gregory King's estimate of social transfers in England in 1688. The poorer half of the population (51.4 per cent) were estimated to spend more than they earned by an amount equivalent to 1.4 per cent of national income. This includes dissaving, but most of it was presumably transfers. See Barnett (1936: 31).
8 See Deutscher Bundestag (1981) and the annual U.S. reports on this topic.
9 See Joint Economic Committee (1982), which argues that more comprehensive measures of government produce a less alarmist view of budget deficits.
10 See O.E.C.D. (1982: 12).
11 See Kuznets (1955) and Kraus (1981) for an extensive review of the literature on distribution and of causal influences.
12 See note 11.
13 For an interpretation of Japanese experience from this perspective, see Minami (1973). The abandonment of classical (subsistence) wage theory in favour of marginal productivity theory may well have occurred at about the time of the Lewis transition in European countries.
14 See Myrdal (1960) and Bell (1960) as well as the 1956 books of Crosland and Strachey quoted in note 4.
15 See Glazer and Moynihan (1963) for a realistic survey of blacks, Puerto Ricans, Jews, Italians and Irish in New York City.
16 See also the rather oddball Marxist analysis by O'Connor (1973), who seems to think that budget deficits may destroy capitalism.
17 See the gloomy assessment of Assar Lindbeck (1981 and 1983), who advances the thesis that a fundamental cause of productivity slowdown is an 'arterio-sclerosis' of the Western economies with a long-term deterioration in the efficiency of their 'basic mechanisms'. See also O.E.C.D. (1981) for useful interpretations of the varieties of disillusion with the welfare state. The most interesting of these is the paper by H.L. Wilensky who bases his analysis on surveys of opinion in a number of

countries, and attempts a threefold classification of countries. His first group of 'corporatist democracies' has effective institutions for consensus on social issues and a low level of discontent with the welfare state. He includes Germany in this group. His third group includes 'fragmented and decentralized political economies' where interest-group conflicts are not institutionally constrained and where there is some disillusion with the welfare state. His middle group includes France, Japan and Switzerland. This book illustrates the difficulty of assessing public moods about the welfare state, particularly in a situation where there is inadequate evidence on the degree of moral hazard in different social transfer systems.

18 See H. Aaron (1982) for a review of recent American discussion on this issue.

19 On 'churning', see the remarks of H. Houthakker (1972): 'we are gradually moving toward a situation where everybody is subsidizing everybody else .... As we all know from birthdays and Christmas Eves, the exchange of gifts, even rather useless gifts, frequently helps stimulate good fellowship and a sense of community. One could be more sanguine about this trend, however, if it did not contain an element of self-deception, in the sense that the beneficiaries of any particular program feel they are getting something for nothing.' On social security reform, see H.J. Aaron (1978) and D.P. Moynihan (1978). On manning in government services see R. Bacon and W. Eltis (1978).

References

Aaron, H.J. (1978), *Politics and the Professors*, Brookings, Washington D.C.

Aaron, H.J. (1982), *Economic Effects of Social Security*, Brookings, Washington D.C.

Allen, W.R. (1977), 'Irving Fisher, F.D.R., and the Great Depression', *History of Political Economy*, vol. 9, Winter, pp. 560–87.

Anderson, C.J. (1965), *A Half-century of Federal Reserve Policy Making, 1914–1964*, Federal Reserve Bank of Philadelphia, Philadelphia, 1977.

Andic, S. and J. Veverka (1964), 'The Growth of Government Expenditure in Germany Since the Unification', *Finanzarchiv*, Band 23, pp. 241–3.

Asimakopulos, A. (1982), 'Keynes' Theory of Effective Demand Revisited', *Australian Economic Papers*, vol. 21, pp. 18–36.

Atkinson, A.B. (1970), *Poverty in Britain and the Reform of Social Security*, Cambridge University Press, Cambridge.

Bacon, R. and W. Eltis (1978), *Britain's Economic Problem: Too Few Producers*, Macmillan, London.

Baran, P.A. and P.M. Sweezy (1966), *Monopoly Capital*, Monthly Review Press, New York.

Barnett, G.E. (1936), *Two Tracts by Gregory King*, Johns Hopkins, Baltimore.

Bartholomew, J. (1932), *The Survey Gazetteer of the British Isles*, 8th edition, John Bartholomew & Sons, Edinburgh.

Beach, E.F. (1971), 'Hicks on Ricardo on Machinery', *Economic Journal*, vol. LXXXI, pp. 916–22.

Beckerman, W., et al. (1979), *Poverty and the Impact of Income Maintenance Programmes in Four Developed Countries*, International Labour Organization, Geneva.

Bell, D. (1960), *The End of Ideology*, Free Press, New York.

Bernstein, Peter L. (1983) *What Does 'Disinflation' Really Mean?*, Peter L. Bernstein Inc., New York.

Berthold, R., H. Harnisch and H.H. Müller (1970), 'Der preuszische Weg der Landwirtschaft und neuere Westdeutsche Forschungen', in *Jahrbuch fuer Wirtschaftsgeschichte*, IV.

Beveridge, W.H. (1909), *Unemployment: A Problem of Industry*, Longmans, London.

Beveridge, W.H. (1942), *Social Insurance and Related Services: Report by Sir William Beveridge*, H.M.S.O., London.

Beveridge, W.H. (1944), *Full Employment in a Free Society*, Allen & Unwin, London.

Beyen, J.W. (1951), *Money in a Maelstrom*, Macmillan, London.

Beyer, P. (1978), *Leipzig und die Anfänge des deutschen Eisenbahnbaus*, Boehlau, Weimar.

Blaug, M. (1958), *Ricardian Economics*, Yale University Press, New Haven.

Blaug, M. (1960), 'Technical Change and Marxian Economics', *Kyklos*, vol. XIII, no. 4, pp. 495–510.

Blaug, M. (1968), *Economic Theory in Retrospect*, 2nd edition, Irwin, Homewood.

Blaug, M. (1978), *Economic Theory in Retrospect*, 3rd edition, Cambridge University Press, Cambridge.

Blitz (1983), see McKeon and Blitz 1983.

Borchardt, K. (1961), 'Zur Frage des Kapitalmangels in der ersten Hälfte des 19. Jahrhunderts in Deutschland', *Jahrbücher fuer Nationaloekonomie und Statistik*, Band CLXXIII, pp. 401–21. Reprinted in Borchardt 1982.

Borchardt, K. (1976), 'Währung und Wirtschaft', in Deutsche Bank (ed.), *Währung und Wirtschaft in Deutschland 1876–1975*, F. Knapp, Frankfurt/Main.

Borchardt, K. (1982), *Wachstum, Krisen und Handlungsspielräume der Wirtschaftspolitik*, Vandenhoeck & Ruprecht, Goettingen.

Boulding (ed.) (1952), see Stigler and Boulding (eds) 1952.

Brandt (1980), see Independent Commission on International Development Issues (eds) 1980.

Bresciani-Turroni, C. (1937), *The Economics of Inflation*, A.M. Kelly, New York.

Broadbridge, S. (1970), *Studies in the Railway Expansion and the Capital Market in England, 1825–1873*, London.

Brockhage, B. (1910), *Zur Entwicklung des preuszisch-deutschen Kapitalexports*, Leipzig.

Bronfenbrenner, M. (1982), 'Schumpeter's Contribution to the Study of Comparative Economic Systems', in Helmut Frisch (ed.) 1982, pp. 99ff.

Buchanan, J.M. and G. Tullock (1962), *The Calculus of Consent*, University of Michigan, Ann Arbor.

Buchanan, J.M. and R.E. Wagner (1977), *Democracy in Deficit. The Political Legacy of Lord Keynes*, Academic Press, New York.

Buckley, W. (1950), *God and Man at Yale*, s.l.

Bukharin, N. (1966), *Imperialism and the World Economy*, Howard Fertig, New York.

Buiter, W.H. (1981), 'Walras' Law and All That: Budget Constraints and Balance Sheet Constraints in Period Models and Continuous Time Models', *International Economic Review*, vol. XXI, pp. 1–16.

Burtle, J. (1973), see Rolfe and Burtle 1973.

Cameron, R. (ed.) (1967), *Banking in the Early Stages of Industrialisation*, Oxford University Press, New York.

Carus Wilson, E. (ed.) (1954), *Essays in Economic History*, Edward Arnold, London.

Casarosa, C. (1978), 'A New Formulation of the Ricardian System', *Oxford Economic Papers*, vol. XXX, no. 1, pp. 38–63.

Cassel, G. (1921), *The World's Monetary Problems*, Constable, London.

Cassel, G. (1936), *The Downfall of the Gold Standard*, Clarendon Press, Oxford.

Cassell & Co. (1899), *The Gazetteer of Great Britain and Ireland*, 3 vols, Cassell & Co., London.

C.B.S. (ed.) (1979), *Tachtig Jaren Statistiek in Tijdreeksen*, Staatsuitgeverij, The Hague.

Chandler, A.D. Jr (1977), *The Visible Hand*, Harvard University Press, Cambridge, Mass.

Chandler, L.V. (1952), *Benjamin Strong, Central Banker*, Brookings, Washington D.C.

Chapman, S. (1979), 'Financial Restraints on the Growth of Firms in the Cotton Industry', *Economic History Review*, vol. XXXII, pp. 50–69.

Clair, O.St. (1965). *A Key to Ricardo*, Kelley Reprints, New York (orig, pub. Routledge, London).

Clapham, J. (1926), *An Economic History of Modern Britain. The Early Railway Age, 1820–1850*, Cambridge University Press, Cambridge.

216   References

Clark, C. (1945), 'Public Finance and Changes in the Value of Money', *Economic Journal*, vol. LV, December, pp. 371–89.

Clemence, R.V. and F.S. Doody (1950), *The Schumpeterian System*, Cambridge University Press, Cambridge.

Cottrell, P. (1980), *Industrial Finance 1830–1914, The Finance and Organisation of English Manufacturing Industry*, Methuen, London.

Coym, P. (1971), *Unternehmensfinanzierung im fruehen 19. Jahrhundert–dargestellt am Beispiel der Rheinprovinz und Westfalens*, Dissertation, University of Hamburg, Hamburg.

Crosland, C.A.R. (1956), *The Future of Socialism*, Cape, London.

Crouch, C. and A. Pizzorno (1978), *The Resurgence of Class Conflict in Western Europe since 1986*, Macmillan, London.

Crouzet, F. (ed.) (1972), *Capital Formation in the Industrial Revolution*, Methuen, London.

Dahrendorf, R. (1959), *Class and Class Conflict in an Industrial Society*, Routledge & Kegan Paul, London.

Deane (1962), see Mitchell and Deane 1962.

Deutsche Bundesbank (ed.) (1976), *Deutsches Geld- und Bankwesen in Zahlen, 1876–1975*, F. Knapp, Frankfurt/Main.

Deutsche Bundestag (ed.) (1981), *Achter Subventionsbericht*, Bonn.

Diewert, W.E. (1978), 'Walras' Theory of Capital Formation and the Existence of a Temporary Equilibrium', in Schwoediauer (ed.) 1978.

Dobb, M. (1940), *Political Economy and Capitalism*, Routledge & Kegan Paul, London.

Doody, F.S. (1950), see Clemence and Doody 1950.

Drummond, J. (1981), *The Floating Pound and the Sterling Area, 1931–1939*, Cambridge University Press, London.

Dudley Baxter, R. (1869), *The Taxation of the United Kingdom*, Macmillan, London.

Eatwell, J.L. (1975), 'Scarce and Produced Commodities', unpublished, Cambridge, Mass.

Eatwell, J.L. and M. Milgate (eds) (1983), *Keynes' Economics and the Theory of Value and Distribution*, London.

Eccles, M. (1951), *Reckoning Frontiers*, Knopf, New York.

Edelstein, M. (1976), 'Realized Rates of Return on U.K. Home and Overseas Portfolio Investment in the Age of High Imperialism', *Explorations in Economic History*, vol. XIII, pp. 283–330.

Eichengreen, B. (1982), 'The Proximate Determinants of Domestic Investment in Victorian Britain', *Journal of Economic History*, vol. XLII, pp. 87–95.

Eichholtz, C. (1962), *Junker und Bourgoisie vor 1848 in der preuszischen Eisenbahngeschichte*, Akademie Verlag, Berlin.

Eltis, W. (1978), see Bacon and Eltis 1978.

Endress, R. (1971), *Unternehmer, Manager oder Staatsfunktionär?* Luchterhand, Neuwied and Berlin.

Engels, F. (1848), see Marx and Engels 1848.

Engels, F. (1937), *Engels on Capital*, International Publishers, New York.

Engels, F. (1964), 'Von der Autoritaet' in *Marx–Engels Werke*, XVIII, Dietz, Berlin.

Fabricant, S. (1952), *The Trend in Government Activity in the United States since 1900*, National Bureau of Economic Research, New York.

Feig, J. (1922), *Unternehmertum und Sozialismus. Eine dogmen- und wirtschaftge-schichtliche Betrachtung*, Jena.

Feinstein, C.H. (1961), 'Income and Investment in the United Kingdom 1856–1914', *Economic Journal*, vol. LXXI, pp. 367–85.

Feinstein, C.H. (ed.) (1967), *Socialism, Capitalism and Economic Growth*, Cambridge University Press, Cambridge.

Feinstein, C.H. (1972), *National Income, Expenditure and Output of the United Kingdom, 1885–1965*, Cambridge University Press, Cambridge.

Feinstein, C.H. (1978), 'Capital Formation in Britain', *Cambridge Economic History of Europe*, vol. VII, Cambridge University Press, Cambridge.

Feiwel, G.R. (1975), *The Intellectual Capital of Michal Kalecki*, University of Tennessee Press, London.

Feldenkirchen, W. (1982a), *Die Eisen-und Stahlindustrie des Ruhrgebiets, 1879–1914*, Steiner, Wiesbaden.

Feldenkirchen, W. (1982b), 'Zur Kapitalbeschaffung und Kapitalverwendung bei Aktiengesellschaften des deutschen Machinenbaus im 19. und beginnenden 20. Jahrhundert', *Vierteljahresschrift fuer Wirtschaftsgeschichte*, Band LXIX, pp. 38–74.

Ferguson, C.E. (1973), 'The Specialisation Gap: Barton, Ricardo and Hollander', *History of Political Economy*, vol. V, pp. 1–13.

Flora, P. and A.J. Heidenheimer (eds.) (1981), *The Development of Welfare States in Europe and America*, Transaction Books, New Brunswick.

Fontvieille, L. (1976), *Evolution et croissance de l'état Française 1815–1969*, I.S.M.E.A., Paris.

Fremdling, R. (1975), *Eisenbalnen und deutsches Wirtschaftswachstum, 1840–1879*, Gesellschaft fuer Westfaelische Wirtschaftsgeschichte, Dortmund.

Frisch, H. (ed.) (1982), *Schumpeterian Economics*, Praeger, New York.

Fritsch, B. (1968), *Die Geld- und Kredittheorie von Karl Marx*, Europaeische Verlagsanstalt, Frankfurt.

Galbraith, J.K. (1952), *American Capitalism*, Penguin, Harmondsworth.

Garegnani, P. (1960), *Il Capitale nelle teorie della distribuzione*, Giuffri, Milan.

Garegnani, P. (1978), 'Notes on Consumption, Investment and Effective Demand: I', *Cambridge Journal of Economics*, vol. II, pp. 325–53.

Gayer, A., W. Rostow and W. Schwartz (1953), *The Growth and Fluctuations of the British Economy, 1790–1850*, 2 vols, Clarendon Press, Oxford.

Gerschenkron, A. (1965), *Economic Backwardness in Historical Perspective*, Praeger, New York.

Giordano, Robert M. (1983), *Record Equity Financing: Lower Risks without Lower Rates*, Goldman Sacks Economic Research, New York.

Glazer, N. and D.P. Moynihan (1963), *Beyond the Melting Pot*, M.I.T. Press, Cambridge, Mass.

Goldsmith, R. (1969), *Financial Structure and Development*, Yale University Press, New Haven.

Goodhart, C. (1972), *The Business of Banking, 1891–1914*, Macmillan, London.

Goodwin, R.M. (1972), 'A Growth Cycle', in Hunt and Schwartz (eds) 1972, pp. 442–9.

Gough, J. (1979), *The Political Economy of the Welfare State*, Macmillan, London.

Haberler, G. (1951), 'Joseph Alois Schumpeter, 1883–1950', in Harris (ed.) 1951, pp. 24–7.

Hagemann, H. and P. Kalmbach (eds) (1983), *Technischer Fortschritt und Beschäftigung*, Campus, Frankfurt.

Hahn, F.H. (1983), *Money and Inflation*, M.I.T. Press, Cambridge, Mass.

Hannah, L. (1974), 'Mergers in British Manufacturing Industry, 1880–1918', *Oxford Economic Papers*, Vol. XXVI, pp. 1–20.

Hannah, L. (ed.) (1976), *Management Strategy and Business Development*, Macmillan, London.

Harnisch (1970), see Berthold, Harnisch and Müller 1970.

Harrington, M. (1962), *The Other America*, Penguin, Harmondsworth.

Harris, D.J. (1978), *Capital Accumulation and Income Distribution*, Stanford University Press, Stanford.

Harris, D.J. (1981), 'Profits, Productivity and Thrift: The Neoclassical Theory of Capital and Distribution Revisited', *Journal of Post-Keynesian Economics*, vol. III, pp. 359–82.

Harris, D.J. (1983), 'Accumulation of Capital and the Rate of Profit in Marxian Theory', *Cambridge Journal of Economics*, vol. VII, no. 3, pp. 31–30.

Harris, D.J. (s.a., s.l.), *The Theory of Uneven Development*, forthcoming.

Harris, S.E. (ed.) (1951), *Schumpeter: Social Scientist*, Harvard University Press, Cambridge, Mass.

Harrod, R.F. (1951), *The Life of John Maynard Keynes*, Macmillan, London.

Hayek, F.A. (1935), *Collectivist Economic Planning*, George Routledge & Sons, London.

Hayek, F.A. (1937), *Monetary Nationalism*, Kelley (reprint), New York.

Hayek, F.A. (1943), 'A Commodity Reserve Currency', *Economic Journal*, vol. LIII, pp. 176–84.

Hayek, F.A. (1944), *The Road to Serfdom*, Routledge & Sons, London.

Hayek, F.A. (1983), 'The Austrian Critique', *The Economist*, June 11, pp. 45–8.

Heertje, A. (ed.) (1981), *Schumpeter's Vision. Capitalism, Socialism and Democracy after 40 years*, Praeger, New York.

Hegel, G.W.F. (1967), *Philosophy of Right* (translated by T.M. Knox), Oxford University Press, Oxford.

Heimann, E. (1945), *History of Economic Doctrines*, Oxford University Press, Oxford.

Heinsohn (s.a., s.l.) see Steiger and Heinsohn.

Hickel, R. (ed.) (1976), *R. Goldscheid-J. Schumpeter, Die Finanzkrise des Steuerstaates*, Suhrkamp, Frankfurt.

Hicks, J.R. (1939), *Value and Capital*, Clarendon Press, Oxford.

Hicks, J.R. (1963), *The Theory of Wages*, 2nd edition, Macmillan, London.

Hicks, J.R. (1969), *A Theory of Economic History*, Clarendon Press, London.

Hicks, J.R. (1971), 'A Reply to Professor Beach', *Economic Journal*, vol. LXXXI, pp. 922–5.

Hicks, J.R. (1973), *Capital and Time*, Clarendon Press, Oxford.

Hicks, J.R. (1982), 'Time in Economics', in J.R. Hicks, *Money, Interest and Wages: Collected Essays in Economic Theory*, II, Blackwell, Oxford, pp. 282–300.

Hilferding, R. (1910), *Das Finanzkapital*, Verlag der Wiener Volksbuchhandlung, Wien.

Himmelweit, S. (1974), 'The Continuing Saga of the Falling Rate of Profit – A Reply to Mario Cogoy', *Bulletin of the Conference of Socialist Economists* No. 9, Autumn.

Hobsbawm, E. (1962), *The Age of Revolution: Europe 1789–1848*, Hertford and Harlow, London.

Hoffmann, W.G. (c.s.) (1965), *Das Wachstum der deutschen Wirtschaft seit der Mitte des 19. Jahrhunderts*, Springer Verlag, Berlin.

Hofstadter, R. (1948), *American Political Tradition*, Knopf, New York.

Hollander, S. (1979), *The Economics of David Ricardo*, University of Toronto Press, Toronto and Buffalo.

Houthakker, H. (1972), see Joint Economic Committee 1972: I.

Howson, S. (1974), see Moggridge and Howson 1974.

Hudson, P. (1981), 'The Role of Banks in the Finance of West Yorkshire Wool Textile Industry, 1780–1850', *Business History Review*, vol. LV, pp. 379–402.

Hughes, J.R.T. (1960), *Fluctuations in Trade, Industry and Finance. A Study of British*

Economic Development, 1850–1860, Clarendon Press, Oxford.

Hunt, E.K. and J.G. Schwartz (eds) (1972), *A Critique of Economic Theory*, Penguin, Harmondsworth.

Illich, I. (1971), *Deschooling Society*, Harper & Row, New York.

Illich, I. (1975), *Medical Nemesis*, Calder & Boyars, London.

Independent Commission on International Development Issues (ed.) (1980) (chairman: Willy Brandt), *North-South: A Programme for Survival*, M.I.T. Press, Cambridge, Mass.

Jeck, A. and H.D. Kurz (1983), 'David Ricardo: Ansichten zur Maschinerie', in Hagemann and Kalmbach (eds) 1983, pp. 38–166.

Jeffreys, J.B. (1938), *Trends in Business Organization in Great Britain since 1856*, Ph.D. Thesis, University of London, London.

Jeidels, O. (1905), *Das Verhaeltnis der Groszbanken zur Industrie*, von Duncker & Humblot, Leipzig.

Jencks, C. (1972), *Inequality*, Harper, New York.

Johansen, L. (1967), 'A Classical Model of Economic Growth', in C.H. Feinstein (ed.) (1967), *Socialism, Capitalism and Economic Growth*, Cambridge University Press, Cambridge, pp. 13–29.

Joint Economic Committee (1972), *The Economics of Federal Subsidy Programs*, Congress of the United States, Washington D.C.

Joint Economic Committee (1982), *The Underground Federal Economy: Off-budget Activities of the Federal Government*, Congress of the United States, Washington D.C., April.

Kaldor, N. (1983), 'Gemeinsamkeiten und Unterschiede in den Theorien von Keynes, Kalecki und Rüstow', *I.F.O. Studien*, vol. XXIX, no. 1, pp. 1–10.

Kaldor, N. (s.a.), *Grenzen der 'Allgemeinen' Theorie*, (ed. B. Schefold), Springer Verlag, Berlin, forthcoming.

Kalecki, M. (1971), *Selected Essays on the Dynamics of the Capitalist Economy (1933–1970)*, Cambridge University Press, Cambridge.

Kalmbach, P. (ed.) (1983) see Hagemann and Kalmbach (eds) 1983.

Kellenbenz, H. (ed.) (1971), *Oeffentliche Finanzen und privates Kapital im spaeten Mittelalter in der ersten Haelfte des 19. Jahrhundert*, Klett-Cotta, Stuttgart.

Kellenbenz, H. (ed.) (1978), *Wirtschaftswachstum, Energie und Verkehr vom Mittelalter bis ins 19. Jahrhundert*, Klett-Cotta, Stuttgart.

Kemmerer, E.W. (1934), *Kemmerer on Money*, Winston, Philadelphia.

Kendrick, J.W. (1961), *Productivity Trends in the United States*, National Bureau of Economic Research, Princeton.

Kendrick, J.W. (1980), 'The National Income and Product Accounts of the United States: an Introduction to the Revised Estimates for 1929–1980', *Survey of Current Business*.

Kennedy, W. (1976), 'Institutional Response to Economic Growth: Capital Markets in Britain to 1914', in Hannah (ed.) 1976.

Kennedy, W. (1982), 'Economic Growth and Structural Change in the United Kingdom, 1870–1914', *Journal of Economic History*, vol. XLIV, pp. 105–14.

Keynes, J.M. (1925), 'Am I a Liberal?', *Nation and Atheneum*, August 8 and 15.

Keynes, J.M. (1926), *The End of Laissez-Faire*, Macmillan, London.

Keynes, J.M. (1936), *The General Theory of Employment, Interest and Money*, Macmillan, London.

Keynes, J.M. (1937), 'The General Theory of Employment', *Quarterly Journal of Economics*, vol. LI, pp. 209–23.

Keynes, J.M. (1943), 'The Objective of International Price Stability', *Economic Journal*, vol. LIII, pp. 185–7.

Keynes, J.M. (1971–83), *The Collected Writings of John Maynard Keynes*, Cambridge

University Press for the Royal Economic Society, vols I-XXX, Macmillan, London.

Keynes, M. (ed.) (1975), *Essays on John Maynard Keynes*, Cambridge University Press, Cambridge.

Kindleberger, C. (1964), *Economic Growth in France and Britain, 1851–1960*, Harvard University Press, Cambridge, Mass.

Kindleberger, C. (1978), *Manias, Panics and Crashes*, Basic Books, New York.

Kindleberger, C.P. and J.P. Lafargue (eds) (1983), *Financial Crisis, Theory, History and Policy*, Cambridge University Press, Cambridge.

Klein, E. (1971), 'Zur Frage der Industriefinanzierung im fruehen 19. Jahrhundert', in Kellenbenz (ed.) 1971.

Kleiner, H. (1914), *Emmissions-Statistikin Deutschland*, Berlin.

Kocka, J. (1978), 'Entrepreneurs and Managers in German Industrialisation', in *Cambridge Economic History of Europe*, vol. VII, pp. 492–589, Cambridge University Press, London.

Kraus, F. (1981), 'The Historical Development of Income Inequality in Western Europe and the United States', in Flora and Heidenheimer (eds) 1981.

Kregel, J. (1980), 'I fondamenti marshalliani del principio della domanda effettiva di Keynes', *Giornali degli Economisti e Annali di Economia*, vol. 39, March and April, pp. 153–68.

Kregel, J. (1983), 'Finanziamento indisavanzo politica economica e preferenza per la liquidata', in Vicarelli (ed.) 1984.

Krüger, Al. (1925), *Das Koelner Bankiergewerbe vom Ende des 18. Jahrhunderts bis 1875*, Essen.

Kurz, H.D. (1978), 'Rent Theory in a Multisectoral Model', *Oxford Economic Papers*, vol. XXXVI, pp. 16–37.

Kurz, H.D. (1979), 'Wahl der Technik und Arbeitswertlehre in einem einfachen Model mit zwei originaeren Faktoren', *Jahrbuch fuer Sozialwissenschaft*, Band XXX, pp. 27–51.

Kurz, H.D. (1983), see Jeck and Kurz 1983.

Kuznets, S. (1955), 'Economic Growth and Income Inequality', *American Economic Review*, vol. XLV, pp. 1–28.

Lafargue (ed.) (1983), see Kindleberger and Lafargue (eds) 1983.

Lavers, G.R. (1951), see Rowntree and Lavers 1951.

Lavington, F. (1921), *The English Capital Market*, London.

Le Grand, J. (1982), *The Strategy of Equality*, Allen & Unwin, London.

Leith, J.C. (1977), see Patinkin and Leith (eds) 1977.

Lekachman, R. (1966), *The Age of Keynes*, Random House, New York.

Lenin, V.J. (1939), *Imperialism, the Highest Stage of Capitalism*, International Publishers, New York.

Leontief, W. (1950), 'Joseph A. Schumpeter (1883–1950)', *Econometrica*, vol. XVIII, April, no. 2, pp. 103–10.

Leontief, W. (1966), *Essays in Economics*, vol. I, Blackwell, London.

Lerner, A. (1946), *The Economics of Control*, Macmillan, New York.

Lerner, A.P. (1937), 'Statics and Dynamics in a Socialist Economy', *Economic Journal*, vol. XLVII, pp. 253–70.

Lewis, W.A. (1954), 'Economic Development with Unlimited Supplies of Labour', *Manchester School of Economic and Social Studies*, vol. XXII.

Lewis, W.A. (1973), *The Deceleration of British Growth, 1873–1913*, mimeo, Princeton.

Lewis, W.A. (1978), *Growth and Fluctudtions 1870–1913*, Allen & Unwin, London.

Lindbeck, A. (1981), 'Work Disincentives in the Welfare State', *National-Oekonomische Gesellschaft Lectures 1979–1980*, Manz, Vienna.

Lindbeck, A. (1983), 'The Recent Productivity Slow Down', *Economic Journal*, vol. XCIII, pp. 13–34.

Lowe, A. (1976), *The Path of Economic Growth*, Cambridge University Press, Cambridge.

Luxemburg, Rosa (1951), *The Accumulation of Capital*, Routledge & Kegan Paul, London.

McClelland, D.D. (1961), *The Achieving Society*, D. van Nostrand Comp., Princeton.

McDonald, R.G. (1960), *A Comparison of the Theories of Entrepreneurial Expectations of Keynes and Schumpeter*, unpublished PhD. dissertation, University of Wisconsin.

McGoldrick, P. (s.a., s.l.), 'Operations of the German Central Bank and the Rules of the Game, 1879–1913', unpublished article.

McKeon, J. and S. Blitz (1983), *Costs of Credit Risk: How Corporate America is Responding*, Solomon Brothers Inc., Bond Market Research, New York, July.

Maddison, A. (1984), 'Origins and Impact of the Welfare State 1883–1983', *Banca Nazionale del Lavoro Quarterly Review*, March.

Magdoff (1983), see Sweezy and Magdoff 1983.

Marget, A.W. (1951), 'The Monetary Aspects of the Schumpeterian System', in Harris (ed.) 1951, pp. 62–71.

Marx, K.H. (1867), *Das Kapital* I, Otto Meissner, Hamburg.

Marx, K.H. (1906), *Capital* I, Modern Library Edition, New York.

Marx, K.H. (1909), *Capital, a Critique of Political Economy*, 3 vols, Charles Kent & Co., Chicago.

Marx, K.H. (1953), *Grundrisse der Kritik der politischen Ökonomie 1857–1859*, Dietz, Berlin.

Marx, K.H. (1954), *Capital* I, Progress Publishers, Moscow.

Marx, K.H. (1958), 'Randglossen zum Programm der deutschen Arbeiterpartei', in *Marx-Engels Ausgewaehlte Schriften*, Dietz Verlag, Berlin, pp. 11–29.

Marx, K.H. (1964), *Das Kapital*, 3 vols, Dietz Verlag, Berlin.

Marx, K.H. (1967), *Capital*, 3 vols, International Publishers, New York.

Marx, K.H. (1968), *Theories of Surplus Value*, vol. II, Progress Publishers, Moscow.

Marx, K.H. (1972), *Capital* II, Progress Publishers, Moscow.

Marx, K.H. (1973a), *The Revolutions of 1848. Political Writings*, vol. I (ed. D. Fernback), Penguin Books, Harmondsworth.

Marx, K.H. (1973b), *Grundrisse der Kritik der politischen Oekonomie 1857–1859*, Penguin Books, Harmondsworth.

Marx, K.H. (1976), *Capital* I, Penguin Books, Harmondsworth.

Marx, K.H. (1977), *Capital* III, Progress Publishers, Moscow.

Marx, K.H. and Friedrich Engels (1848), *Manifest der Kommunistischen Partei*, Burghard, London.

Marx, K.H. and Friedrich Engels (1960), *The First Indian War of Independence 1857–1859*, Lawrence Wishart,London.

Marx, K.H. and Friedrich Engels (1968), *Selected Works*, International Publishers, New York.

März, E. (1964), 'Zur Genesis der Schumpeterschen Theorie der wirtschaftlichen Entwicklung', in *On Political Economy and Econometrics: Essays in Honour of Oscar Lange*, Polish Scientific Publishers, Warszawa, pp. 363–87.

März, E. (1968), *Oesterreichische Industrie- und Bankpolitik der Zeit Franz Josephs I*, Europa Verlag, Wien.

März, E. (1976), *Einfuehrung in die Marxsche Theorie der wirtschaftlichen Entwicklung*, Europa Verlag, Frankfurt.

Mathias, P. (1973), 'Capital, Credit and Enterprise in the Industrial Revolution', *Journal of European Economic History*, vol. II, pp. 121–43.

Mattick, P. (1969), *Marx and Keynes: The Limits of the Mixed Economy*, Porter Sargent, Boston.

Meade, J.F. (1948), *Planning and the Price Mechanism*, Allen & Unwin, London.

Messner, J. (1968), *Das Unternehmerbild in der katholischen Soziallehre*, Koeln.

Mill, J.S. (1965), *Principles of Political Economy* (ed. J.M. Robson), University of Toronto Press, Toronto.

Minami, R. (1973), *The Turning Point in Economic Development: Japan's Experience*, Kinkuniya, Tokyo.

Minsky, H.P. (1975), *John Maynard Keynes*, Columbia University Press, New York.

Minsky, H.P. (1978), 'The Financial Instability Hypothesis: A re-statement', *Thames Papers in Political Economy*, Autumn.

Minsky, H.P. (1982a), *Can 'It' Happen Again?* M.E. Sharpe and C.A.R. Monk, New York.

Minsky, H.P. (1982b), 'The Breakdown of the 1960's Policy Synthesis', *Telos*, Winter 1981–1982, no. 50, pp. 49–58.

Minksy, H.P. (1983), 'The Financial Instability Hypothesis: Capitalist Processes and the Behaviour of the Economy', in C.P. Kindleberger and J.P. Lafargue (eds) (1983), *Financial Crisis, Theory, History and Policy*, Cambridge University Press, Cambridge.

Mitchell, B.R. and Phyllis Deane (1962), *Abstract of British Historical Statistics*, Cambridge University Press, Cambridge.

Mnacko, L. (1970), *Der Vorgang*, Kindler, Munich.

Moggridge, D. and S. Howson (1974), 'Keynes on Monetary Policy, 1910–1946', *Oxford Economic Papers*, vol. XXVI, pp. 226–47.

Moggridge, D.E. (1975), 'The Influence of Keynes on the Economics of his Time', in M. Keynes (ed.) (1975), pp. 73–81.

Moll, G. (1972), 'Kapitalistische Bauernbefreiung und Industrielle Revolution: Zur Rolle des "Loskaufs"', *Jahrbuh fuer Wirtschaftsgeschichte*, Band VI.

Morishima, M. (1964), *Equilibrium, Stability and Growth*, Clarendon Press, Oxford.

Morishima, M. (1973), *Marx's Economics: A Dual Theory of Value and Growth*, Cambridge University Press, Cambridge.

Mosser, A. (1980), *Die Industrieaktiengesellschaften in Oesterreich, 1880–1913*, Oesterreichische Akademie der Wissenschaften, Wien.

Moynihan, D.P. (1963), see Glazer and Moynihan 1963.

Moynihan, D.P. (1978), *The Politics of a Guaranteed Income*, Vintage Books, New York.

Müller (1970), see Berthold, Harnisch and Müller 1970.

Musgrave, R.A. (1959), *The Theory of Public Finance*, McGraw-Hill, New York.

Musgrave, R.A. and A.T. Peacock (eds) (1967), *Classics in the Theory of Public Finance*, Macmillan, London.

Myrdal, G. (1960), *Beyond the Welfare State*, Duckworth, London.

Niskanen, W.A. (1971), *Bureaucracy and Representative Government*, Aldric, Chicago.

Nuti, M. (1972), 'On Incomes Policy', *Science and Society* (1969), reprinted in Hunt and Schwartz (eds) 1972, pp. 431–41.

O'Connor, J. (1973), *The Fiscal Crisis of the State*, St Martins Press, New York.

O.E.C.D. (1981), *The Welfare State in Crisis*, O.E.C.D., Paris.

O.E.C.D. (1982), *Employment in the Public Sector*, O.E.C.D., Paris.

O.E.C.D. (1950–83). *National Accounts of O.E.C.D. Countries, 1950–1983*, (yearly issues), O.E.C.D., Paris.

O.E.E.C. (ed). (1957), *Statistics of National Product and Expenditure*, no. 2, O.E.E.C., Paris.

Ohkawa, K. and M. Shinohara (1979), *Patterns of Japanese Development*, Yale University Press, New Haven/London.

Okishio, N. (1972), 'A Formal Proof of Marx's Two Theorems', *Kobe University Economic Review*, no. 18, pp. 1–6.

Parinello, S. (1983), *The Marshallian Core of the General Theory*, mimeographed copy, s.l.

Parquez, A. (1981), 'Ordre social, monnaie et regulation', *Economie Appliquée*, vol. XXXIV, no. 283, p. 382–448.

Pasinetti, L.L. (1974), *Growth and Income Distribution*, Cambridge University Press, Cambridge.

Pasinetti, L.L. (1977), *Lectures on the Theory of Production*, Columbia University Press, New York.

Patinkin, D. (1979), 'Keynes and Chicago', *The Journal of Law and Economics*, vol. XXII, pp. 213–32.

Patinkin, D. and J.C. Leith (eds) (1977), *Keynes, Cambridge and the General Theory*, Macmillan, London.

Peacock, A.T. (ed.) (1967), see Musgrave and Peacock (eds) 1967.

Peacock, A.T. and J. Wiseman (1961), *The Growth of Public Expenditure in the United Kingdom*, National Bureau of Economic Research, Princeton.

Pigou, A.C. (1943), 'The Classical Stationary State', *Economic Journal*, vol. LIII, pp. 343ff.

Pizzorno, A. (1978), see Crouch and Pizzorno 1978.

Pohl, M. (1982), *Konzentration im deutschen Bankwesen (1848–1980)*, Frankfurt/Main.

Pollard, S. (1964), 'Fixed Capital in the Industrial Revolution in Britain', *Journal of Economic History*, vol. XXIV, pp. 299–314.

Pressnell, L. (1956), *Country Banking in the Industrial Revolution*, Oxford.

Redlich, F. (1949), 'The Business Leader in Theory and Reality', *American Journal of Economics and Sociology*, no. 3.

Rettig, R. (1978), *Das Investitions- und Finanzierungsverhalten deutscher Groszunternehmer 1880–1911*, Dissertation, University of Munich, Munich.

Ricardo, D. (1951–73), *The Works and Correspondence of D. Ricardo* (ed. Piero Sraffa, with the collaboration of M.H. Dobb), vols I–X, Cambridge University Press, London.

Riesser, J. (1910), *Die deutschen Groszbanken und ihre Konzentration*, Jena.

Robbins, L. (1934), *The Great Depression*, Macmillan, London.

Robertson, D.H. (1936), 'The Snake and the Worm', in *Essays in Money and Interest*, Collins Fontana Library, London, 1966.

Robinson, Joan (1937), 'Full Employment', in *Essays in the Theory of Employment*, Macmillan, London, pp. 3–39.

Robinson, Joan (1974), 'History versus Equilibrium', *Thames Papers in Political Economy*, reprinted in Joan Robinson (1979), *Collected Economic Papers*, vol. V, Basil Blackwell, Oxford, pp. 48–58.

Robinson, Joan (1975), 'What Has Become of the Keynesian Revolution?', in M. Keynes (ed.) 1975.

Robinson, Joan (1976), 'Michal Kalecki. A Neglected Prophet', *New York Review of Books*, March 4.

Rodbertus, Johann C. (1899), *Schriften von Johann Carl Rodbertus* (ed. Adolph Wagner, Theophil Kozak and Moritz Wirth), vols I–IV, Puthammer & Muehlbrecht, Berlin.

Rolfe, S. and J. Burtle (1973), *The Great Wheel*, McGraw-Hill, New York.

Rosenberg, N. (1976), *Perspectives on Technology*, Cambridge University Press, New York.

Rostow (1953), see Gayer, Rostow and Schwartz 1953.

Rostow, W.W. (1978), *The World Economy, History and Prospect*, University of Texas Press, Austin.

Rowntree, B.S. and G.R. Lavers (1951), *Poverty and the Welfare State*, Longmans, London.

Rowse, A.C. (1936), *Mr. Keynes and the Labour Movement*, Macmillan, London.

Rudolph, R. (1972), *Austria 1800–1914*, in R. Cameron (ed.) (1967), *Banking in the Early Stages of Industrialisation*, Oxford University Press, New York.

Salant, W. (1977), 'Keynes as Seen by his Students in the 1930's', in D. Patinkin and J.C. Leith (eds) (1977), *Keynes, Cambridge and the General Theory*, Macmillan, London, pp. 39–63.

Salin, E. (1967), *Politische Oekonomie*, 5th edition, J.C.B. Mohr (Paul Siebeck), Tuebingen.

Samuelson, P.A. (1943), 'Dynamics, Statics and the Stationary State', *The Review of Economics and Statistics*, vol. XXV, no. 1 (February), pp. 58–68.

Samuelson, P.A. (1947), *Foundations of Economic Analysis*, Harvard University Press, Cambridge, Mass.

Samuelson, P.A. (1948), *Economics: An Introduction*, McGraw-Hill, New York.

Samuelson, P.A. (1951), 'Schumpeter as a Teacher and Economic Theorist', *The Review of Economics and Statistics*, vol. XXXIII, no. 2 (May), pp. 98–103.

Samuelson, P.A. (1978), 'The Canonical Classical Model of Political Economy', *Journal of Economic Literature*, vol. XVI, pp. 1415–34.

Schefold, B. (1976), 'Different Forms of Technical Progress', *The Economic Journal*, vol. LXXXIII, pp. 806–19.

Schefold, B. (1983), 'Kahn on Malinvaud', in Eatwell and Milgate (eds) 1983, pp. 229–46.

Schneider, E. (1970), *Joseph A. Schumpeter*, J.C.B. Mohr (Paul Siebeck), Tuebingen.

Schumpeter, J.A. (1908), *Das Wesen und Hauptinhalt der theoretischen Nationaloekonomie*, von Duncker und Humblot, Leipzig.

Schumpeter, J.A. (1913a), 'Zinsfusz und Geldverfassung', in Schumpeter 1952a, pp. 1–28.

Schumpeter, J.A. (1913b), 'Eine dynamische Theorie des Kapitalzinses', in Schumpeter 1952a, pp. 411–51.

Schumpeter, J.A. (1914), 'Epochen der Dogmen- und Methodengeschichte' in *Grundriss der Sozialoekonomik*, I. Abteilung, J.C.B. Mohr (Paul Siebeck), Tuebingen, pp. 19–124.

Schumpeter, J.A. (1917/18), 'Das Sozialprodukt und die Rechenpfennige', in Schumpeter 1952a, pp. 29–117.

Schumpeter, J.A. (1919), *Rede des Staatssekretaers der Finanzen*, 9. Sitzung der konstituierenden National-Versammlung am 4. April 1919, Reichsarchive, Vienna.

Schumpeter, J.A. (1927), 'Die goldene Bremse an der Kreditmaschine', in Schumpeter 1952a, pp. 158–84.

Schumpeter, J.A. (1928), 'The Instability of Capitalism', in Schumpeter 1951a, pp. 47–72.

Schumpeter, J.A. (1931), 'The Present World Depression', in Schumpeter 1951a, pp. 96–9.

Schumpeter, J.A. (1934), *The Theory of Economic Development*, Harvard University Press, Cambridge, Mass. (translated from the German language by Redvers Opic, German publication of 1912).

Schumpeter, J.A. (1936), 'Review of Keynes' General Theory', *Journal of the American Statistical Association*.

Schumpeter, J.A. (1939), *Business Cycles. A Theoretical Historical and Statistical*

Analysis of the Capitalist Process, vols I-II, McGraw-Hill Book Co., New York.

Schumpeter, J.A. (1942), *Capitalism, Socialism and Democracy*, Allen & Unwin, London.

Schumpeter, J.A. (1950a), 'The March into Socialism', in *American Economic Review*, vol. XV, Papers and Proceedings, pp. 446–56.

Schumpeter, J.A. (1950b), *Capitalism, Socialism and Democracy*, Harper & Row, New York.

Schumpeter, J.A. (1951a), *Essays* (ed. R.C. Clemence), Cambridge University Press, Cambridge.

Schumpeter, J.A. (1951b), *Imperialism. Social Classes*, Noonday Press, New York.

Schumpeter, J.A. (1952a), *Aufsätze zur oekonomischen Theorie* (ed. E. Schneider and A. Spiethoff), J.C.B. Mohr (Paul Siebeck), Tuebingen.

Schumpeter, J.A. (1952b), *Ten Great Economists, from Marx to Keynes*, Allen & Unwin, London (1st edition: New York 1951).

Schumpeter, J.A. (1954), *History of Economic Analysis*, Allen & Unwin, London.

Schumpeter, J.A. (1955), *Imperialism, Social Classes: Two Essays*, Meridan Books, New York.

Schumpeter, J.A. (1961), *The Theory of Economic Development*, Oxford University Press, Oxford.

Schumpeter, J.A. (1970), *Das Wesen des Geldes*, aus dem Nachlasz herausgegeben von F.K. Mann, Vandenhoeck und Ruprecht, Goettingen.

Schumpeter, J.A. (1976), 'Die Krise des Steuerstaats', in Hickel (ed.) 1976, pp. 329–79.

Schwartz, J. (ed.) (1977), *The Subtle Anatomy of Capitalism*, Goodyear, Santa Monica, Cal.

Schwartz, J.G. (ed.) (1972), see Hunt and Schwartz (eds) 1972.

Schwartz, W. (1953), see Gayer, Rostow and Schwartz 1953.

Schwoediauer, G. (ed.) (1978), *Equilibrium and Disequilibrium in Economic Theory*, D. Reidel Publishing Co., Boston.

Seers, D. (1950), *Bulletin of the Oxford Institute of Statistics*, vol. XII, no. 10.

Seidl, C. (1982), 'Joseph Alois Schumpeter in Graz', *Research Memorandum*, no. 8201, August, Department of Economics, University of Graz (mimeographed copy), Graz.

Seidl, C. (ed.) (1984), *Lectures on Schumpeterian Economics*, Springer, Berlin.

Shaikh, A. (1978), 'Political Economy and Capitalism: Notes on Dobb's Theory of Crisis', *Cambridge Journal of Economics*, vol. II, no, 2, pp. 233–51.

Shannon, H.A. (1954), 'The Coming of General Limited Liability', in E. Carus Wilson (ed.) 1954. pp. 358–79.

Sheppard, D.K. (1971), *The Growth and Role of U.K. Financial Institutions 1880–1962*, Methuen, London.

Shinohara, M. (1979), see Ohkawa and Shinohara 1979.

Simon, M. (1967), 'The pattern of new British Portfolio investment, 1865–1914', in A.R. Hak (ed.), *The Export of Capital from Britain, 1870–1914*, London.

Skidelsky, R. (1979), 'Keynes and the Reconstruction of Liberalism', *Encounter*, April, pp. 29–39.

Spiethoff, A. (1949/50), 'Joseph Schumpeter in Memoriam', *Kyklos*, vol. III, pp. 289–93.

Spiethoff, A. (1955), *Die wirtschaftlichen Wechsellagen*, 2 vols, J.C.B. Mohr (Paul Siebeck), Tuebingen.

Sraffa, P. (1920), *L'inflazione monetaria in Italia durante e dopo la guerra*, Scuola Tipografia Salesiana, Milan.

Sraffa, P. (1932), 'Dr. Hayek on Money and Capital', *Economic Journal*, vol. LXII, pp. 42–54.

Sraffa, P. (1951), 'Introduction', in D. Ricardo 1951–73, vol. 1, pp. xiii–lxii.

Sraffa, P. (1960), *Production of Commodities by Means of Commodities*, Cambridge University Press, Cambridge.

Steiger, O. and G. Heinsohn (s.a.), 'Private Property, Debts and Interest or the Origin of Money and the Rise and Fall of Monetary Economics', *Studia Economica*, forthcoming.

Stein, H. (1969), *The Fiscal Revolution in America*, University of Chicago Press, Chicago.

Steitz, W. (1974), *Die Enstehung der Koeln-Mindener Eisenbahngesellschaft*, Rheinisch Westfaelisches Wirtschaftsarchiv, Koeln.

Stigler, J. and K. Boulding (eds) (1952), *Readings in Price Theory*, D. Irwin, Chicago.

Stoleru, L. (1977), *Vaincre la Pauvreté dans les Pays Riches*, Flammarion, Paris.

Strachey, J. (1956), *Contemporary Capitalism*, Gollancz, London.

Sweezy, P.M. (1942), *Theory of Capitalist Development*, Oxford University Press, Oxford.

Sweezy, P.M. (1956), *The Theory of Capitalist Development*, Monthly Review Press, New York.

Sweezy, P.M. (1966), see Baran and Sweezy 1966.

Sweezy, P.M. (1971), *Theorie der kapitalistischen Entwicklung*, Suhrkamp, Frankfurt.

Sweezy, P.M. (1981), *Four Lectures on Marxism*, Monthly Review Press, New York.

Sweezy, P.M. and H. Magdoff (1983), 'Listen Keynesians', *Monthly Review*, vol. XXXIV, no. 8, pp. 1–11.

Thweatt, W. (s.a., s.l.), *Keynes and Marx's Das Kapital*, Vanderbilt University.

Tilly, R. (1966), *Financial Institutions and the Industrialisation of the Rhineland*, University of Wisconsin Press, Madison.

Tilly, R. (1973), 'Zeitreihen zum Geldumlauf in Deutschland 1870–1913', *Jahrbuecher fuer Nationaloekonomie und Statistik*, Band CLXXXVII.

Tilly, R. (1978a), 'Capital Formation in Germany in the Nineteenth Century', *Cambridge Economic History of Europe*, vol. VII, pp. 382–429, Cambridge University Press, London.

Tilly, R. (1978b), 'Das Wachstum industrieller Groszunternehmen in Deutschland, 1880–1911', in Kellenbenz (ed.) 1978.

Tilly, R. (1980a), 'Zur Entwicklung des Kapitalmarktes im 19. Jahrhundert', in R. Tilly, *Kapital, Staat und sozialer Protest in der deutschen Industrialisierung*, Vandenhoeck und Ruprecht, Goettingen.

Tilly, R. (1980b), 'Banken und Inustrialisierung in Deutschland: Quantifizierungsversuche', in F.W. Henning (ed.), *Entwicklung und Aufgaben von Versicherung und Banken in der Industrialisierung*, Duncker und Humblot, Berlin, pp. 165–94.

Tilly, R. (1982), 'Mergers, External Growth and Finance in the Development of Large-Scale Enterprises in Germany 1880–1913', *Journal of Economic History*, vol. XLII, pp. 629–58.

Titmuss, R.H. (1962), *Income Distribution and Social Change*, Allen & Unwin, London.

Tobin, J. (1982), 'Money and Finance in the Macroeconomic Process', *The Journal of Money, Credit and Banking*, vol. XIV, pp. 171–204.

Townshend, H. (1937), 'Liquidity-premium and the Theory of Value,' *Economic Journal*, vol. XLVII, March, pp. 157–69.

Tucker, G. (1960), *Progress and Profits in British Economic Thought, 1650–1850*, Cambridge University Press, Cambridge.

Tullock, G. (1962), see Buchanan and Tullock 1962.

Veverka, J. (1963), 'The Growth of Government Expenditure in the United Kingdom since 1790', *Scottish Journal of Political Economy*, vol X, pp. 111–27.

Veverka, J. (1964), see Andic and Veverka 1964.

Vicarelli, F. (ed.) (1984), *Attualità di Keynes*, Laterza, Roma–Bari. English translation: *Keynes' Relevance Today*, Macmillan, London.

Viner, J. (1952), 'Cost Curves and Supply Curves', in Stigler and Boulding (eds) 1952, pp. 198–233.

Wagner, A. (1967), 'Three Extracts on Public Finance', in Musgrave and Peacock (eds) 1967, pp. 1–15.

Wagner, R.E. (1977), see Buchanan and Wagner 1977.

Walras, L. (1954), *Elements of Pure Economics* (translated by W. Jaffe), Irwin, Homewood.

Weber, A. (1922), *Depositionsbanken und Spekulationsbanken*, von Duncker und Humblot, Leipzig.

Weber, W. (1973), *Der Unternehmer, Eine umstrittene Sozialgestalt zwischen Ideologie und Wirklichkeit*, Köln.

Wicksell, K. (1934), *Lectures on Political Economy*, vol. I, Routledge, London.

Wiener, N. (1948), *Cybernetics or Control and Communication in the Animal and the Machine*, M.I.T. Press, Cambridge, Mass.

Winkel, H. (1968), *Die Abloesungskapitalien aus der Bauernbefreiung in West-und Sued-Deutschland*, Gustav Fischer, Stuttgart.

Winkel, H. (1970), 'Kapitalquellen und Kapitalverwendung am Vorabend des industriellen Aufschwungs in Deutschland', *Schmollers Jahrbuch*, Band XC, pp. 275–301.

Wiseman, J. (1961), see Peacock and Wiseman 1961.

Wright, E. (1977), 'Alternative Perspectives in Marxist Theory of Accumulation and Crisis', in Schwartz (ed.) 1977.

Name Index

Aaron, H.J., 213
Alexander, J., 174–5
Allen, W.R., 43–6, 48
Anderson, C.J., 48
Andic, S., 198
Aquinas, St. Thomas, 23
Asimakopulos, A., 107
Atkinson, A.B., 203
Ayres, C.E., 154

Bacon, R., 213
Bakunin, M., 23
Balzac, H., 39
Baran, P.A., 30
Barnett, G.E., 212
Bartholomew, J., 185
Barton, J., 82, 92
Bauer, O., 93, 152
Beach, E.F., 92
Beckermann, W., 204, 210
Bell, D., 212
Bernstein, P.L., 122
Berthold, R., 153
Beuchat, Jac., 138
Beveridge, W.H., 200, 202
Beyen, J.W., 48
Beyer, P., 129
Bismarck, O. von, 12, 197–213
Blaug, M., 5, 60, 63, 90, 92
Blitz, S., 122
Böhm-Bawerk, E. van, 17, 93, 99, 125, 152
Booth, Ch., 200
Brand, R.H., 122
Brandt, W. 27
Brenner, R., 184
Brenner, Y.S., 4–5, 29
Broadbridge, S., 124, 127, 153
Brockhage, B., 129, 153
Bronfenbrenner, M., 4, 22–30
Buchanan, J.M., 12, 210
Buckley, W., 5

Buiter, W.H., 8
Bukharin, N., 158, 161
Burtle, J., 43–4

Calhoun, J.C., 22, 28
Calvin, J., 23–4
Cameron, R., 152
Casarosa, C., 63
Caspari, V., 109, 111
Cassel, G., 34
Cassell, 185
Chamberlain, N., 159–60
Chandler, L.V., 63
Chapman, S., 126, 153
Chenery, H.B., 209
Christy, J., 174
Clair, O. St., 92
Clapham. J., 153
Clark. C., 209
Clark, J., 174–5
Clemence, R.V., 102
Cohen, L.L., 174
Cottrell, P., 124, 126–8, 142–4, 153–5
Coym, P., 153
Crosland, C.A.R., 212
Crouch, C., 208
Crouzet, F., 152

Dahrendorf, R., 200
Dalgety, F.G., 174
Darwin, C., 14
Davis, L.E., 10, 156–85
Deane, Ph., 133
Delius, 128
Denison, E., 209
Dickler, R., 111
Diewert, W.E., 104
Dobb, M., 60, 161
Doody, F.S., 102
Drummond, J., 34

228

Subject Index

accelerator, 4, 16, 21
accumulation, 17, 19, 50–5, 59, 61, 77, 80,
    84, 86, 88, 104, 120, 132, 158, 177,
    190–1, 193
adjustment, 37
agents, 61–2
animal spirits, 5, 76, 194
Austria, 94, 125, 191
Austrian School, 97
Austro-Marxism, 152
automation, 20
axiom of reals, 8, 118–19, 122

backwardness, 151, 160, 191, 212
bank (s), 100, 103, 116, 119, 142, 144, 146,
    150
  central bank notes, 112, 121, 144, 146–7,
    150
  shares, 144, 146
bankers, 39, 46, 124, 130
banking, 10, 102, 117, 123, 125, 132, 146
  current business, 144, 148
  growth, 145, 150
  mixed, 129–30, 144, 147–8, 150, 152, 155
  system, 114, 118, 120–1, 127, 143, 151
banking school, 124, 152
bankrupt, 39
bargaining power, 207, 211
basics (basic commodities), 50, 109
Berlin capital market, 129, 133–5, 137
Bloomsbury Group, 194
boards of directors, 129
Boer War, 159
bonds, 126–7
  rate, 142, 144
book of blueprints, 75–6, 113
bourgeoisie, 160, 197
breakdown theory, 18, 61
budget
  balanced, 42–3, 47
  deficits, 208
businessmen, 170, 173–4, 178–80, 182

capital, 80, 84, 126, 160, 163
  assets, 112, 115–20, 126
  export, 128–9, 159, 162
  formation, 102
  individual, 62
  logic of, 62
  long term, 126
  marginal efficiency of, 99, 119
  market, 10, 114, 127, 130–2, 135–8, 141,
    143–4, 148, 151, 177
  merchant, 157, 161
  stock, 108–9
  theory of, 82–3, 107
  two-price system of, 115–16
  see also accumulation, composition of
    capital
capitalism, 1, 3, 8, 10, 13–15, 20, 61, 96,
    113–15, 123, 152, 158, 187, 190–1, 194,
    197–213
  development of, 3, 6, 14–15, 53, 60, 62,
    68–9, 88, 113, 123, 131, 157, 207, 209
  industrial, 14–15, 20
  managerial, 192, 204
capitalist, 11, 125, 128, 131, 186–96
capitalist mode of production, 9, 190
  society, 187, 192, 206
Cambridge Debate, 102
captains of industry, 5
cash-flow, 116–17, 120
centralisation of capital, 153
change, technical, 48, 54–5, 57, 60, 71, 74,
    81–2, 84, 88, 90, 98, 191
'churning', 210, 213
class, (social), 11–12, 27, 44, 189, 156–85
  capitalist, 190–1, 193
  conflict, 20, 152, 207
  middle, 203, 207
  of labourers, 72, 197, 207
Classical Political Economy, 50–2, 64, 78,
    94, 96, 187, 197, 199
classical theory 37, 52, 54, 82, 94, 100
colonies, 157, 162, 165
colonisation, 158–60